ST. MARY'S UNIVERSITY COLLEGE LIBRARY
A COLLEGE OF THE QUEENS UNIVERSITY OF BELFAST

Tel. 028 90268 316/237
Web site www.stmarys-belfast.ac.uk
email: library@stmarys-belfast.ac.uk

Fines will be charged for overdue and recalled books not returned by notified
date **Recalled books will be given a new date different from the one here.**

Date Due	Date Due	Date Due
6 OCT 2014		
1 5 OCT 2014		
1 0 OCT 2016		

UKLA is a registered charity, which has as its sole object the advancement of education in literacy. UKLA is concerned with literacy education in school and out-of-school settings in all phases of education and members include researchers, teacher educators, local authority inspectors, advisers and consultants, classroom practitioners, teaching assistants, school literacy co-ordinators, publishers and librarians.

The Association was founded in 1963 as the United Kingdom Reading Association. Its founding journal was the *Journal of Research in Reading*. In 2003 it changed its name to the United Kingdom Literacy Association in order to reflect more accurately its wider range of concerns. Through the work of its various committees and Special Interest Groups, the Association is active in a wide variety of areas, both nationally and internationally. The Association is committed to the funding and dissemination of high-quality national and international research projects that include practitioner-researchers. UKLA also works with a range of government and non-governmental agencies on issues of national interest in literacy.

UKLA provides a forum for discussion and debate through a wide range of conferences – international, national, regional and local – and publications, which as well as the *Journal of Research in Reading* include the journal *Literacy* and the professional magazine, *English 4-1*.

See the UKLA website: http://www.ukla.org

Visual Factors in Reading

Edited by

Piers L. Cornelissen and Chris Singleton

First published as a special issue of 'Journal of Research in Reading' (volume 28, number 3).

BLACKWELL PUBLISHING
350 Main Street, Malden, MA 02148-5020, USA
9600 Garsington Road, Oxford OX4 2DQ, UK
550 Swanston Street, Carlton, Victoria 3053, Australia

First published 2007 by Blackwell Publishing Ltd

Library of Congress Cataloging-in-Publication Data has been applied for

ISBN-13: 978-1-4051-6091-9

A catalogue record for this title is available from the British Library.

Set in 10pt Times
by Macmillan, India
Printed and bound in the United Kingdon
by TJ International, Padstow, Cornwall

The publisher's policy is to use permanent paper from mills that operate a sustainable forestry policy, and which has been manufactured from pulp processed using acid-free and elementary chlorine-free practices. Furthermore, the publisher ensures that the text paper and cover board used have met acceptable environmental accreditation standards.

For further information on
Blackwell Publishing, visit our website:
www.blackwellpublishing.com

Contents

Notes on Contributors

Dr Peter Bailey is a Reader in Psychology at the University of York, UK. He graduated in experimental psychology from the University of Sussex in 1970 and then gained his Ph.D. from the University of Cambridge, UK, on the topic of speech perception. After post-doctoral research at the Queen's University, Belfast, Northern Ireland, and Haskins Laboratories in New Haven, USA, he moved to York in 1977. His research interests include the perceptual processing of phonetic contrasts, auditory perceptual grouping, auditory spectral and spatial attention, the perception of 'aversive' sounds and the auditory perceptual capabilities of people with dyslexia.

Dr John R. Beech is a Senior Lecturer in the School of Psychology, University of Leicester, UK, and was Editor of *Journal of Research in Reading* for volumes 24–27 and is currently a Co-Editor. He is author/editor of a dozen books including *Learning to Read, Cognitive Approaches to Reading* and *Psychological Assessment of Reading* (the last co-edited with Chris Singleton). Kate Mayall and John Beech were awarded a grant from the BBSRC, which was completed in 2004, to examine the external feature advantage in word recognition. His research interests are in cognitive, biological and educational approaches to reading and reading development.

Professor Marc Brysbaert is Professor of Cognitive Psychology at Royal Holloway, University of London, UK. Previously, he held appointments at the Universities of Leuven and Ghent in Belgium. His research mainly deals with word and number recognition. The article presented in the current special issue is the culmination of a 15-year discussion between Nazir and Brysbaert on how to understand the OVP phenomenon in visual word recognition.

Andrea Canning is a speech-language pathologist who received her master's degree from the Curry School of Education at the University of Virginia, USA.

Dr Piers Cornelissen is a Reader in Psychology at the University of York, UK. As an undergraduate he studied medicine at Worcester College, Oxford, UK, continuing his clinical training at St Thomas's Hospital in London. He studied for a D.Phil. with Professor John Stein at the University Laboratory of Physiology, Oxford, funded by the Wellcome Trust. After three years as a McDonnell-Pew postdoctoral Fellow, he moved to Newcastle upon Tyne to take up a lectureship, and most recently to the University of York as a Reader. The main thrust of his research is to understand the neural basis of reading using a combination of psychophysical and neuroimaging techniques (MEG and fMRI).

Dr Bruce Evans is Director of Research at the Institute of Optometry and Visiting Professor to City University in London, UK. He is a Fellow of the College of Optometrists and holds their higher qualifications of Diploma in Contact Lens Practice and Diploma in Orthoptics. His main areas of research are children's vision, dyslexia and orthoptics and he was awarded a Ph.D. for research into vision and dyslexia in 1991. He has published about 130 papers and book chapters and has authored three books, including one on dyslexia and vision. He has a private optometric practice in Brentwood, Essex.

Dr Laura Justice directs the Preschool Language and Literacy Lab in the Curry School of Education at the University of Virginia, USA. She is a clinically-certified speech-language pathologist with a joint faculty appointment in the McGuffey Reading Center and the Communication Disorders Program.

Isla Kriss studied psychology at Manchester Metropolitan University, UK, and became interested in reading disabilities after working in a learning support unit. After graduating she completed a Post Graduate Certificate in Primary Education at Goldsmiths College, University of London. She subsequently taught English and children with special needs in Peru and is currently teaching in a primary school in London.

Chris Lankford is a systems engineer with doctoral training at the University of Virginia, USA. He is currently involved with research and systems development of the ERICA system through his work at ERICA, Inc., USA

Dr Michal Lavidor is a Reader in Psychology at the University of Hull, UK. During her D.Phil., which she carried out in Israel, she specialised in visual word recognition, in particular hemispheric differences in processing written words. She moved to the University of York, UK, as a Marie Curie Research Fellow and developed further her research interests to investigate brain structures involved in orthographic processing of words and letters. She now has her own Transcranial Magnetic Stimulation (TMS) laboratory in the Psychology Department at Hull, with the aim of investigating the neural pathways of word processing, from the retina to the frontal cortex.

Professor Gordon Legge received an S.B. degree in physics from MIT in 1971 and an M.S. in astronomy and Ph.D. in experimental psychology from Harvard University in 1972 and 1976, respectively. In 1977, he joined the Faculty of the University of Minnesota in Minneapolis, USA, where he is currently a Professor of Psychology and Neuroscience and Director of the Minnesota Laboratory for Low-Vision Research. His research deals with visual perception and cognition, currently focusing on the roles of vision in reading and spatial navigation, with a special interest in the problems encountered by people with impaired vision.

Dr Scott McDonald is a Research Fellow in the Department of Psychology at the University of Edinburgh, UK. His current research centres on eye movements in reading, with emphasis on statistical and computational modelling of saccade generation during normal reading. He is also interested in developing models of the visual and reading impairments characteristic of hemianopia and dyslexia.

Dr Steve Mansfield is an Assistant Professor in the Department of Psychology at the State University of New York College at Plattsburgh, USA. He earned his B.Sc. in Psychology from the University of St. Andrews, UK, and his D.Phil. from the University of Oxford, UK. He was a postdoctoral research associate at the Minnesota Laboratory for Low Vision Research at the University of Minnesota in Minneapolis, USA, where he helped develop the MNREAD Acuity Charts. His research interests concern the perceptual and cognitive processes involved in reading, and the cognitive factors underlying plagiarism in student work.

Dr Kate Mayall is an honorary lecturer at the School of Psychology, University of Leicester, UK. Her research investigates the cognitive processes involved in naming visually presented words and objects. Her recent projects, funded by BBSRC and Wellcome Trust, have examined the visual features important to word recognition using functional imaging and cognitive experiments with normal adults, children and patients with peripheral dyslexia.

Dr Tatjana Nazir is head of the Brain & Language laboratory at the National Center of Scientific Research (CNRS) in Lyon, France. She is an expert on visual aspects of word recognition. The article presented in the current special issue is the culmination of a 15-year discussion between Nazir and Brysbaert on how to understand the OVP phenomenon in visual word recognition.

Dr Beth O'Brien received a B.A. degree in psychology from the College of the Holy Cross in 1987 and an M.S. and Ph.D. in cognitive science from Tulane University in 1994 and 1996, respectively. She received a postdoctoral fellowship from 1996 to 1999 at the University of Minnesota's Laboratory for Low-Vision Research, and is currently a Research Assistant Professor in the Eliot Pearson Department of Child Development and Center for Reading and Language Research at Tufts University, USA. Her research focus is on visual and orthographic processing in reading development and in developmental reading disabilities.

Dr Kristen Pammer studied first at the University of Wollongong, Australia, where she did her Ph.D. in visual psychophysics. She began her research into dyslexia at the department of psychology at the Australian National University, Canberra. Through research positions at the University of Newcastle, UK and at the Helsinki University of Technology, Finland, she became interested in the use of magnetoencephalographic neuroimaging to investigate the cortical events involved in cognitive processes such as reading and attention. On returning to the Australian National University, she is pursuing her interests in the neuropsychology of dyslexia and early attentional processes.

Dr Richard Shillcock has a joint appointment in Informatics and in Psychology at the University of Edinburgh, UK. Since his D.Phil. at the University of Sussex, he has been involved in research on the processing of spoken and written language within a variety of paradigms, from experimental psycholinguistics to connectionist modelling, and is currently part of the *Language at Edinburgh* research community.

Dr Chris Singleton is a Chartered Psychologist and Senior Lecturer in Educational Psychology at the University of Hull, UK. His research interests centre on the identification and assessment of dyslexia and other learning problems, and his research team has developed a range of computer-based assessment systems that are currently in use in over 7,000 UK schools, colleges and universities, and which have been translated to several other languages. He has been a member of the editorial board of the *Journal of Research in Reading* since 1994 and was Editor of the journal from 1997–2000. His publications include *The Psychological Assessment of Reading* (Routledge, 1997), which he edited jointly with John Beech.

Lori Skibbe is a doctoral candidate in the Curry School of Education's Interdisciplinary Doctoral Training Program in Risk and Prevention at the University of Virginia, USA.

Susannah Trotter graduated in psychology from the University of Hull, UK, in 2002. She currently works as an Assessment Officer in the Psychological Assessment Unit at the University of Hull, and is pursuing doctoral research on comorbidities in specific developmental disorders of childhood.

Dr Trichur Vidyasagar began his investigations of the visual system during his undergraduate years in the medical school at University of Madras, India. He pursued them further during his graduate studies at the University of Manchester, UK, thereafter at the Max-Planck-Institute for Biophysical Chemistry, Goettingen, Germany, and since 1989 in Australia, first at the Australian National University and presently at University of Melbourne. His interests have ranged from neural mechanisms of perception, attention and memory in animals to human psychophysical studies, with a recent interest in applying our understanding of parallel visual pathways and visual attention to elucidating the aetiology of dyslexia.

Dr Carol Whitney is an Assistant Research Scientist in the Linguistics department at the University of Maryland, USA. Her pre-doctoral education was in Computer Science, and she holds a Ph.D. in Neural and Cognitive Sciences from the University of Maryland, where she studied under Dr. Amy Weinberg. Her research focuses on formulating and experimentally testing computational theories of brain representations in visual word recognition and sentence parsing.

Preface

As you read this, your brain is adeptly converting visual images of letter strings into words, together with their meanings. To paraphrase Ian McEwan:

> 'reading is a form of telepathy. By means of inking symbols onto a page, you are able to send thoughts and feelings from your mind to the reader's. It is a magical process, so commonplace that no one stops to wonder at it. Reading a sentence and understanding it are the same thing; as with the crooking of a finger, nothing lies between them. There is no gap during which the symbols are unravelled. You see the word castle, and it is there'. (McEwan, 2001)

For the majority of adults, this apparently effortless skill underpins daily existence; it determines an individual's ability to earn a living and survive as a fully functioning, independent member of society. Moreover, much of our cultural identity and ability to communicate using abstract thought depends on the ability to read. It is very easy to take this for granted. So much so, that disembarking at an airport where the local writing system is completely unfamiliar provides us with, not just a culture shock, but immediate practical problems. It is no surprise, therefore, that in our society, people who do not learn to read well, or who lose the ability through illness or accident, suffer emotional, intellectual and financial consequences. The ability to read fluently matters hugely; arguably, a better understanding of how we read matters just as much.

A century of reading research has taught us much. A multitude of psychophysical, neuro-imaging, longitudinal and genetic studies have given us significant insight into aspects of how we read and how we learn to read. In particular, the critical role of phonological skills in reading, having been recognised, has been used to justify the emphasis on phonics teaching – learning the relationships between letters and the sounds they represent – in the USA and the UK. However, despite this, recent UK Government reports state that almost one third of 11- and 12-year-olds fail to meet basic standards in reading and spelling (OFSTED, 2004). This raises the question as to whether the scientific basis for current educational policy is flawed. One possibility is that by over-emphasising the role of phonological processing in reading, we have underestimated the importance of the role of vision; that reading is inherently a learnt specialisation which depends on the dynamic integration between a highly practised visual system and the language system. More specifically, I suggest that current research has paid insufficient attention to what visual and linguistic computations are fundamental to reading, and how these are implemented in the brain.

In this special edition we present samples of recent work which are relevant in addressing four important questions concerning the role of vision in reading:

What basic constraints does the visual system and eye movement control set on visual word recognition?

If you have read this far, your eyes have been foraging the text by making an alternating sequence of fixation and saccadic eye movements. In this special edition, there are no contributions about how this oculo-motor sequence is controlled in expert readers. For those interested, I recommend Rayner (1998) for an exhaustive review. However, the paper by Justice, Skibbe, Canning and Lankford does present new data on the extent to which pre-school children visually attend to print when looking at storybooks – hence they provide fresh insight into the early development of reading eye-movements.

When expert readers fixate a word, the visual system samples the letter string, thereby initiating visual word recognition. Brysbaert and Nazir provide a useful overview of the main constraints that our visual systems impose on this process. They emphasise several critical factors including the fact that, because of the differential density of retinal sampling, not all letters are equally visible to the reader. The letter that is most visible is the letter that is fixated, and the visibility of other letters in a string depends on (a) the distance between the letters and the fixation location, (b) whether the letters are outer or inner letters of the word, and (c) whether the letters lie to the left or to the right of the fixation location. Because of these three factors, the efficiency of word recognition depends on viewing position. In languages read from left to right, the optimal viewing position (OVP) is situated between the beginning and the middle of the word. Brysbaert and Nazir go on to point out that the OVP is the result of an interplay between the distance between the viewing position and the farthest letter, the fact that the word beginning is usually more informative than the word end, the fact that during reading words have been recognised a lot of times after fixation on this letter position and the fact that stimuli in the right visual field have direct access to the left cerebral hemisphere. This last point is of particular interest because it relates to my next question.

What is the role of the left and right visual field, together with the right and left hemispheres, in visual word recognition?

In natural reading, the word currently being fixated straddles the fixation point. This is thought to mean that the letters falling to the left of fixation project initially to the right cerebral hemisphere while letters to the right of fixation fall initially to the left cerebral hemisphere. Words to the right of the fixated word fall entirely in the right visual field (RVF) and so are projected entirely to the left hemisphere (LH) while words to the left of the fixated word fall entirely in the left visual field (LVF) and so are projected entirely to the right hemisphere (RH). Recent evidence strongly suggests that this division between LVF/RH and RVH/LH is very sharp, with almost no overlap. Assuming this to be the case, Shillcock, Ellison & Monaghan (2000) have shown (and Shillcock and McDonald pursue the argument here) that a range of observed reading behaviours may be interpreted in terms of the equitable division of labour between the two hemispheres. They argue that the problem of visual word recognition can be reconceptualised in terms of the problem of co-ordinating the relevant information in the two hemispheres. For example, they reinterpreted the tendency of readers to fixate towards the more informative beginning of English words as a tendency to divide the orthographic information evenly between the hemi-fields, by minimising the confusion between the left part of all of the words in a large lexicon and between the right parts of all of the words in the lexicon.

Shillcock and McDonald's argument depends to a great extent on the idea that each hemisphere has its own mode of lexical access. Support for this so-called 'dual-mode' of lexical access has come from studies requiring the processing of words displayed briefly in the LVF or RVF. For example, if familiar words are presented in the conventional format in the LVF or RVF, then recognition accuracy and reaction time are relatively unaffected by variations in length in the RVF/LH while in the LVF/RH, accuracy declines, and reaction time increases as the number of letters in the word increases. This is true for accuracy of report after brief presentations as well as for reaction time measures in lexical decision, semantic judgements and rapid word naming (Ellis, 2004). Sensitivity to letter length in the processing of familiar words in normal formats has been taken as an index of right-hemisphere involvement in the early stages of visual word recognition.

In contrast, word recognition in the RVF/LH is more strongly affected by changes in format (e.g. CaSe AlTeRnAtIoN or stepped format) than word recognition in the LVF/ RH (Lavidor, Ellis & Pansky, 2002). Hence, sensitivity to format distortion in the recognition of familiar words can be regarded as an index of left-hemisphere involvement in the early stages of visual word recognition. In this special issue, Lavidor and Bailey provide further data concerning the details of the word length × visual field interaction.

What information does the brain compute when we read a word?

Amongst reading researchers, there is a majority opinion that abstract letter identity, independent of font type and case, represents the basic perceptual unit underlying visual word recognition (Besner & McCann, 1987; Grainger & Jacobs, 1996). Recent support for this view was provided by Pelli, Farrell and Moore (2003), who showed that the efficiency of visual word recognition (i.e. the ratio of an ideal observer's word identification threshold to that of a human observer) is inversely proportional to word length. This means that, for a page of text, contrast energy (i.e. the product of squared contrast and 'ink' area) in the image must be divided equally amongst the letters, so that every letter is as visible as every other letter. The alternative possibility, which Pelli, Farrell and Moore refuted, was that contrast energy be shared equally at the word level regardless of word length. This would mean that individual letters within a word become less visible as words get longer. By comparing these psychophysical results to an ideal observer model, Pelli, Farrell and Moore showed that human performance in visual word recognition never exceeds that attainable by strictly letter- or feature-based models. Thus, individual letter identification appears to provide the gateway to more complex sub-lexical and lexical processes, such as phonological and morphological processing.

In this issue, Beech and Mayall provide some evidence consistent with a comple-mentary view – that word shape is also important for word recognition. The word-shape hypothesis is based on the idea that the overall shape of words plays a role in visual word recognition above and beyond the identity of individual letters. I think the real problem with this hypothesis, from an object recognition point of view, is what does word shape really mean here? What is implied is some kind of enveloping function which wraps around the outside of a word, like a silhouette. But, from an image-processing point of view, this would only really work if the word image itself was low-pass filtered, since otherwise, all the inner workings of a letter string are either available for view, or can (largely) be inferred from the outer word fragments used by Beech and Mayall. Perhaps future experimental approaches might test the ability of low-pass spatial frequency filtered primes (where individual letters cannot actually be recognised) to facilitate visual word recognition.

If we accept the letter-identity-as-basic-perceptual-unit dogma, what then does the brain compute during visual word recognition? Current evidence suggests that our visual systems extract information about the relative position of letters in words, and this view is supported by priming studies (Humphreys, Evett & Quinlan, 1990; Peressotti & Grainger, 1999). Accordingly, the string 'GRDN' can prime the target 'GARDEN' just as much as 'G-RD-N'. However, 'GDRN' does not prime 'GARDEN'. Thus, when letter order is preserved, even when absolute position is not, there is priming, but when order is not preserved there is no priming. Whitney (2001) has derived a computational model of this process called SERIOL (Sequential Encoding Regulated by Inputs to Oscillations within Letter units). The SERIOL model (see also Colin Davis' SOLAR model: ⟨http:// www.maccs.mq.edu.au/∼colin/⟩) offers a comprehensive theory of the representational transformations carried out by a skilled reader in the processing stream extending from primary visual cortex to orthographic lexical access. A key property of SERIOL, consistent with recent neuro-imaging data (Cohen et al., 2000; Pammer et al., 2004), is that it is capable of accounting for visual field × word length interactions, for example, *without* the demand for dual modes of lexical access between the cerebral hemispheres. Therefore, the reader should be aware that this represents a strong alternative theoretical position regarding what visual information the brain computes during visual word recognition. In this issue, Whitney and Cornelissen apply the SERIOL model of orthographic processing to dyslexia, and also extend the model to include a phonological route (i.e. sub-lexical route) as well as considering how the model applies to reading acquisition.

What, if any, contribution does the visual system make towards reading disability?

In 1987, at the Third World Congress on Dyslexia in Chania, Crete, the late Isabelle Liberman began her plenary talk with a statement to the effect that 'Vision has nothing to do with developmental dyslexia'. There are many reasons why I found this statement distressing, not least of which was the fact that no evidence whatsoever was offered in support of such an extreme position. Furthermore, it was particularly ironic, since Bill Lovegrove and colleagues in Wollongong, Australia, had consistently demonstrated during the preceding five years that children with developmental dyslexia do perform differently from age-matched, normally reading controls, when carrying out low-level dynamic visual tasks. Perhaps more than anything, Liberman's statement reflected the pervasive sense of 'us versus them' in the world of dyslexia research at the time; the 'vision crowd' versus the 'phonology crowd'. Since that time, as reviewed in this issue by Pammer and Vidyasagar as well as by O'Brien, Mansfield and Legge, there is a preponderance of evidence in favour of the idea that people with developmental dyslexia do indeed show different patterns of performance in dynamic visual tasks, and that a substantial proportion of (unique) variance in reading accuracy/speed in both children and adults can be predicted by such visual tasks. At the risk of labouring the point, the vision protagonists have never suggested that the phonology advocates were wrong, nor have they asserted that developmental dyslexia is really a visual problem after all. Instead, the thrust of this research effort has been to test whether there may be a dimension to the reading problems experienced by (some) dyslexics that was being missed. It was certainly reassuring at the Fourth World Congress on Dyslexia, Halkidiki,

Greece, 1997, when the inimitable Frank Wood (Wake Forest University Health Sciences, North Carolina) publicly declared, in response to the then-latest vision research, 'my phonological armour has been pierced'. So perhaps the accumulation of evidence has helped to soften attitudes and territorial boundaries.

I accept that the role of vision in explaining reading disability is still far from clear. In interpreting the literature there are important caveats; most prominently: How is 'developmental dyslexia' defined in any given sample? Are there referral biases? Are the differences in performance in a visual task related to individual differences in vigilance or attentional behaviour? Have sufficient cognitive controls been implemented? Intriguingly, with regard to the latter issue, in some studies it turns out that co-varying for full-scale IQ (e.g. Hulslander et al., 2004) tends to weaken the strength of the relationship between a visual task and reading. Sometimes the response to such a finding (though not in the case by Hulslander et al.) – perhaps echoing the old 'us versus them' mind-set – is that this must mean that observed visual differences are merely epiphenomenal. But it seems to me that to interpret the data in this way misses the main point, namely: what on earth does one's ability to detect coherent motion in a patch of moving dots, for example, have to do with performance on an IQ test? What brain mechanisms associated with reading are responsible for linking such disparate tasks? Why is the variance shared? This should be telling us something.

The last point I would like to make in this section is one which is elegantly illustrated in the discussions by Kriss and Evans, and by Singleton and Trotter, concerning the association between Mears-Irlen syndrome and developmental dyslexia. It is this: rather than worrying over the somewhat restrictive question of whether developmental dyslexia is or is not associated with visual deficits, surely there is a much more important and pragmatic question. Are there reasons to do with visual processing why some children, despite our best efforts, have an impossibly difficult time learning how to read and write? For what it is worth, my bet is that the 'phonology crowd' and the 'visual crowd' are both right, but they are also both wrong. I predict that in the next decade, detailed psychophysical, computational and neuro-imaging work will show that the key mechanisms driving visual word recognition depend on much closer ties between the vision and language domains than has previously been appreciated (see Whitney and Cornelissen, this issue, for one theoretical treatment). So it is simply inappropriate to think about reading, and the ways it can fail, in terms of (Vision) OR (Phonology). The answer, I think may be found in the intimate linkage: (Vision-AND-Phonology). Therefore, in as much as synthetic phonetics seems to encourage letter-sound binding and sequencing right at the start of reading instruction, it may well prove to be more successful than analytic phonics in the classroom (⟨http://www.standards.dfes.gov.uk/pdf/literacy/rjohnston_phonics.pdf⟩).

Technical warning

In the papers by O'Brien, Mansfield and Legge, Pammer and Vidyasagar, and Whitney and Cornelissen, the term 'relative position' is used on several occasions. The reader should be aware that this phrase refers to different concepts depending on the research context. For cognitive scientists interested in constraining their computational models by psychophysical experimentation (see e.g. Peressotti & Grainger, 1999) it is important to distinguish between *absolute* versus *relative* position encoding schemes. For words, absolute position encoding means that there exist separate representations of each letter in each position in a string, that is, there are separate units representing 'A' in the first position, 'A' in the second position and so on. Therefore, for a given input, an optimal match can only occur for the same letter in the same position. Relative-position encoding means that the order of letters is encoded, without specification of their absolute positions, although anchoring of the initial and final letters is often assumed (see the example above how the string 'GRDN' can prime the target 'GARDEN'). For vision scientists, who think more in terms of object recognition, relative position is often used to refer to the idea that blob X in the visual field is either to the left or to the right of blob Y – and of course this is closer to (though not quite the same as) the notion of absolute position coding for the cognitive scientists.

Conclusion

Clearly, the sample of papers we present cannot provide anything like a complete set of answers to the questions I have posed, let alone air all the relevant issues. However, they do give a flavour of how those of us who are interested in vision and reading think, and what sort of problems we currently find exciting and challenging. For the interested reader, it is also important to point out what is not represented here, but which is, I think, of significance. Specifically, there is important recent work from the mainstream visual psychophysics literature about how letters and letter strings are processed, e.g. the work from the laboratories of Denis Pelli (http://www.psych.nyu.edu/pelli/) and Gordon Legge (http://gandalf.psych.umn.edu/ ∼ legge/legge.html). Lastly, in this era of interdisciplinary research, I believe it is critical to consider the ways in which neurobiology and, particularly, recent findings from the functional neuroimaging literature are starting to constrain our thinking about how vision interacts with the language system when we read (e.g. see http://www.unicog.org/biblio/Author/COHEN-L.html; http://nbr.physiol.ox. ac.uk/nbr_research.html; http://www.haskins.yale.edu/Haskins/STAFF/pugh.html).

Piers Cornelissen
University of Newcastle, UK

References

Besner, D. & McCann, R. (1987). Word frequency and pattern distortion in visual word identification and production: An examination of four classes of models. In M. Coltheart (Ed.), *Attention and performance XII: The psychology of reading*. Hillsdale, NJ: Erlbaum.

Cohen, L., Dehaene, S., Naccache, L., Lehericy, S., Dehaene-Lambertz, G., Henaff, M.A. & Michel, F. (2000). The visual word form area, spatial and temporal characterization of an initial stage of reading in normal subjects and posterior split-brain patients. *Brain*, 123, 291–307.

Ellis, A.E. (2004). Length, formats, neighbours, hemispheres, and the processing of words presented laterally or at fixation. *Brain and Language*, 88, 355–366.

Grainger, J. & Jacobs, A. (1996). Orthographic processing in visual word recognition: A multiple read-out model. *Psychological Review*, 103, 518–565.

Hulslander, J., Talcott, J., Witton, C., DeFries, J., Pennington, B., Wadsworth, S., Willcutt, E. & Olson, R. (2004). Sensory processing, reading, IQ, and attention. *Journal of Experimental Child Psychology*, 88(3), 274–295.

Humphreys, G.W., Evett, L.J. & Quinlan, P.T. (1990). Orthographic processing in visual word identification. *Cognitive Psychology*, 22, 517–561.

Lavidor, M., Ellis, A.W. & Pansky, A. (2002). Case alternation and length effects in lateralized word recognition: Studies of English and Hebrew. *Brain and Cognition*, 50, 257–271.

McEwan, I. (2001). *Atonement*. London: Jonathan Cape.

OFSTED (2004). *Reading for purpose and pleasure: An evaluation of the teaching of reading in primary schools*. London: Office for Standards in Education.

Pammer, K., Hansen, P.C., Kringelbach, M.L., Holliday, I., Barnes, G., Hillebrand, A., Singh, K.D. & Cornelissen, P.L. (2004). Visual word recognition: The first half second. *Neuroimage*, 22, 1819–1825.

Pelli, D.G., Farrell, B. & Moore, D.C. (2003). The remarkable inefficiency of word recognition. *Nature*, 423, 752–756.

Peressotti, F. & Grainger, J. (1999). The role of letter identity and letter position in orthographic priming. *Perception and Psychophysics*, 61, 691–706.

Rayner, K. (1998). Eye movements in reading and information processing: 20 years of research. *Psychological Bulletin*, 124(3), 372–422.

Shillcock, R., Ellison, T.M. & Monaghan, P. (2000). Eye-fixation behaviour, lexical storage and visual word recognition in a split processing model. *Psychological Review*, 107, 824–851.

Whitney, C. (2001). How the brain encodes the order of letters in a printed word. The SERIOL model and selective literature review. *Psychonomic Bulletin & Review*, 8, 221–243.

1

Visual constraints in written word recognition: evidence from the optimal viewing-position effect

Marc Brysbaert and Tatjana Nazir

It is now clear that reading and visual word recognition are not simply based on orthographic information but involve the activation of phonological codes. This has been shown both at the level of individual-word processing (e.g. Drieghe & Brysbaert, 2002; Harm & Seidenberg, 2004) and at the level of sentence and discourse understanding (e.g. Brysbaert, Grondelaers & Ratinckx, 2000; Inhoff et al., 2004). In addition, children with deficient phonological awareness (i.e. awareness that spoken words consist of sequences of sounds, phonemes) are at risk for not acquiring good reading skills (e.g. Schatschneider et al., 2004).

Unfortunately, the recent emphasis on phonological coding in reading has overshadowed the fact that a written or printed word is a visual stimulus in the first place, and that limitations of the human visual system put strong constraints on the speed and the accuracy with which words can be recognised. To redress the balance, we will review these constraints in the present paper.

The drop of visual acuity outside the fixation location

The most important variable that limits visual word recognition is the steep drop of visual acuity outside the centre of fixation. Even at an eccentricity of 1 degree, there is already a reduction in visual acuity to about 60% of maximum (Wertheim, 1894). This means that humans find it difficult to recognise words presented a few letter positions to the left or to the right of the fixation location (unless these words are large enough). In such situations, participants have a strong tendency to move their eyes so that the stimulus word becomes fixated.

Starting from the observation that in reading participants mainly fixate words between the beginning and the middle of the word, O'Regan (1981) wondered whether the drop of acuity outside the fixation location not only had implications for the processing of parafoveally presented words (i.e. words presented a few letter positions away from the fixation location) but also for the processing of foveally presented words. His reasoning was that if the drop in visual acuity is important enough, it should be easier to recognise words after fixation on the middle letter than after fixation on the first or the last letter. Central fixation makes maximal use of the high acuity region around the fixation location, whereas fixation on the first letter makes the last letters fall more than 1 degree away

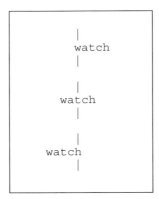

Figure 1. Example of how the initial fixation position is manipulated in the optimal viewing position paradigm.

Note: The participant is asked to fixate the gap between two vertically aligned lines. Words are presented in such a way that the participants initially look at different letter positions within the words.

from the fixation location (under usual reading conditions there are some three to four letters per degree of visual angle). The same is true for fixations on the last letter: they make the first letters fall in parafoveal vision.

To test this idea, O'Regan and colleagues (1984) systematically manipulated the participants' initial fixation location within a word by displaying words in such a way that they were shifted horizontally relative to an imposed fixation location. More specifically, participants had to fixate a gap between two vertically aligned fixation lines placed just above and below the horizontal position where the words were presented. Then a word appeared shifted so that a different letter position fell between the two fixation lines (see Figure 1).

An impressive series of experiments has established a consistent pattern of results because of fixation position manipulation. This pattern is present in word naming, lexical decision and perceptual identification, and has been observed in many different languages (French, Dutch, Hebrew, Arabic, Japanese). Figure 2 shows this pattern, which has been called the *Optimal Viewing Position (OVP) effect*, for words of five and seven letters in three different tasks: word naming, lexical decision and perceptual identification. In all tasks, word identification was best when the words were fixated between the beginning and the middle, and performance declined when participants were forced to fixate on the extreme letters of the words. The processing cost was larger for fixations on the end letters than for fixations on the beginning letters.

To directly test the idea that the drop of visual acuity is equally important for foveally presented and parafoveally presented words, Brysbaert, Vitu and Schroyens (1996) investigated perceptual identification for five-letter words presented so that the observers looked either four character spaces in front of the word, two character spaces in front of the word, on the first letter of the word, on the middle letter of the word, on the last letter of the word, two character spaces after the word or four character spaces after the word. Presentation duration of the words varied from 14 ms to 70 ms. Figure 3 shows the results. As can be seen, there was no discontinuity between the performance to foveally and parafoveally presented words. Performance levels at all fixation positions were captured well by a Gaussian curve that was shifted slightly to the left (accounting for the

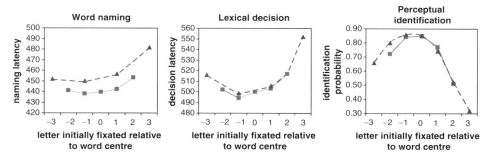

Figure 2. OVP effect for 5-letter (squares) and 7-letter (triangles) words.

Notes: For these two panels, not all letter positions within the seven-letter words were tested. Right panel: perceptual identification (data from Stevens & Grainger, 2003). Left panel: word naming; middle panel: lexical decision (data from Brysbaert, 1992, 1994).

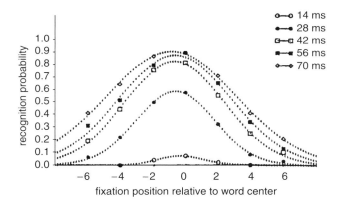

Figure 3. The continuity of the drop of performance for foveally presented and parafoveally presented five-letter words.

Note: Five different presentation durations were used. The data for each duration fell on a Gaussian distribution that was slightly shifted to the left of the word centre. (Data from Brysbaert, Vitu & Schroyens, 1996.)

fact that performance was better when words were presented in the right visual field than in the left visual field).

Measuring the drop of perceptibility for embedded letters

To get a more precise measure of the drop of letter perceptibility as a function of stimulus eccentricity, Nazir, O'Regan and Jacobs (1991) inserted lower-case target letters in tachistoscopically presented strings of eight letter ks (e.g. kkkkckkkk) and asked participants to identify the target letter. The strings were presented in such a way that participants either fixated on the first or the last k. Target letters could be presented at each location of the k-string. Figure 4 shows the findings of the study, as a function of fixation position (beginning versus end) and position of the target letter.

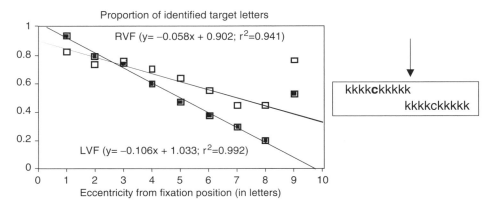

Figure 4. Recognition probability of letters presented within a sequence of ks, either fixated on the first letter (open symbols) or on the last letter (closed symbols).

Source: Nazir, O'Regan and Jacobs (1991).

Nazir, O'Regan and Jacobs (1991) observed three important effects. First, identification of the most extreme letter (i.e. the last letter when fixated at the beginning or the first letter when fixated at the end) was better than identification of the nearby inner letters. This is because of the well-known phenomenon of lateral inhibition (Bouma, 1970): letters are more difficult to recognise when they are embedded within other letters than when they are presented against an empty background. Second, when the most extreme letter was discarded, the drop of performance could be approximated successfully with a linear regression (notice that a large part of the slopes of the normal distributions in Figure 3 can also be approximated by a linear regression line). Lastly, Nazir, O'Regan and Jacobs (1991) observed that the drop of perceptibility was stronger in the left visual field (when participants fixated on the last k) than in the right visual field (when participants fixated on the first k). The slope of the linear regression line was 1.8 times steeper in the left visual field than in the right visual field.

Simulating OVP curves on the basis of letter perceptibility measures

Subsequently, Nazir, O'Regan and Jacobs (1991) examined whether they could predict the OVP curves obtained in perceptual identification, on the basis of the perceptibility of the individual letters and by assuming that a word is recognised only when all its constituent letters are recognised. Table 1 illustrates the reasoning. The first row shows the probability of identifying each letter when the participant fixates on the first letter. The probability of identifying the first letter when the eyes are on this letter is 1.00. The probability of identifying the second letter is 0.94 (a drop of 0.06). The probability of identifying the third letter is 0.88 (another drop of 0.06), and so on. Likewise, when the eyes are looking at the last letter (the last line of Table 1), the probability of identifying this letter is 1.00. The probability of identifying the second last letter is 0.89. This is a drop of 0.11, because the perceptibility of letters decreases 1.8 times more rapidly as a function of eccentricity in the left visual field than in the right visual field. The chances of

Table 1. Probability of identifying a word under various assumptions.

Position of fixated letter	Probability of letter identification					Probability of recognising a chain of five letters
	1	2	3	4	5	
1	1.00	0.94	0.88	0.82	0.76	0.52
2	0.89	1.00	0.94	0.88	0.82	0.60
3	0.78	0.89	1.00	0.94	0.88	0.57
4	0.68	0.78	0.89	1.00	0.94	0.44
5	0.57	0.68	0.78	0.89	1.00	0.27

Note: Assumptions: (1) that all letters must be identified, (2) that the chances of perceiving a letter drop linearly as a function of the distance from the fixation location, and (3) that the drop of perceptibility is 1.8 times higher in the left visual field than in the right visual field.

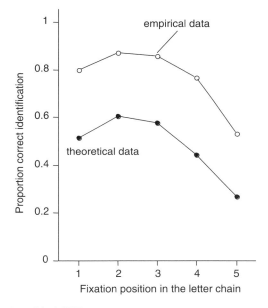

Figure 5. Theoretical and empirical OVP curves.

Note: Theoretical data based on the model presented in Table 1; empirical data from Nazir, O'Regan and Jacobs (1991).

identifying the third last letter when the eyes are looking at the last letter are 0.78 (i.e. another drop of 0.11), and so on.

Figure 5 shows the results of the simulation and compares them with empirical data obtained for five-letter words. As can be seen, the simulation captures the asymmetry in the OVP curve very well, but underestimates the overall recognition probability of the words. Further simulations indicated that the model predicts a strong word-length effect (poorer performance for long words than for short words), which is not observed in the empirical data of adults either (although it is present in the data of beginning readers; Aghababian & Nazir, 2000).

There are two reasons why the Nazir, O'Regan and Jacobs's (1991) simulation underestimated the overall word recognition probability. The first is that it did not take into account the higher perceptibility of the first and the last letter (see the rightmost data points in Figure 4). The second is that the model assumed that all letters must be recognised before a word can be identified. The latter assumption is not realistic, given that many words can be guessed on the basis of a subset of the letters that make the word (e.g. tabl-, h-us-).

Stevens and Grainger (2003) examined whether it was possible to predict the empirical OVP curves on the basis of individual letter recognition probabilities by taking into account the probabilities of recognising words on the basis of incomplete information. They were able to do so, if they used a coding scheme in which not the absolute letter positions were used (1st, 2nd, 3rd, ...) but relative letter positions (first, last or middle letter). The latter observation agrees with the fact that words can be recognised rather easily when the positions of middle letters have been swapped (Grainger & Whitney, 2004; Perea & Lupker, 2004). Ben-Boutayab (2004) recently also showed that it is possible to simulate empirical OVP curves on the basis of individual letter recognition probabilities and the probability of producing the target word on the basis of partial input.

Accounting for the asymmetry in the OVP effect

In the previous sections, we have seen that because of the drop of visual acuity outside the fixation location and because of the existence of lateral inhibition not all letters of a word are equally visible. This means that a word is more rapidly recognised when readers fixate on the centre letters than when readers fixate on the outer letters. Two factors are involved in the word processing quality (either accuracy or speed): (1) the perceptibility of the individual letters as a function of the fixation location, and (2) the extent to which the most visible letters isolate the target word from its competitors.

One element that still has to be accounted for, however, is the asymmetry in the OVP curve. Why are words recognised better after fixation on the first letters than after fixation on the last letters? Three factors seem to be involved.

The first factor is the observation that, in general, the initial letters of a word carry more information about the identity of the word than the last letters. Some authors have argued that this is because of the way spoken words are recognised (for a review, see Shillcock, Ellison & Monaghan, 2000). Because the production of a spoken word takes a few hundred milliseconds (depending on the length), it is more efficient and communicatively effective to pack the maximum possible information at the beginning of the word. Then spoken words can be recognised before the speaker has ended the pronunciation, leaving more time for other (syntax and discourse-related) processes.

The effect of the information distribution within words has been examined in a number of papers (Brysbaert, Vitu & Schroyens, 1996; Farid & Grainger, 1996; O'Regan et al., 1984; Pynte, Kennedy & Murray, 1991) and the results have been consistent. The information distribution has some influence, but on its own it does not reverse the asymmetry of the OVP effect. Figure 6 shows the results of Brysbaert, Vitu and Schroyens (1996). Five-letter words were used that had a high informative beginning (the words had a chance of 84% of being correctly produced by participants given the first three letters, against a chance of only 9% when given the last three letters) or that had a high informative end (71% correct target production on the basis of the last three letters versus 8% correct target production on the basis of the first three letters). The task was perceptual identification after tachistoscopic presentation.

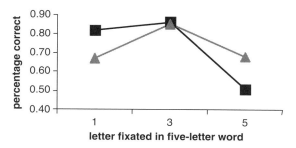

Figure 6. Identification probability for five-letter words as a function of initial fixation (first, middle, last letter) and information distribution within the word (informative beginning [squares] versus informative end).

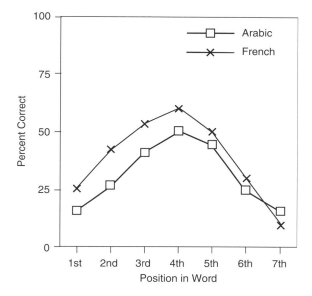

Figure 7. The OVP effect for Arabic and French seven-letter words; perceptual identification.

Source: Farid & Grainger (1996).

As can be seen in Figure 6, the OVP pattern indeed changed as a function of the most informative word part, but whereas for words with a high informative beginning performance was much better after initial fixation on the first letter than after initial fixation on the last letter, no comparable word-end advantage was observed for words with a high informative end. For these words, performance was equal after fixation on the first letter and fixation on the last letter.

A second factor that plays a role in the left–right asymmetry of the OVP effect is the reading direction. The OVP curve is much more symmetric for languages read from right to left (Arabic and Hebrew) than for languages read from left to right (French and Dutch). Figure 7 shows perceptual identification data for tachistoscopically presented Arabic and French words (Farid & Grainger, 1996). As can be seen, the OVP curve for Arabic has become symmetric; it has not turned into an advantage for fixations on the rightmost (initial) letter of the word. A similar pattern has been observed in Hebrew (Nazir et al., 2004).

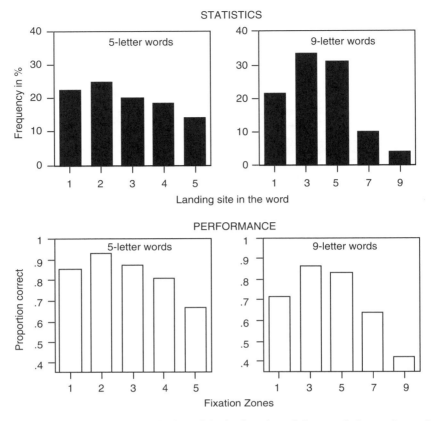

Figure 8. Correlation between the distribution of the landing sites of the eyes during reading and word recognition performance.

Notes: Top panel. Distribution of landing positions in five- and nine-letter Roman words, observed during reading. Bottom panel. Probability of correct responses for five- to nine-letter words as a function of the location of the eyes on the word (from Nazir, 2000).

The main reason why the reading direction influences the OVP effect probably has to do with low-level perceptual learning. Nazir (2000; Nazir et al., 2004) argued that left-to-right text reading results in many words being recognised in the right visual field (either when they are in parafoveal vision or after fixation on the initial letters). There is evidence that repeated presentation of a visual stimulus in the same region of the visual field leads to enhanced discrimination of that stimulus at that particular region (Nazir & O'Regan, 1990) but not at other nearby parts of the visual field. Given this location-dependent perceptual learning, words will be more easily recognised after fixation on the first letters than after fixation on the last letters, because during reading the eyes land more often on the first part of a word than on the last part of a word (see Figure 8).

Notice that the perceptual learning factor, just like the information distribution factor, predicts that the OVP effect in a language read from right to left (Arabic, Hebrew) should be the mirror image of the effect observed in languages read from left to right (French, Dutch). So, one final factor must be invoked to explain why the OVP effect is more

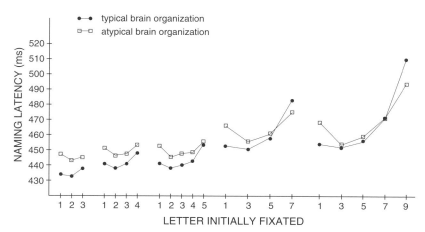

Figure 9. Naming latencies for words of 3, 4, 5, 7 and 9 letters as a function of the initial fixation location and the cerebral dominance of the participants.

Source: Brysbaert (1984).

asymmetric for languages that are read from left to right than for languages read from right to left.

Brysbaert (1994, 2004) argued that this factor is the asymmetry of the brain for language processing. For the vast majority of people, the left cerebral hemisphere is more important for language processing than the right cerebral hemisphere. Because information in the right visual half-field is projected directly onto the left cerebral hemisphere whereas information in the left visual half-field requires inter-hemispheric transfer to reach the left cerebral hemisphere, word recognition will be slightly easier after fixation on the leftmost letter of a word than after fixation on the rightmost letter. This will be true both for languages read from left to right and for languages read from right to left (remember that the leftmost letter is the first letter of a word when the word is read from left to right, but the last letter of the word when the word is read from right to left).

Brysbaert (1994) tested the laterality hypothesis by comparing the OVP effect in participants with left hemisphere language dominance and participants with atypical language dominance.[1] Participants named words of three, four, five, seven and nine letters. Figure 9 shows the results.

As can be seen in Figure 9, the word-beginning advantage observed in unselected participants (the vast majority of whom are left-dominant for language) did not turn into a word-end advantage for participants with right-hemisphere dominance, but the effect of cerebral dominance on the asymmetry of the OVP curve was significant. So, a third reason for the strong word-beginning advantage in words that are read from left to right is related to the fact that fixation on the leftmost letter makes the whole word fall in the right visual half-field, which has direct connections to the dominant left hemisphere. This finding also implies that the fovea does not project information bilaterally to both hemispheres, as is sometimes assumed (see Brysbaert, 2004; Lavidor & Walsh, 2004; Leff, 2004; Monaghan, Shillock & McDonald, 2004; Whitney, 2004 for further discussion of this issue).

To further test the laterality hypothesis, Nazir et al. (2004) examined the letter perceptibility as a function of eccentricity for Hebrew letters. Remember from Figure 4,

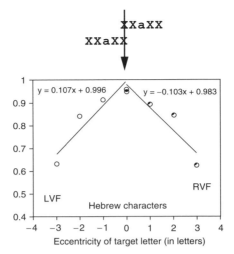

Figure 10. Recognition probability of Hebrew letters in a homogeneous string of characters, as a function of letter eccentricity and fixation location (left character of the string or right character).

Source: Nazir et al. (2004).

that for French participants the drop of letter visibility as a function of letter eccentricity is 1.8 times steeper in the left visual field than in the right visual field. If perceptual learning is the only factor that contributes to this left–right asymmetry, then for Hebrew readers and Hebrew letters, the pattern should be reversed with a 1.8 times steeper drop in letter perceptibility for letters presented in the right visual field than for letters presented in the left visual field. On the other hand, if the right visual-field advantage for French participants is the sum of perceptual learning and cerebral asymmetry, then the asymmetry should be much smaller for Hebrew participants, because for them perceptual learning (which favours the left visual field) and cerebral dominance (which favours the right visual field) should cancel each other out. This is exactly the pattern Nazir et al. (2004) obtained (see Figure 10). There was no difference between the regression lines in the left and the right visual field.

Conclusion

In this paper we have reviewed the literature on visual constraints in written-word processing. We have seen that not all letters are equally visible to the reader. The letter that is most visible is the letter that is fixated. The visibility of the other letters depends on (1) the distance between the letters and the fixation location, (2) whether the letters are outer or inner letters of the word, and (3) whether the letters lie to the left or to the right of the fixation location. Because of these three factors, word recognition depends on the viewing position. In languages read from left to right, the optimal viewing position is situated between the beginning and the middle of the word. This optimal viewing position is the result of an interplay of four variables: (1) the distance between the viewing position and the farthest letter, (2) the fact that the word beginning is usually more informative than the word end, (3) the fact that during reading, words have been recognised a lot of times after fixation on this letter position, and (4) the fact that stimuli in the right visual field have direct access to the left cerebral hemisphere. For languages read from right to left, the first three variables pull the optimal viewing position towards the right side of the word (which is the word beginning), but the fourth variable counteracts these forces to some extent. Therefore, the asymmetry of the OVP curve is less clear in Hebrew and Arabic than in French and Dutch.

Our review has concentrated entirely on the recognition of individual words. This raises the question to what extent the OVP phenomenon has implications for text reading, given that in this situation several words are presented on a line of text. We venture that the implications of the OVP phenomenon will be particularly strong for beginning readers, because for quite some time they read text materials word by word. The situation is slightly more complicated for proficient readers, because they pick up information from the parafoveal word $n+1$ while they are still fixating on word n. This can be concluded from the fact that the reading rate slows down when letter information from the parafoveal word is denied (e.g. because the word remains masked until the eyes land on it) and also from the fact that skilled adult readers skip about one-third of the English words (predominantly the short ones; Brysbaert, Drieghe & Vitu, forthcoming). This means that in text reading proficient readers quite often have rudimentary information about the word, in particular the word beginning, when they land on a word. This advance knowledge is likely to attenuate the OVP effect in text reading relative to isolated word recognition, as has indeed been observed by Vitu, O'Regan and Mittau (1990). However, it seems unlikely that the advance knowledge could nullify the visual constraints discussed in this paper. Indeed, McDonald and Shillcock's research group recently showed that several of these constraints are needed for a good understanding of eye movement control both in normal (McDonald & Shillcock, 2005) and in dyslexic readers (Kelly et al., 2004).

Note

1. Assessment procedures available at the time did not allow the author to be completely sure that participants were right hemisphere language dominant; some participants could have had a symmetric language representation. Therefore, the data of Figure 9 are likely to slightly underestimate the effect due to cerebral dominance. We intend to repeat the study in the near future using brain imaging to assess the cerebral dominance (Knecht et al., 2000).

References

Aghababian, V. & Nazir, T.A. (2000). Developing normal reading skills: Aspects of the visual processes underlying word recognition. *Journal of Experimental Child Psychology*, 76, 123–150.

Ben-Boutayab, N. (2004). Interactions des facteurs visuels et lexicaux au cours de la reconnaissance des mots écrits. University of Lyon: Unpublished PhD thesis.

Bouma, H. (1970). Interaction effects in parafoveal letter recognition. *Nature*, 226, 177–178.

Brysbaert, M. (1992). *Interhemispheric transfer in reading*. University of Leuven: Unpublished PhD Thesis.

Brysbaert, M. (1994). Interhemispheric transfer and the processing of foveally presented stimuli. *Behavioural Brain Research*, 64, 151–161.

Brysbaert, M. (2004). The importance of interhemispheric transfer for foveal vision: A factor that has been overlooked in theories of visual word recognition and object perception. *Brain and Language*, 88, 259–267.

Brysbaert, M., Drieghe, D. & Vitu, F. (forthcoming). Word skipping: Implications for theories of eye movement control in reading. In G. Underwood (Ed.), *Cognitive processes in eye guidance*. Oxford: Oxford University Press.

Brysbaert, M., Grondelaers, S. & Ratinckx, E. (2000). Sentence reading: Do we make use of orthographic cues in homophones? *Acta Psychologica*, 105, 31–56.

Brysbaert, M., Vitu, F. & Schroyens, W. (1996). The right visual field advantage and the optimal viewing position effect: On the relation between foveal and parafoveal word recognition. *Neuropsychology*, 10, 385–395.

Drieghe, D. & Brysbaert, M. (2002). Strategic effects in associative priming with words, homophones, and pseudohomophones. *Journal of Experimental Psychology: Learning, Memory, and Cognition*, 28, 951–961.

Farid, M. & Grainger, J. (1996). How initial fixation position influences visual word recognition: A comparison of French and Arabic. *Brain and Language*, 53, 351–368.

Grainger, J. & Whitney, C. (2004). Does the huamn mnid raed wrods as a wlohe? *Trends in Cognitive Science*, 8, 58–59.

Harm, M.W. & Seidenberg, M.S. (2004). Computing the meaning of words in reading: Cooperative division of labor between visual and phonological processes. *Psychological Review*, 111, 662–720.

Inhoff, A.W., Connine, C., Eiter, B., Radach, R. & Heller, D. (2004). Phonological representation of words in working memory during sentence reading. *Psychonomic Bulletin & Review*, 11, 320–325.

Kelly, M.L., Jones, M.W., McDonald, S.A. & Shillcock, R.C. (2004). Dyslexics' eye fixations may accommodate to hemispheric desynchronization. *Neuroreport*, 15, 2629–2632.

Knecht, S., Drager, B., Deppe, M., Bobe, L., Lohmann, H., Floel, A., Ringelstein, E.G. & Henningsen, H. (2000). Handedness and hemispheric language dominance in healthy humans. *Brain*, 123, 2512–2518.

Lavidor, M. & Walsh, V. (2004). Magnetic stimulation studies of foveal vision. *Brain and Language*, 88, 331–338.

Leff, A. (2004). A historical review of the representation of the visual field in primary visual cortex with special reference to the neural mechanisms underlying macular sparing. *Brain and Language*, 88, 268–278.

McDonald, S.A. & Shillcock, R.C. (2005). The implications of foveal splitting for saccade planning in reading. *Vision Research*, 45, 801–820.

Monaghan, P., Shillcock, R. & McDonald, S. (2004). Hemispheric asymmetries in the split-fovea model of semantic processing. *Brain and Language*, 88, 339–354.

Nazir, T.A. (2000). Traces of print along the visual pathway. In A. Kennedy, R. Radach, D. Heller & D. Pynte (Eds.), *Reading as a perceptual process*. (pp. 3–22). Oxford: Elsevier.

Nazir, T.A., Ben-Boutayab, N., Decoppet, N., Deutsch, A. & Frost, R. (2004). Reading habits, perceptual learning, and recognition of printed words. *Brain and Language*, 88, 294–311.

Nazir, T.A. & O'Regan, J.K. (1990). Some results on the translation invariance in the human visual system. *Spatial Vision*, 3, 81–100.

Nazir, T.A., O'Regan, J.K. & Jacobs, A.M. (1991). On words and their letters. *Bulletin of the Psychonomic Society*, 29, 171–174.

O'Regan, J.K. (1981). The convenient viewing position hypothesis. In D.F. Fisher, R.A. Monty & J.W. Senders (Eds.), *Eye movements, cognition, and visual perception*. (pp. 289–298). Hillsdale, NJ: Erlbaum.

O'Regan, J.K., Lévy-Schoen, A., Pynte, J. & Brugaillère, B. (1984). Convenient fixation location within isolated words of different length and structure. *Journal of Experimental Psychology: Human Perception and Performance*, 10, 250–257.

Perea, M. & Lupker, S.J. (2004). Can CANISO activate CASINO? Transposed letter similarity effects with nonadjacent letter positions. *Journal of Memory and Language*, 51, 231–246.

Pynte, J., Kennedy, A. & Murray, W. (1991). Within-word inspection strategies in continuous reading: Time course of perceptual, lexical and contextual processes. *Journal of Experimental Psychology: Human Perception and Performance*, 17, 458–470.

Schatschneider, D., Fletcher, J.M., Francis, D.J., Carlson, C.D. & Foorman, B.R. (2004). Kindergarten prediction of reading skills: A longitudinal comparative analysis. *Journal of Educational Psychology*, 96, 265–282.

Shillcock, R., Ellison, T.M. & Monaghan, P. (2000). Eye-fixation behavior, lexical storage, and visual word recognition in a split processing model. *Psychological Review*, 107, 824–851.

Stevens, M. & Grainger, J. (2003). Letter visibility and the viewing position effect in visual word recognition. *Perception & Psychophysics*, 65, 133–151.

Vitu, F., O'Regan, J.K. & Mittau, M. (1990). Optimal landing position in reading isolated words and continuous text. *Perception & Psychophysics*, 47, 583–600.

Wertheim, T. (1894). Uber die indirekte Sehschärfe. *Zeitschrift für Psychologie*, 7, 172.

Whitney, C. (2004). Hemisphere-specific effects in word recognition do not require hemisphere-specific modes of access. *Brain and Language*, 88, 279–293.

2

Pre-schoolers, print and storybooks: an observational study using eye movement analysis

Laura M. Justice, Lori Skibbe, Andrea Canning and Chris Lankford

The years preceding the transition to kindergarten are an important time in which young children develop emergent knowledge about the forms and functions of written language. This knowledge base has been described variously during the last two decades as 'print awareness', 'written language awareness' and 'concepts about print' (e.g. Goodman, 1986; Hiebert, 1981; Justice & Ezell, 2001; Lomax & McGee, 1987; Mason, 1980). In this manuscript, we adopt the term 'print awareness' to describe pre-literate children's attainments from roughly birth to the kindergarten transition that include the following understandings: (a) print is an object worthy of interest; (b) print carries meaning; (c) print is organised in specific ways; (d) print units can be differentiated and named, and (e) print units can be combined to make other print units (Justice & Ezell, 2004). Measures reflecting children's knowledge in these areas correlate, moderately to strongly, with other contemporary aspects of pre-literacy skill, such as phonological awareness and developmental writing, as well as later conventional literacy achievements, including word recognition and spelling (e.g. Bryant et al., 1990; Chaney, 1998; Lonigan et al., 1998; Stuart, 1995; Welsch, Sullivan & Justice, 2003).

Several papers have presented descriptions of major print-awareness achievements, including work completed by Hiebert (1981), Justice and Ezell (2001), Lomax and McGee (1987) and van Kleeck (1998). Along with identifying key print achievements in young children, these papers have also worked to place print awareness within a broader framework of the development of reading skill. For instance, in a paper that consolidated the place of print awareness in the framework of early reading development, Lomax and McGee (1987) showed that for 3- to 6-year-olds, print awareness, alphabet knowledge, phonemic awareness, grapheme-phoneme knowledge and word reading formed an overall sequential model of early reading development. Lomax and McGee's influential findings demonstrated the importance of print awareness as an early and necessary component of reading development. Convergent findings supporting the contribution of print awareness to early reading, and the documentation of integrative relationships between print awareness and other aspects of literacy have since been reported in numerous papers (e.g. Badian, 1998, 2001; Chaney, 1998; Justice & Ezell, 2001; Storch & Whitehurst, 2002; Welsch, Sullivan and Justice, 2003). And while the actual strength of the contribution of print awareness to the subsequent achievement of fluent, skilled word-reading ability has yet to be established (e.g. Anthony et al., 2002), it is clear that print awareness – representing a child's understanding of and interest in the forms and functions of written language – is a necessary prerequisite for the achievement of word reading.

Empirically grounded theoretical descriptions of the nature by which print awareness develops are relatively few in number, albeit of great interest in light of current research showing the importance of emergent literacy development for explaining individual differences in children's later reading achievements. Of the few that have been presented in the literature, these have generally been derived from ethnographic and qualitative descriptions of children's interactions with, and discussions about, print during the pre-school years (e.g. Mason, 1980; Snow, 1983). These papers describe pre-school children's interactions with print within the content of scaffolded, contextualised interactions with adults in authentic literacy contexts; for instance, Snow (1983) examined a young child's explorations of print (e.g. questions concerning print) when reading favoured storybooks with his mother. Goodman (1986) drew from a compendium of observational studies to posit that children's print awareness moves along a continuum from highly contextualised understanding of print forms and functions to de-contextualised and conventional awareness. Many of these early qualitative reports describe children's achievements of print awareness through a 'print experience model', in which children's print awareness is developed through their 'informal and naturalistic interactions with print during supportive, mediated opportunities' (Justice & Lankford, 2002, p. 11). This prevailing perspective is derived from emergent literacy and social constructivist perspectives that are currently the predominant theoretical frameworks used by early childhood literacy theorists (Crawford, 1995). The emergent literacy perspective views children's pre-literacy development as a developmental and dynamic process in which children are actively involved. As with the acquisition of oral language, children 'emerge as readers by immersion in a print-rich environment, through a series of learning experiences that encourage active engagement with both spoken and written language' (Crawford, 1995, p. 79). The social constructivist perspective extends emergent literacy theory by emphasising literacy as a social tool, whereby literacy knowledge is gradually internalised from external events by the child through mediated interactions with knowledgeable peers (see Justice & Ezell, 1999).

The literacy event viewed by the preponderance of theorists and practitioners as a particularly fertile context for the development of print awareness is adult–child shared storybook reading. The frequency of adult–child storybook reading accounts for approximately 15 to 24% of the variance in young children's print awareness (see Scarborough & Dobrich, 1994). When considering *how* children's print awareness develops in this context, emergent literacy and social constructivist accounts suggest that adult–child shared storybook reading sessions would show some evidence of (1) deliberate adult mediation of children's print awareness, and (2) children's active engagement with print. Empirical studies of adult–child storybook reading have nonetheless shown little evidence of either of these manifestations. For instance, in a series of descriptive studies, Justice and colleagues showed that adult facilitation of children's interactions with print was a rare occurrence in the storybook reading interactions of adults and young children (see Ezell & Justice, 2000; Justice et al., 2002; also see Phillips & McNaughton, 1990; Yaden, Smolkin & Conlon, 1989; Yaden, Smolkin & MacGillivray, 1993). When reading storybooks with four-year-old children, adults were found infrequently to ask questions about print, seldom to make comments about print and rarely to point to or track the print. While these behaviours have been recommended for use by adults to encourage children's print awareness (e.g. Snow, Burns & Griffin, 1998), there is little evidence that such behaviours are a commonplace occurrence when adults read with children. Additionally, like the adults who are reading to them, young children themselves also show little active engagement with print when looking at storybooks. Pre-literate children – even those with well-developed literacy skills – rarely talk about print (Ezell & Justice, 2000) or look at print (Justice & Lankford, 2002) when reading books with adults, even when the storybook selections feature print-salient characteristics such as large print and print embedded within the illustrations (Smolkin, Conlon & Yaden, 1988). Yaden, Smolkin and MacGillivray (1993) concluded from their longitudinal book reading study of nine children that print forms and functions 'are of far less interest to the children than the meaning of the story [and] its visual impression via the illustrations' (p. 44). Such findings raise questions concerning theoretical perspectives that view storybook reading interactions as fertile contexts for print awareness development, particularly notions that young children actively internalise knowledge about print that arises from mediated interactions with their adult partners.

The research described in this manuscript was conducted to inform theory and practice in print awareness by using eye-movement analysis to characterise pre-literate children's visual attention to print when looking at storybooks. Descriptive and applied studies of the development of print awareness and its contribution to reading have primarily used three methods of inquiry: parental report (e.g. Marvin & Mirenda, 1993), behavioural testing (e.g. Justice & Ezell, 2000) and systematic observation (e.g. Martin, 1998). We recently used a fourth method of inquiry for studying print awareness in young children, namely eye-movement analysis (Justice & Lankford, 2002), a method that has been used to study story comprehension (Takahashi, 1991) and word learning (Yoshida, 1984) for pre-school-aged children. Using technologies to monitor children's visual attention presents an ideal online means for exploring the extent to which children engage with print during literacy activities and for informing theories on print awareness. Eye-movement analysis has provided a valid and useful online measure of information processing during reading for older children, and decades of research have confirmed that an individual's sustained visual attention reflects information processing (for review, see Rayner, 1998). For these reasons, eye-movement analysis has provided a rich (albeit occasionally controversial) source of information concerning reading development and disability.

The present work was conducted to replicate our pilot use of eye-movement analysis for studying print awareness in typically developing four- and five-year-old children. In our pilot work, four children were found to attend minimally to storybook print when being read storybooks. Although the percentage of print fixations increased from 1% for a traditional narrative storybook to nearly 6% when children were read a print-salient storybook, we concluded that young children show an overwhelming preference for anything *but* print when looking at books. We hypothesised that young children, even those with considerable pre-literacy knowledge, are unlikely to interact with print of their own accord regardless of whether print is a salient feature of the storybook. This hypothesis has important implications for current practices in pre-school literacy interventions, by suggesting the need for explicit and deliberate scaffolding by educators and parents to support young children's visual attention to print when looking at storybooks.

Interestingly, recent findings from a laboratory independent of ours provide further support for the present hypotheses. Evans and Saint-Aubin (forthcoming) examined visual attention to print for typically developing French-speaking pre-schoolers in

Canada. Their findings showed that four- and five-year-old children rarely looked at text *and* that even when looking at books with enticing print features (e.g. a single word printed in uppercase font), children's visual attention focused almost exclusively on illustrations. Importantly, a hallmark of science is the accumulation of evidence across independent laboratories using different approaches; thus it is relevant that Evans and Saint-Aubin's findings are so similar to ours.

The specific aims of the present work included: (a) to determine the extent to which pre-school children visually attended to print when looking at two storybooks, (b) to contrast visual attention to print for a print-salient versus a picture-salient storybook, and (c) to consider the extent to which individual differences are present in pre-schoolers' visual attention to print in storybooks. Respectively, it was hypothesised that children would infrequently attend to print when looking at storybooks, that visual attention would be greater for a print-salient relative to picture-salient storybook, and that there would be little individual variation in pre-school visual attention to storybook print.

Method

Participants

Participants were ten typically developing pre-school children (seven boys, three girls) and data was included from four children described in Justice and Lankford (2002). Using the means and standard deviations from pilot work (for which the effect-size estimates for the difference were consistent with a very large effect), we determined that a sample size of ten children was needed in order to detect the difference between two story-book stimuli, with power = 0.90 and $\alpha = 0.01$ (for power analysis, see Sokel & Rolf, 1981).

Children were recruited through flyers dispersed at local daycare centres and pre-school programmes and through personal contacts in the community. All children were required to meet five eligibility requirements to participate, namely:

1. to pass a bilateral audiological screening at 30dB for 500, 1000, 2000 and 4000 hertz;
2. to pass binocular near-field (40 cm) vision screening (the *Massachusetts Visual Acuity Test*, Mayer & Moore, nd) at 20/50 or better;
3. to be a native English speaker;
4. to have no history of neurological, gross-motor, hearing or vision problems;
5. to exhibit typical language and literacy skills, as measured by performance on two sub-tests of the *Clinical Evaluation of Language Fundamentals-Preschool*, namely, Linguistic Concepts and Recalling Sentences in Context (CELF-P; Wiig, Secord & Semel, 1992), and three sub-tests of the *Phonological Awareness Literacy Screening-PreKindergarten*, namely, rhyme awareness, beginning sound knowledge and alphabet knowledge (PALS-PreK; Invernizzi, Sullivan & Meier, 2001).

The criteria for eligibility were standard scores of 8 or better on both of the CELF sub-tests (i.e. scores greater than $-1SD$ of the mean) and raw scores corresponding to 25% accuracy or higher on the three PALS sub-tests.

Table 1 provides an overview of characteristics of the participants, who ranged in age from 50 to 69 months ($M = 58$ months; $SD = 7$ months). All ten children were Caucasian and resided in middle-class two-parent households in a small mid-Atlantic city. All

Table 1. Characteristics of child participants (n = 10).

Characteristics	M	SD	Range
Age (in months)	58	7	50–69
Linguistic concepts	12.4	1.8	10–16
Recalling sentences in context	13.4	1.3	11–15
Rhyme awareness	8.5	2.3	3–10
Beginning sound knowledge	9.0	1.1	7–10
Alphabet knowledge	20.3	5.6	7–26

Note: Scores for Linguistic Concepts and Recalling Sentences in Context (sub-tests of the CELF-P, Wiig, Secord & Semel, 1992) are standard scores, based on a mean of 10 and a standard deviation of 3. Scores for Rhyme Awareness and Beginning Sound Knowledge (sub-tests of the PALS-PreK, Invernizzi, Sullivan & Meier 2001) are percentages, based on number-correct-out-of-10 tasks. Score for Alphabet Knowledge, also from PALS-PreK, is a percentage based on number correct for naming the 26 upper-case alphabet letters.

parents had a high-school diploma, with the majority (80% of mothers and 70% of fathers) having a four-year college degree as well. The children were reported by their parents to enjoy reading books; specifically, parents were asked to rate their children's enjoyment of storybook reading on a scale of 1 to 5, where 1 = *not at all* and 5 = *very much*; all children received a score of 5.

Materials

Materials included two children's storybooks and eye-gaze recording technologies. Two children's books were chosen for this study and then scanned to create electronic versions. *The Very Hungry Caterpillar* (Carle, 1986) contained 9 slides and *Spot Bakes a Cake* (Hill, 1994) contained 12 slides. They are hereafter referred to as 'Caterpillar' and 'Spot', respectively. These books were selected to reflect distinct print genre, with *Spot* a *print-salient* text and *Caterpillar* a *picture-salient* text (see Justice & Lankford, 2002, for specific details about each book). Print-salient texts are those for which 'artists' illustration and design decisions result in print being displayed in a visually salient fashion which influences children's attention to print' (Smolkin et al., 1992, p. 291). Picture-salient texts are those in which illustrations are displayed in a salient fashion to influence children's attention to pictures. Print-salient books promote children's visual attention to print (Justice & Lankford, 2002) and their participation in print-oriented discourse (Ezell & Justice, 2000; Smolkin, Conlon & Yaden, 1988; Smolkin et al., 1992).

Apparatus

The eye-gaze technologies used for this study were the Eye-gaze Response Interface Computer Aid (ERICA) and Gazetracker software (ERICA, Inc., 2001). The ERICA eye-tracking system was used to study children's viewing patterns when looking at storybooks. ERICA is a non-invasive, compact technology that requires no attachments to be worn by participants. The ERICA technology comprises an eye-tracking camera and a light-emitting diode (LED) that directs an infrared light to a participant's eye. ERICA tracks eye gazes at a sampling rate of 60 hertz, with an accuracy of 0.5 to 1 degree visual angle, which is roughly 0.5–1 cm accuracy on the computer monitor at a normal viewing distance. Eye-tracking data generated by ERICA were stored on a peripheral computer's hard drive (a Dell Dimension XPS T500). Gazetracker software (ERICA, Inc., 2001) was used for

Figure 1. Examples of eye-gaze patterns of second author for a line-drawing illustration. The black circles represent fixations, and the lines between fixations represent saccades. The print zone is bounded by a box.

stimulus presentation and eye-movement analysis, specifically the generation of descriptive statistics concerning children's eye movements within identified regions of interest, or 'print zones'. Gazetracker software was also used to demarcate 'print zones' on each page of the storybooks, separating regions of print from that of other page matter (pictures and white space). The print zones comprised regions of both narrative print (the print that tells the story) and print embedded within the illustrations (see Figure 1 for an example).

Caterpillar contained 13 individual print zones marked by Gazetracker software, all of which bounded narrative text. *Spot* contained 21 individual print zones: 14 bounded narrative text, 4 bounded print embedded within the illustrations (e.g. a sign in a grocery store that said 'Special Today Chocolate') and 3 bounded speech bubbles.

General procedures

Eligibility sessions were conducted in a research laboratory on the university campus in 45-minute sessions, during which children were individually administered the eligibility protocol (i.e. hearing, vision, language and literacy testing). An individual 20-minute eye-gaze session was then scheduled for each child within a one-week period. During the eye-gaze session, children sat facing a computer monitor with their heads resting fully against the back cushion of the chair. In two instances, children sat on their mothers' laps. Children were told that they were going to look at two storybooks on the computer, and that they would need to sit very still. After practising sitting still, the ERICA system was calibrated in an approximate 10-second session during which children were asked to stare directly at the computer screen and to look at a series of six sequential icons. (Note that once the ERICA system is calibrated, if it becomes 'uncalibrated' from the user's eyes it stops functioning, which occurred for none of the children in this study.) Then, children were read the two electronic storybooks by an adult reader (the first or third author), with the order of storybooks counterbalanced across the ten children.

Approximate viewing time for the two books together was about seven minutes, and no break was provided between the two storybooks. For each book, the adult read the text on each page verbatim and then waited approximately two seconds before turning to the next page. Children were given a set of storybooks as a gift.

Eye-gaze measures

The eye-gaze measures of specific interest in this study were (a) the number of times children fixated in print zones, and (b) the amount of time children spent in print zones. A fixation is the amount of time that children's eyes are relatively still, allowing them to attend to particular stimuli. The ERICA system coded fixations for gaze durations of 50 ms or longer, based on data showing that new information is brought into the sensory system when the eye is fixated using this parameter (Rayner, 1985). Fixations follow saccades, referring to rapid movement of the eye from one focal point to another, the purpose of which is to bring a particular visual stimulus into foveal vision for processing (Rayner, 1985).

Results

Preliminary analyses

Table 2 presents the total number of fixations and total reading time for the two storybooks. Children averaged 233.1 fixations ($SD = 19.6$) for *Caterpillar* and 229.7 fixations ($SD = 31.0$) for *Spot*. Total reading time averaged 107.5 seconds ($SD = 7.3$) for *Caterpillar* and 90.8 seconds ($SD = 10.0$) for *Spot*. The latter difference is probably attributable to the greater amount of text in *Caterpillar* that was read by the adult, averaging 19 words per page for *Caterpillar* compared to 7 words per page for *Spot*.[1] *Caterpillar* thus took about 16 seconds longer to read. Two paired-samples *t* tests showed that the total number of fixations was similar across the books, $t(9) = 0.32$, $p = 0.76$ (*Caterpillar* $M = 233.1$, $SD = 19.6$; *Spot* $M = 229.7$, $SD = 31$), but that reading sessions were longer for *Caterpillar* compared to *Spot*, $t(9) = 3.9$, $p < 0.01$ (*Caterpillar* $M = 107.5$, $SD = 7.3$; *Spot* $M = 90.8$, $SD = 10$). As the sessions differed for length, the two storybooks were considered separately in all subsequent analyses or, when appropriate, raw data were divided by the length of sessions to control for reading time differences.

Main analyses

Results are presented to address the three research questions: (a) To what extent do pre-school children visually attend to print when looking at storybooks? (b) Do pre-school children show greater visual attention to print when looking at a print-salient storybook relative to a picture-salient storybook? (c) To what extent are individual differences apparent for visual attention to print? The dependent variables of interest for addressing these questions were the number of fixations in print zones and the amount of time in print zones (see Table 2).

Descriptive findings showed that children's print fixations and time spent in print zones were infrequent for both of the storybooks studied. Table 2 shows that children averaged

Table 2. Children's visual attention to print for two storybooks: raw data.

Variables	Book					
	Caterpillar			Spot		
	M	SD	Range	M	SD	Range
Print-zone fixations	6.6	4.7	0–13	16.6	7.2	8–29
Other fixations	226.5	17.7	196–256	213.1	27.6	176–252
Total fixations	233.1	19.6	204–269	229.7	31	187–272
Print-zone time (in sec)	2.7	2.4	0.03–7.31	5.2	2.1	2.1–8.7
Other time	104.8	7.2	96.4–119.5	85.6	9.6	68.9–97
Total time	107.5	7.3	100.1–121.7	90.8	10	73–102

Table 3. Comparison of visual attention to print to other page matter.

Dependent measures Book Category (Title)	Zones		
	Print zones	All zones	Proportion print focus
Fixations			
Picture salient (*Caterpillar*)	6.6	233.1	0.027
Print salient (*Spot*)	16.6	229.7	0.071
Duration (in sec)			
Picture salient (*Caterpillar*)	2.7	107.5	0.025
Print salient (*Spot*)	5.2	90.8	0.057

approximately seven print-zone fixations for *Caterpillar*, and about 17 print-zone fixations for *Spot*. Proportionally, 0.03 of children's visual fixations ($SD = 0.02$) focused on print when reading *Caterpillar*, whereas 0.07 of children's fixations ($SD = 0.03$) focused on print for *Spot*. Children spent about 2.7 seconds in print zones for *Caterpillar*, and about 5.2 seconds in print zones for *Spot*. Thus, 0.03 of children's time ($SD = 0.02$) was spent in print zones for *Caterpillar*, compared to 0.06 ($SD = 0.02$) for *Spot*. Although the number of print-zone fixations and time spent in print zones showed a twofold increase when comparing *Spot* to *Caterpillar*, these data indicate that children's visual attention to print was overall quite modest for both books.

Two paired samples *t*-test were computed to determine the extent to which children showed greater visual attention to print for the print-salient storybook compared to the picture-salient storybook. The proportion of print-zone fixations and the proportion of time spent in print zones served as the dependent measures; the use of proportional rather than raw indices controlled for the number of print zones and the length of reading time, both of which differed across the two books. These indices were compared for *Spot* (print-salient) to *Caterpillar* (picture-salient) (see Table 3). Results showed that a greater proportion of children's fixations were focused on print for the print-salient book ($M = 0.07$, $SD = 0.03$) compared to the picture-salient book ($M = 0.03$, $SD = 0.02$), $t(9) = 6.6$, $p < 0.01$. Likewise, children spent a greater proportion of their time in print zones when reading a print-salient book ($M = 0.06$, $SD = 0.02$) compared to a picture-salient book ($M = 0.02$, $SD = 0.02$), $t(9) = 4.6$, $p < 0.01$. Thus, children's visual attention to print was significantly higher for the print-salient storybook relative to the picture-salient book.

Table 4. Individual differences in print attention for *Spot Bakes a Cake*.

Child	Proportion of print-zone fixations	Proportion of time in print zones
1	0.07	0.05
2	0.07	0.06
3	0.04	0.04
4	0.07	0.06
5	0.07	0.07
6	0.04	0.02
7	0.11	0.08
8	0.12	0.10
9	0.06	0.05
10	0.06	0.04

Effect size estimates for these differences were made using Cohen's *d* (Cohen, 1988) on the proportional means (see Table 3). The effect size estimate for the difference in print zone fixations was 1.93; 79.4% of observations did not overlap in the two distributions. Likewise, the effect size estimate for the difference in time spent in print zones was 1.48; 70.7% of observations did not overlap in the two distributions. These outcomes show that the magnitude of difference across the two storybook stimuli was appreciable.

For the next analyses, we considered individual differences among pre-school children's visual attention to print by creating a visual depiction of the data. Table 4 presents case-level data detailing the proportion of fixations and time spent in print zones (relative to other page matter) for *Spot*. The *Spot* data are highlighted because print attention was significantly higher for this book, and thus it may provide a more enlightening glimpse of individual differences in children's attention to print. As can be seen in Table 4, there was little variation across children in terms of print-zone fixations and print-zone duration. For visual depictions of individual differences, see Figure 2. For 80% of children, the proportion of fixations in print zones ranged only within the lowest tenth percentile; only two children appeared to be 'outliers' with higher proportions of time on print, at 0.11 and 0.12 (Children 7 and 8, respectively). Similarly, when considering the duration data, the range of scores for all children was within the lowest tenth percentile. Seventy percent of children spent between 4% and 7% of viewing time in print zones; one child was below this range (Child 6, with 2% of time focused on print) and two children were above this range (Children 7 and 8, with 8% and 10% of time focused in print zones, respectively).

Our observation of little individual differences among children's visual attention to print suggested that children's pre-literacy knowledge had little association with their attention to print. By way of illustration, Child 5 knew all 26 letters of the alphabet and Child 4 knew only 7 letters of the alphabet. For both children, however, 7% of their fixations for *Spot* focused on print. We conducted correlational analyses between alphabet knowledge and the following variables: *Spot* print fixations ($r = 0.29$, $p = 0.42$), *Spot* time in print ($r = 0.37$, $p = 0.29$), *Caterpillar* print fixations, ($r = 0.45$, $p = 0.19$) and *Caterpillar* time in print, ($r = 0.44$, $p = 0.21$). As can be seen, none of these correlations were significant, suggesting that emergent literacy knowledge was not significantly associated with visual attention to print.

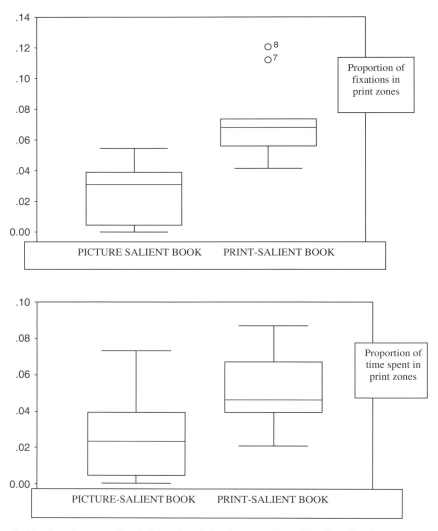

Figure 2. Boxplots demonstrating individual variation in proportion of fixations in print zones and time spent in print zones (relative to other page matter) for picture- versus print-salient storybook.

Discussion

Major findings of the present work were as follows. First, pre-school children spent little time attending to print when looking at a picture-salient storybook. A total of 2.7% of their fixations focused on print and 2.5% of their time was spent in regions of print. These findings left us to speculate, as did Yaden, Smolkin and MacGillivray, 'about the efficacy of this activity to generate substantial knowledge about written language symbols, despite assertions to the contrary' (1993, p. 64). Second, pre-school children fixated more frequently on print and spent more time looking at print when looking at a print-salient storybook relative to a picture-salient book. In the former context, about 7% of children's fixations focused on print and they spent nearly 6% of their time looking in print zones, compared to 2.7% and 2.5%, respectively, in the latter context. Third, little variation in visual attention to print was observed when studying individual differences across the ten children. Although both print attention variables for the two books could have ranged from 0 to 1.00, only in two instances did children's print attention extend beyond the lowest tenth percentile of this range. Correlational analyses investigating the relationship between children's alphabet knowledge and the print attention variables suggested that the emergent literacy skills of the children did not explain a meaningful level of variance in individual differences in print attention.

In sum, the pattern of results gives evidence that (a) pre-literate children spend little time attending to print during storybook reading, (b) their print attention increases when looking at a print-salient book, (c) children are generally similar in their visual preferences, and (d) emergent literacy skills have little influence on children's visual attention to print. This study replicated our previous findings from eye-gaze analyses (Justice & Lankford, 2002) and converge with those of Evans and Saint-Aubin (forthcoming), both finding that pre-school children overwhelmingly prefer looking at illustrations even when the children have well-developed emergent literacy knowledge and when the storybooks feature salient print characteristics. Research using eye-gaze analyses provide further support to observations of what children talk about when looking at storybooks, which has suggested they prefer discussing aspects of the illustrations than talking about print (e.g. Ezell & Justice, 2000; Yaden, Smolkin & MacGillivray, 1993). As Evans and Saint-Aubin note, the use of eye-gaze measurements provides yet another window through which to examine children's attention during shared storybook reading and to question prevailing theories concerning children's construction of knowledge about print within this important literacy context.

Current theories concerning the development of print awareness in pre-literate children are guided by emergent literacy and social constructivist perspectives (see Crawford, 1995). These perspectives view print awareness specifically and pre-literacy skills generally as developing through children's socially embedded mediated interactions with adults in meaningful literacy contexts. Importantly, within these interactions children are viewed as active 'meaning-making' participants and adults are viewed as dynamic facilitators of children's literacy engagement. Several studies of adult–child interactions within the literacy-rich storybook reading context have, however, raised questions about this perspective, namely the extent to which children actively construct meaning about print and the extent to which adults actively facilitate children's engagement with print (e.g. Ezell & Justice, 2000; Justice & Ezell, 2000; Justice & Lankford, 2002; Phillips & McNaughton, 1990; Yaden, Smolkin & MacGillivray, 1993). These studies have suggested that adults rarely include an explicit focus on print forms or functions within the shared-book reading context, and that children themselves rarely talk about print or look at print, even when reading storybooks in which print is a salient quality.

The present work converges with this body of empirical work by showing that pre-literate children rarely attend to print when looking at storybooks. The present findings also show that storybook stimuli are a potentially powerful force in eliciting children's attention to print. However, even when looking at print-salient books children's print attention was quite low, with less than 10% of the reading session involving print engagement by the child. The present findings substantiate Yaden, Smolkin and MacGillivray's observation that young children looking at storybooks are not interested in 'formal aspects of written letters and words, page formats and even the conventional procedures for reading a book (i.e. left-to-right sequence)' (1993, p. 44).

A number of correlational studies have consistently demonstrated moderate associations between the frequency of adult–child shared storybook reading and children's print awareness (for review, see Scarborough & Dobrich, 1994). For instance, Crain-Thoreson and Dale (1992) showed the frequency of parent–child storybook reading to explain about 8% of the variance in children's knowledge about print concepts, a moderate to large effect size in the social science disciplines. This well-documented effect provides support to emergent literacy and social interactionist theories that view children's pre-literacy skills as developing through their active engagement with print during mediated literacy-learning opportunities with adults. The present work shows, nonetheless, that the link between adult–child storybook reading and children's print awareness is not straightforward, as children are unlikely to attend to print of their own accord.

While adult use of print-referencing behaviours has been shown to be efficacious for increasing children's print awareness (Justice & Ezell, 2000, 2002), the *processes* inherent to this model – or the mechanisms by which adults scaffold children's internalisation of print knowledge – have yet to be studied. Likewise, researchers have yet to identify the factors that influence the extent to which adults use these print-referencing behaviours. Work by Bennett, Weige and Martin (2002) has suggested that adult beliefs about their role in literacy teaching may make an important contribution to how they interact with children during book-reading interactions, influencing whether this time is used to teach children explicitly about print forms and functions. Thus, it is not the storybook reading interaction *per se* that facilitates children's print awareness, but rather the adult behaviours during those interactions that manifest from their beliefs concerning their role in pre-literacy development.

The current findings have several useful implications for educators. First, findings show that young children – albeit those with considerable pre-literacy knowledge – are unlikely to attend to print when looking at storybooks. This finding suggests the need for adults deliberately and actively to encourage children's engagement with print when an awareness of print forms and functions is an educational goal. Educators (teachers and parents) are thus encouraged to use interactive techniques that explicitly focus children's attention on print forms and functions. Several evidence-based techniques include asking questions about print, commenting about print, tracking the print when reading and pointing to print (Justice & Ezell, 2000, 2002). Educators should provide ample interactive supports to guide children's engagement with print, as the acquisition of pre-literacy is a lengthy and gradual process that involves many abstract concepts. Second, findings also show that print-salient storybooks summon children's visual attention to print at significantly greater rates than picture-salient storybooks. While many picture-salient storybooks may be useful for supporting children's linguistic achievements, these may not be particularly useful for facilitating print awareness. Smolkin, Conlon and Yade (1988) provided a useful description of five aspects of print-salient storybooks: (a) print included as part of an illustration (e.g. speech balloons, labels); (b) print displaying a change of type (e.g. changes of colour, size, style, orientation); (c) print in which the text itself forms a pattern (e.g. print arranged in a circle); (d) print where words are presented three dimensionally; and (e) print where letters appear in isolation (as in alphabet books). Educators are encouraged to use storybooks with these characteristics to encourage children's print awareness. Yaden, Smolkin and MacGillivray (1993) have also written on the importance of alphabet books for facilitating children's engagement with print; however, these researchers note that alphabet books constrain the discourse of adult–child storybook reading interactions, and thus should be used in combination with a wide variety of other genres.

Acknowledgements

Many thanks are due to the parents and children who participated in this work. Portions of this work were presented at the 2003 Annual Convention of the American Speech-Language-Hearing Association, Chicago, IL.

Note

1. Note that the actual reading sessions themselves were longer; the numbers here represent the actual time children's visual attention was focused on the book pages, thus eliminating periods when pages were turning or children were looking away from the pages of the book.

References

Anthony, J.L., Lonigan, C.J., Burgess, S.R., Driscoll, K., Phillips, B.M. & Cantor, B.G. (2002). Structure of preschool phonological sensitivity: Overlapping sensitivity to rhyme, words, syllables, and phonemes. *Journal of Experimental Child Psychology*, 82, 65–92.

Badian, N.A. (1998). A validation of the role of preschool phonological and orthographic skills in the prediction of reading. *Journal of Reading Disabilities*, 31, 472–581.

Badian, N.A. (2001). Phonological and orthographic processing: Their roles in reading prediction. *Annals of Dyslexia*, 51, 179–202.

Bennett, K.K., Weigel, D.J. & Martin, S.S. (2002). Children's acquisition of early literacy skills: Examining family contributions. *Early Childhood Research Quarterly*, 17, 295–317.

Bryant, P.E., Maclean, M., Bradley, L.L. & Crossland, J. (1990). Rhyme and alliteration, phoneme detection, and learning to read. *Developmental Psychology*, 26, 429–438.

Carle, E. (1986). *The very hungry caterpillar*. New York: Putnam.

Chaney, C. (1998). Preschool language and metalinguistic skills are links to reading success. *Applied Psycholinguistics*, 19, 433–446.

Cohen, J. (1988). *Statistical power analysis for the behavioral sciences* (2nd edn). Hillsdale, NJ: Lawrence Erlbaum Associates.

Crain-Thoreson, C. & Dale, P.S. (1992). Do early talkers become early readers? Linguistic precocity, preschool language, and emergent literacy. *Developmental Psychology*, 28, 421–429.

Crawford, P.A. (1995). Early literacy: Emerging perspectives. *Journal of Research in Childhood Education*, 10, 71–86.

Erica, Inc. (2001). *Gazetracker* (version 2001.2.9.18) [Computer software]. Charlottesville, VA: Erica, Inc.

Evans, M.A. & Saint-Aubin, J. (forthcoming). What children are looking at during shared storybook reading: Evidence from eye movement monitoring. *Psychological Science*.

Ezell, H.K. & Justice, L.M. (2000). Encouraging the print focus of shared reading sessions through observational learning. *American Journal of Speech-Language Pathology*, 9, 36–47.

Goodman, Y.M. (1986). Children coming to know literacy. In W.H. Teale & E. Sulzby (Eds.), *Emergent literacy*. (pp. 1–16). Norwood, NJ: Ablex.

Hiebert, E.H. (1981). Developmental patterns and interrelationships of preschool children's print awareness. *Reading Research Quarterly*, 16, 236–260.

Hill, E. (1994). *Spot bakes a cake*. New York: Puffin Books.

Invernizzi, M., Sullivan, A. & Meier, J.D. (2001). *Phonological awareness literacy screening: Pre-kindergarten*. Charlottesville, VA: University of Virginia.

Justice, L.M. & Ezell, H.K. (1999). Vygotskian theory and its application to language assessment: An overview for speech-language pathologists. *Contemporary Issues in Communication Science and Disorders*, 26, 111–118.

Justice, L.M. & Ezell, H.K. (2000). Enhancing children's print and word awareness through home-based parent intervention. *American Journal of Speech-Language Pathology*, 9, 257–269.

Justice, L.M. & Ezell, H.K. (2001). Descriptive analysis of written language awareness in children from low income households. *Communication Disorders Quarterly*, 22, 123–134.

Justice, L.M. & Ezell, H.K. (2002). Use of storybook reading to increase print awareness in at-risk children. *American Journal of Speech-Language Pathology*, 11, 17–29.

Justice, L.M. & Ezell, H.K. (2004). Print referencing: An emergent literacy enhancement strategy and its clinical applications. *Language, Speech, and Hearing Services in Schools*, 35, 185–193.

Justice, L.M. & Lankford, C. (2002). Preschool children's visual attention to print during storybook reading: Pilot findings. *Communication Disorders Quarterly*, 24, 11–21.

Justice, L.M., Weber, S.M., Ezell, H.K. & Bakeman, R. (2002). A sequential analysis of children's responsiveness to parental print references during shared book-reading interactions. *American Journal of Speech-Language Pathology*, 11, 30–40.

Lomax, R.G. & McGee, L.M. (1987). Young children's concepts about print and reading: Toward a model of word reading acquisition. *Reading Research Quarterly*, 22, 237–256.

Lonigan, C.J., Burgess, S.R., Anthony, J.S. & Barker, T.A. (1998). Development of phonological sensitivity in 2- to 5-year old children. *Journal of Educational Psychology*, 90, 294–311.

Marvin, C. & Mirenda, P. (1993). Home literacy experiences of preschoolers in Head Start and special education programs. *Journal of Early Intervention*, 17, 351–367.

Mason, J.M. (1980). When do children begin to read: An exploration of four year old children's letter and word reading competencies. *Reading Research Quarterly*, 15, 203–227.

Martin, L.E. (1998). Early book reading; How mothers deviate from printed text for young children. *Reading Research and Instruction*, 37, 137–160.

Mayer, L. & Moore, B. (nd). *Massachusetts Visual Acuity Test*. La Salle, IL: Precision Vision.

Phillips, G. & McNaughton, S. (1990). The practice of storybook reading to preschool children in mainstream New Zealand families. *Reading Research Quarterly*, 25, 196–212.

Rayner, K. (1985). The role of eye movements in learning to read and reading disability. *Remedial and Special Education*, 6, 53–60.

Rayner, K. (1998). Eye movements in reading and information processing: 20 years of research. *Psychological Bulletin*, 124, 372–422.

Scarborough, H.S. & Dobrich, W. (1994). On the efficacy of reading to preschoolers. *Developmental Review*, 14, 245–302.

Smolkin, L.B., Conlon, A. & Yaden, D.B. (1988). Print salient illustrations in children's picture books: The emergence of written language awareness. In J.E. Readance & R.S. Baldwin (Eds.), *Thirty-Seventh Yearbook of the National Reading Conference: Dialogues in literacy research*. (pp. 59–68). Chicago: National Reading Conference.

Smolkin, L.B., Yaden, D.B., Brown, L. & Hofius, B. (1992). The effects of genre, visual design choices, and discourse structure on preschoolers' responses to picture books during parent–child read-alouds. In C.K. Kinzer & D.J. Leu (Eds.), *Forty-Fifty Yearbook of the National Reading Conference: Literacy research, theory, and practice: Views from many perspectives*. (pp. 291–301). Chicago: National Reading Conference.

Snow, C. (1983). Literacy and language: Relationships during the preschool years. *Harvard Educational Review*, 53, 165–189.

Snow, C., Burns, M.S. & Griffin, P. (Eds.) (1998). *Preventing reading difficulties in young children*. Washington, DC: National Academy Press.

Sokel, R.R. & Rolf, F.J. (1981). *Biometry*. NY: WH Freeman & Company.

Storch, S. & Whitehurst, G. (2002). Oral language and code-related precursors to reading: Evidence from a longitudinal structural model. *Developmental Psychology*, 38, 934–947.

Stuart, M. (1995). Prediction and qualitative assessment of five- and six-year old children's reading: A longitudinal study. *British Journal of Educational Psychology*, 65, 287–296.

Takahashi, N. (1991). Developmental changes of interest to animated stories in toddlers measured by eye movement while watching them. *Psychologia*, 34, 63–68.

van Kleeck, A. (1998). Preliteracy domains and stages: Laying the foundations for beginning reading. *Journal of Children's Communication Development*, 20, 33–51.

Welsch, J.G., Sullivan, A.K. & Justice, L.M. (2003). That's my name!: What preschoolers' name writing can tell us about emergent literacy knowledge. *Journal of Literacy Research*, 35, 757–776.

Wiig, E.H., Secord, W. & Semel, E. (1992). *Clinical Evaluation of Language Fundamentals – Preschool*. San Antonio, TX: The Psychological Corporation.

Yaden, D.B., Smolkin, L.B. & Conlon, A. (1989). Preschoolers' questions about pictures, print conventions and story text during reading aloud at home. *Reading Research Quarterly*, 24, 188–214.

Yaden, D.B., Smolkin, L.B. & MacGillivray, L. (1993). A psychogenetic perspective on children's understanding about letter associations during alphabet book readings. *Journal of Reading Behavior*, 25(1), 43–68.

Yoshida, N. (1984). Is a visual search changed by training labels? *Japanese Journal of Educational Psychology*, 32, 174–181.

3

Hemispheric division of labour in reading

Richard C. Shillcock and Scott A. McDonald

For a word to be read it must be fixated and the visual information projected to the primary visual cortex, and thence to other parts of the brain, for analysis. Recently there have been suggestions that the anatomical details of this initial projection to the cortex can help us to understand the process of word identification (see, e.g., Shillcock, Ellison & Monaghan, 2000). It has been known for a long time that contra-lateral projection is a major anatomical principle of the nervous system, with each hemisphere directly monitoring and controlling the opposite side of the body. In the visual system, the right hemisphere (RH) directly receives the projection from the left visual field (LVF); conversely, the left hemisphere (LH) monitors the right visual field (RVF). This issue has been argued to be critical for reading because in functional terms the division between the two visual hemifields seems to be very precise: it seems that when a word is fixated, the left part of the word is projected to the RH and the right part to the LH (see Figure 1), even though the word falls into the fovea. The processing of foveated stimuli supports the conclusion that the human fovea is precisely vertically split (for further discussion, see Brysbaert, 2004; Lavidor & Walsh, 2004; Shillcock, Ellison & Monaghan, 2000). If the visual representation of a word is initially divided between the two hemispheres, then we need to be able to say something about how the two halves of the brain interact to achieve effective cognition. Hemispheric interaction is complex and is not well understood; the issue is crosscut by other issues such as hemispheric specialisation, individual differences, gender differences and the analysis of complex tasks – particularly language tasks – into simpler sub-tasks. Although a simple task may be performed more effectively when the relevant stimuli are directly projected to just one hemisphere, the normal brain typically performs more complex tasks more effectively when both hemispheres are able to collaborate in a task, sharing the labour between them (see, e.g., Monaghan & Pollman, 2003). In the current paper we consider the issue of visual word recognition and discuss some implications of the fact that both hemispheres are immediately implicated in the processing of a fixated word.

Shillcock, Ellison and Monaghan (2000) have shown that a range of observed reading behaviours can be interpreted in terms of the equitable division of labour between the two hemispheres. They argued that a fixated word is projected across the fovea, from where the information to the left of fixation is initially projected to the right hemisphere (RH) and the information to the right of fixation to the left hemisphere (LH), so that part of the problem of visual word recognition can be re-conceptualised in terms of the problem of co-ordinating the relevant information in the two hemispheres. They reinterpreted the tendency of readers to fixate towards the (typically more informative) beginning of English words (cf. O'Regan et al., 1984) as a tendency to divide the orthographic

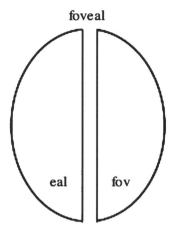

Figure 1. Schematic picture of the projection of the parts of a word to the left and right of fixation to the contralateral hemispheres.

Note: We abstract away from the inversion and the lateral inversion of the visual stimulus.

information evenly between the hemifields. Shillcock, Ellison and Monaghan described an algorithm that divided words at the point that simultaneously minimised the confusion between the left part of all of the words in a large lexicon and between the right part of all of the words in the lexicon, and showed that the algorithm accurately reproduced a number of fixation behaviours observed in the reading of words presented in isolation and in text. Thus, the assumption that the brain was optimally fixating words so as to divide the labour equally between the LH and the RH led to an accurate characterisation of real reading behaviour. More realistically, the study was a demonstration that fixating the centre-left of unidentified English words approximates optimal fixation behaviour for a large proportion of words in the lexicon. In the present paper, we develop a fuller picture of the implications of foveal splitting for visual word recognition.

Further research has reinforced two aspects of this claim regarding the hemispheric division of labour. First, a growing number of studies have confirmed the claim that the human fovea is precisely vertically divided, with subsequent contralateral projection to the primary visual cortex (e.g., Lavidor, 2003; Lavidor, Ellison & Walsh, 2004; Lavidor et al., 2004; Leff, 2004). If there is any direct bilateral projection from the human retina, then it is very small and appears to be of no functional importance (Gazzaniga, 2000). Recognition of a fixated word entails the co-ordination of the information in each hemisphere. We will refer only to the 'co-ordination' of information in the two hemispheres, compared with more explicit terms such as 'transfer'.

The second development to have reinforced the claim regarding the equitable division of labour across the hemispheres comes from the demonstration that the initial fixations on words in normal reading do accurately divide the information contained in a written word (McDonald & Shillcock, 2005). We now describe this demonstration in some detail, as it forms the point of departure for the research we present in this paper. We reproduce the relevant graphs in Figure 2. These graphs were obtained from a corpus of fixation behaviour produced from the reading of English newspaper text (for full details, see McDonald & Shillcock, 2003). To understand these graphs, consider the factors that

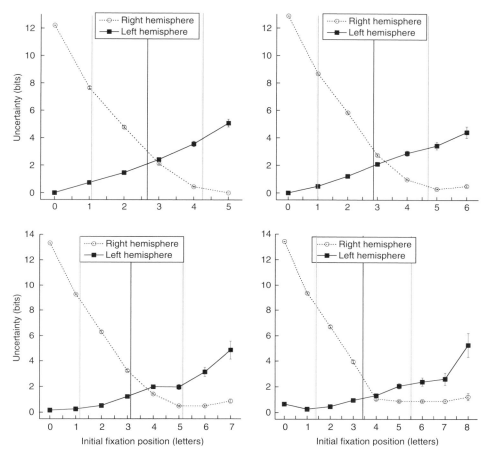

Figure 2. Hemispheric uncertainty (orthographic) plotted against initial fixation position within the word, for words of length five, six, seven and eight letters respectively.

Notes: Bars indicate standard error of the mean (and throughout the following figures). For the first graph (words of length 5), position 0 on the x-axis corresponds to fixation on the space before 'chair', position 1 to fixation on the 'c' of 'chair', position 2 to the 'h', and so on. The black vertical line marks the mean fixation position and the grey vertical lines mark 1 s.d. from the mean (see text for details).

might determine the information profile of English words. Overall, the beginnings of English words tend to be more informative than the latter parts (Bryden et al., 1990; Farid & Grainger, 1996), with the relative complexities of onsets and codas and the relative numbers of prefixes and suffixes contributing to the pattern. Figure 2 shows the effects of fixating words in text in normal reading. Consider the dotted line in Figure 2, representing the RH's uncertainty about the identity of the fixated word (calculated for fixations at the relevant points in five-letter words in a corpus of eye movements, and with respect to a large lexicon). (Details of the calculation of uncertainty are provided below.) When participants fixated on the space immediately before a five-letter word, then uncertainty is very high: the RH cannot yet have directly received any information about the critical word at all. For other cases in which five-letter words were fixated progressively further rightwards (with a six-letter forward visual span for letter identification), the RH knows more and more about the word, as the beginning letters are progressively revealed. When the final letter position is fixated, then the RH knows the identity of all of the last four letters of the word (the backwards visual span is four character spaces wide) and RH uncertainty is very low. Thus, the RH curve in Figure 2 summarises the uncertainty in the RH about the five-letter words when they were fixated at different positions by participants in the course of reading the corpus.

Conversely, uncertainty grows in the LH the further the fixation point is from the left end of the word. Critically, the data summarised in these graphs assume trans-saccadic integration of letter information: any information that either hemisphere knows about the critical word from the previous fixation(s) is integrated with the information that hemisphere gains from the current fixation; the graphs in Figure 2 summarise uncertainty about lexical identity for words of particular length for real reading of the text, as opposed to considering the words in isolation. Thus, the LH can take advantage of any parafoveal preview of the beginning of the word; without such trans-saccadic integration the slope of the LH uncertainty would be steeper and displaced slightly to the left. The overall effect of calculating hemispheric uncertainty with a large lexicon and with a psychologically-plausible estimate of visual span (and hence parafoveal preview) is to keep the cross-over point – at which LH and RH uncertainty are equal – just to the left of the centre of the word, resembling the informational midpoint calculated with isolated words (Shillcock, Ellison & Monaghan, 2000).

In the graphs in Figure 2, the vertical line represents the observed mean initial fixation position for that set of words. Overall, we see that the observed mean fixation location is close to the cross-over point.[1] The claim regarding an equal hemispheric division of labour is confirmed by these graphs. We can also see that there is a consistent tendency across all four word lengths for the mean initial fixation position to fall to the left of the cross-over point, thereby favouring the LH with slightly lower uncertainty. The LH has typically been seen as the more important hemisphere for visual word recognition (see Cohen et al., 2000, for a recent restatement of this observation); the preference for slightly lower uncertainty in the LH may therefore be seen as adaptive.

In the current paper we elaborate on this picture of the hemispheric division of labour in the reading of English. The calculations we have described above, and illustrated in Figure 2, effectively take the orthographic identity of the word as a shorthand representation for the lexical entry: if the RH has the letters 'syz' of a six-letter word, then it has solved the problem of lexical access and knows that the word is 'syzygy'. The studies we have described ignore the phonological and semantic processing that may be occurring on the basis of the orthographic information in each hemisphere.

We assume that normal recognition of a word entails both halves of the brain having established the identity of the word, perhaps with reference to their own particular processing propensities. There is considerable scope for variation in the processing that co-ordinates the orthographic, phonological and semantic identity of the fixated word, both within and between the hemispheres, reflecting variation between individuals in the lateralisation of different types of processing, variation between languages in the complexity of orthographic and phonological form, variation in the inherent speed and ease of these different types of processing and variation in the efficiency of inter-hemispheric (primarily callosal) transfer. In the current study, we aim to clarify some of the principles by which orthographic, phonological and semantic information are co-ordinated inter-hemispherically during reading. We explore the nature of the hemispheric division of labour in these three domains in a population of skilled readers of English in a naturalistic reading task. Lastly, we will explore some of the implications concerning impaired reading.

The null hypothesis in this study is illustrated by considering the processing that might be elicited by the word 'proud'. It is clear that, as we consider each possible view of the word that each hemisphere might receive, depending on where it was fixated – p, pr, pro, prou, proud, roud, oud, ud, d – that more information about the orthographic identity of the word leads to more information about the phonological and semantic identities of that word. Under the null hypothesis, the semantic and phonological identities of the word – when viewed from the two hemispheres – are equally tied to the orthographic identity of the word and there is no relation between the cross-over points in their uncertainty-by-position–by–hemifield curves and the observed mean initial fixation position.

We know from the grapheme-phoneme rules of English that there are complexities in the letter-by-letter mapping from letters to phonemes: several letters may comprise a single grapheme, 'sw' becoming /s/ in 'sword', for instance. It is an empirical question as to how these complexities feature in the hemifield processing windows proposed in the model of visual word recognition we are currently exploring. Similarly, there is obscure structure at and below the morphological level when we consider how words behave semantically and syntactically. The letters 'pro' in 'proud' fortuitously correspond to a prefix, but it is again an empirical question as to how the different 'pro'-initial words, both prefixed and pseudo-prefixed, cluster in semantic terms. Suffixing begs similar questions: compare *sing* and *talking, walking, speaking* .... The analyses we present below are the first exploration of how psychologically plausible semantic representations pattern with orthographic and phonological representations, and of the implications for reading. If the resulting hemifield profiles of the semantic and phonological information are dissimilar in relation to the observed mean fixation position, then they may suggest alternative ways in which readers whose orthographic processing is sub-optimal may co-ordinate lexical information across the hemispheres.

Method

We calculated each hemisphere's uncertainty (cf. Underwood, Clews & Everatt, 1990) regarding the orthographic, the phonological and the semantic representation of the word or part word falling in the relevant hemifield. When these measures of uncertainty were applied to the words in the text of the EMBRA corpus, a corpus of eye movements recorded from 23 native speakers of British English, reading some 2300 words of contemporary journalism (see McDonald & Shillcock, 2003, for further details), they allowed us to compare the observed behaviour with the profiles of orthographic, phonological and semantic uncertainty as defined for each hemisphere under explicit plausible assumptions concerning the size of the visual span, foveal splitting, the rapid availability of word-length information to both hemispheres and the integration of letter information across saccades.

The calculation of orthographic uncertainty used information about the length of the word and the identity of the visible letters.[2] Thus, if the RH can see the first three letters 'dwa' of a five-letter word, then the word 'dwarf' is identified if it is the only word-initial match in the lexicon, and uncertainty is zero; if 'dwale' were also in the lexicon, then the number of matching candidates would be two and uncertainty about its identity would be non-zero. The lexicon used was the CELEX English database (Baayen, Pipenbrock & Gulikers, 1995). The uncertainty (H), measured in bits, was calculated as the $\log_2$ of the number of candidates in the lexicon that could match the letter and length information available to a particular hemisphere. Thus, for instance, H is 0 when there is enough information to identify uniquely the word, and it is 1 when there are two alternatives, as in our 'dwarf/dwale' example. Trans-saccadic integration of letter information was implemented by pooling the letters available on successive fixations, as, for instance, when the initial letters of a word are perceptible via parafoveal preview prior to fixation on that word (a visual span of six character spaces to the right of fixation and four character spaces to the left of fixation was used, within which letters were assumed to be perceptible).

The calculation of phonological uncertainty was based on the number of possible pronunciations of the part word visible to a particular hemisphere. This measure was computed as the base-2 logarithm of the number of real words that are consistent with the possible phoneme sequences that map to the available orthographic information. Specifically, the set of grapheme-to-phoneme correspondence rules employed in the DRC model (Coltheart et al., 2001) were implemented in conjunction with the citation-form pronunciations present in CELEX (i.e. including the irregular correspondences not in the GPC rules) to produce a set of potential pronunciations for a given letter sequence (e.g. at least three mappings are possible for the sequence 'ough' isolated in one hemifield: the vowels in *thorough*, *through* and *enough*). Note that context-sensitive, one-to-many and many-to-one mappings between grapheme(s) and phoneme(s) characteristic of English meant that although coverage of our rule set was high, it was not complete. (By analysing the phonological implications of the letters projected to the LH and RH, we are not making any assumptions about the phonological knowledge that may or may not reside in either hemisphere; rather, we are exploring the nature of the problem.)

The calculation of semantic uncertainty was based on lexical co-occurrence vectors derived from the British National Corpus (see McDonald, 2000, for further methodological details). Briefly, a co-occurrence vector is a representation of a word's contexts of use, compiled by counting the number of times each of a designated set of 'context words' occurs within the immediate vicinity of the word of interest, over millions of words of text. Co-occurrence vectors for words similar in meaning tend to be similar, as assessed using standard geometric similarity or distance measures (cf. Lund & Burgess, 1996; McDonald, 2000). We use the term 'semantic' to refer to the information encoded in these vectors, recognising that they embody a blend of semantic and syntactic information. Thus, if only the initial letter d of a five-letter word is visible to the RH, for instance, the semantic constraint is negligible, as the 'meaning' of the word can be that of any five-letter word beginning with d. As possible fixation positions further to the right are considered, the coherence of the contextual information will reflect both the size of the 'cohort' of word candidates, and any (quasi-)morphological structure in that cohort.

Semantic uncertainty was expressed in terms of the mean normalised cluster coherence of the vectors corresponding to the words that matched the letter information present in a particular hemifield. Coherence was computed separately for each hemisphere as the average of the normalised cosine[3] of the angle between each candidate word's vector and a centroid vector formed by summing the vectors for the entire candidate set. Thus, coherence will tend to be higher – and thus semantic uncertainty will be lower – for a set of candidates sharing aspects of meaning (i.e. appearing in similar contexts) than for candidates with little overlap in meaning. Lastly, we excluded cases in which only one word from the lexicon matched the visible letters, to avoid artificially inflating the coherence measure.

Results and discussion

Figure 3 shows hemispheric semantic uncertainty, in terms of the mean normalised cluster coherence measure, plotted against fixation position for words of length five to eight respectively.[4] The four graphs show the predictable pattern of intersecting curves; as more of the word is revealed to a hemisphere, uncertainty tends to fall (indicated by a rise in mean normalised cluster coherence). A comparison of the four graphs reveals the effects of increasing morphological complexity interacting with the size of the visual span available to the hemisphere. The curves for the shortest, five-letter words change monotonically, resembling the corresponding curves for orthographic identity in the first graph of Figure 1; this resemblance may be grounded in the relationship between semantic coherence and number of words involved, for these shorter words. This quality is lost in the curves for the longer words, which include a larger proportion of

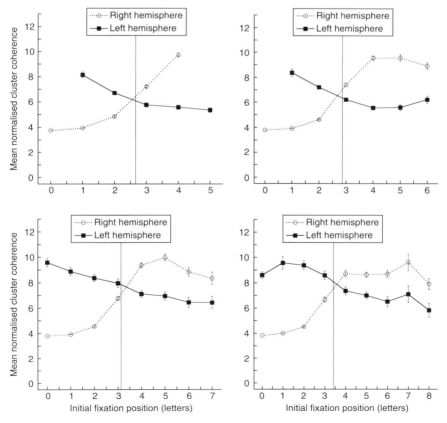

Figure 3. Hemispheric uncertainty (semantic) plotted against initial fixation position within the word, for words of length five, six, seven and eight letters, respectively.

morphologically complex words and for which the end letters are beyond the visual span for letter recognition. The pairs of curves are each asymmetrical. There is greater disparity between the two curves on the left-hand side of each graph, compared with the right-hand side, reflecting the fact that in the left-hand fixation positions the RH has little information about the identity of the word compared with the LH, which has a good view of the word, whereas in the right-hand fixation positions the RH has a good view of the word but the LH has information about the word from parafoveal preview from the previous fixation(s). This asymmetry, and the reasons for it, applies across all the graphs shown, for all three different domains of processing.

The most striking aspect of Figure 3 is the fact that the mean fixation point is again close to the cross-over point between the two curves. At the point of the cross-over, uncertainty in the two hemispheres is equal and hemispheric co-ordination of information is by definition optimised. In the case of the five- and six-letter words, the disparity between the mean fixation point and the cross-over point is in the direction of providing the RH with less uncertainty (i.e. greater cluster coherence). Thus the shorter words – which Figures 2 and 3 show are associated with greater uncertainty at the cross-over – have complementary LH and RH advantages for orthographic and semantic representations respectively. In contrast, Figure 3 shows that mean fixation point of the seven- and eight-letter words is to the left of the cross-over, favouring the LH. Overall, there is an equitable division of semantic labour between the hemispheres, resembling the division in the orthographic domain, and with a slight asymmetry in the direction seen in the orthographic domain for the longer two words and in a complementary direction for the shorter two words.

Figure 4 shows the curves of hemispheric uncertainty against letter position for uncertainty about the phonological interpretation of the letters visible to each hemisphere.[5] The graphs all show closely convergent, low levels of phonological uncertainty in the right-hand part of the word (apart from the unrepresentative final letter position) and a bump in the left-hand part of the word, in which there is increased phonological uncertainty in the RH. This bump represents the unfolding, across letter position, of the structure of the nucleus of the first syllable of the word; in our earlier *proud* example, there is marginal phonological ambiguity regarding the *p* (the first letter of the onset could be /p/, whether or not it is part of a cluster, or it could be /f/ or /s/ as in *ph* and *psy*, respectively) but there is substantial ambiguity in the pronunciation of the *o* of the nucleus. For the LH, the level of phonological uncertainty tends to increase slightly across letter position, from left to right across the word. The vertical line again shows the mean fixation position, and in each of the graphs of Figure 4, it falls to the left – often substantially so – of the cross-over point (or region) in the right of the word. (Note that the first letter of the word may also be construed as a cross-over point, at least for some word lengths.) At each of the mean fixation points, there is less uncertainty in the LH than the RH.

Overall, then, we reject the null hypothesis that the semantic and phonological domains pattern similarly and equally distantly from the orthographic domain, in these characteristic graphs charting the hemispheric division of labour. The orthographic and semantic graphs resemble each other closely, particularly in the closeness of the cross-over point to the mean fixation location. There is a limited indication of a complementary division of labour between these two domains. In contrast, the curves for the phonological domain differ from the other two domains. Overall, there is a tendency to provide the LH with lower uncertainty in each of the domains.

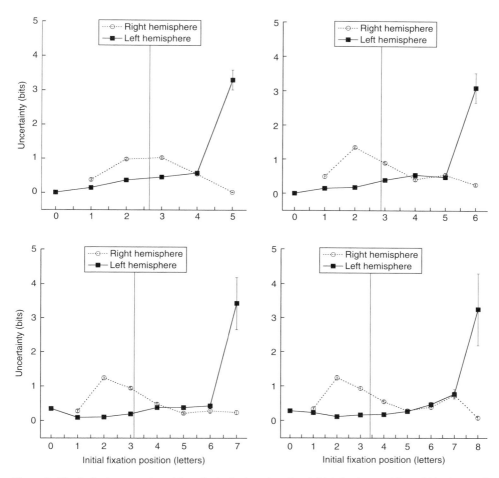

Figure 4. Hemispheric uncertainty (phonological) plotted against initial fixation position within the word, for words of length five, six, seven and eight letters, respectively.

What are the implications for reading impairment? First, the fact that the orthographic and semantic curves pattern so similarly is reason for claiming that if there is any impairment in the inter-hemispheric co-ordination of orthographic information, a natural compensatory strategy is to rely on the semantic domain. One interpretation of phonological dyslexia is that there is impaired inter-hemispheric co-ordination of orthographic information due to hemispheric de-synchronisation and a subsequent reliance on integrating the relevant partially activated semantic representations in the two hemispheres to establish the identity of the fixated word; this model of phonological dyslexia resembles that proposed in the connectionist tradition (e.g. Plaut et al., 1996) in which the mapping between orthographic and phonological representations is impaired, but it grounds the impairment in callosal transfer (cf. Davidson & Saron, 1992). There is far greater 'bandwidth' available in the human corpus callosum for the transfer of semantically-related information compared with visual information. Figures 2 and 3 indicate that this 'semantic strategy' is a natural back-up strategy given the contours of the problem, potentially leading to apparently high functioning reading behaviour for known words, but the characteristic inability to compile the pronunciation of unknown words or nonwords; indeed, it is reasonable to see such inter-hemispheric co-ordination of semantic information as a component of normal reading behaviour (cf. the division of labour in connectionist models of word naming (see Seidenberg, 1995, for discussion)).

A second implication for dyslexic reading concerns the word-initial convergence in hemispheric uncertainty seen in Figure 4. We have recently reported a tendency among dyslexics to fixate significantly further to the left in words, and to have initial single fixation durations comparable with those of normal readers at fixation positions just before the word and on the first letter of the word, but significantly longer fixations further rightwards into the word (Kelly et al., 2004). These behaviours are consistent with a number of models of reading impairment, in which processing is advantaged in the LH/RVF, and disadvantaged in the RH/LVF, and in which hemispheric interaction is sub-optimal. What would be the implications of a leftward shift in initial fixation position in the current analyses? In the orthographic and the semantic domains, a leftward shift would predictably decrease uncertainty in the LH and increase it in the RH. The longer fixation durations produced by the dyslexic readers for more rightward fixation positions correspond to increased uncertainty in the LH, and to decreased uncertainty in the RH. If the LH typically has some degree of priority in lexical processing (see, e.g., Cohen et al., 2000), then it may be advantageous to provide the LH with less uncertainty in a sub-optimal processor. In the phonological domain, the shallow slopes of LH uncertainty in Figure 4 suggest a limited advantage to be found in decreased uncertainty in the LH. A leftward movement in the distribution of initial fixation position would move some of the fixations onto the first letter of the word, projecting relatively unambiguous phonological implications to the LH and also coinciding with the word-initial cross-over point in Figure 4; the rest of the distribution of fixations would result in increased phonological uncertainty in the RH. (There may also be some advantage in denying the RH any purchase on a phonological interpretation, from the perspective of Orton (1937), in which reading development is seen as a progressive disengagement of the RH from processing.)

Lastly, we have concentrated on the nature of the problem of identifying visually presented words and we have only referred briefly to the fact that there is a complex, often idiosyncratic pattern of lateralisation of function in the human brain. Do such lateralisations render irrelevant the differences in hemispheric information we have described? For instance, does the fact that phonological processing is typically seen as being substantially left lateralised mean that there is no point in discussing the RH's uncertainty about the phonological representations implied by the part of the fixated word that it can see? We claim that the initial projection of information from the divided fovea to the divided brain fundamentally conditions the nature of the problem of word recognition. The information that is projected to the precisely divided primary visual cortex is the most authentic, authoritative representation available to the visual system about what is being fixated. Visual processing seems to involve both very fast conduction through the visual system and access to frontal areas (e.g. Foxe & Simpson, 2002; Thorpe, Fize & Marlot, 1996) and slower recurrent processing (e.g. VanEssen & Felleman, 1991) (see, e.g., Lamme, 2003, for further discussion). This view of the processing of visually presented words is compatible with a model in which the initial division of information between the hemifields exerts a continuing influence on the processes of word recognition. There is evidence for early contact with areas associated with phonological processing in visual word recognition (see, e.g., Pammer et al., 2004), and in reading (e.g. Inhoff & Topolski, 1994), and early contact with semantic areas in visual processing (Thorpe, Fize & Marlot, 1996), and it is reasonable to assume that direct projection to the relevant hemisphere facilitates processing in that hemisphere. Thus, even if phonological processing were seen as completely located in the LH we could still distinguish between phonological processing based on information directly projected to that hemisphere and phonological processing based on information derived from callosal interaction, in effect importing the hemifield split into intra-hemispheric processing. Thus, it is potentially illuminating to determine the nature of the problem of visual word recognition as it relates to the hemifields, distinct from any consideration of special processing priorities that the hemispheres might have in particular representational domains. It remains an empirical question as to how hemifield specialisations in orthographic processing (e.g. Cohen et al., 2000), phonological processing (e.g. Ivry & Lebby, 1998) and semantic processing (e.g. Beeman et al., 1994) might impinge upon the solution to the problem of visual word recognition.

Conclusions

We have used hemifield/hemisphere-based measures of uncertainty about the orthographic, phonological and semantic identity of the fixated word to theorise about the relationship between these domains in reading. We began with the principle that an equitable hemispheric division of labour is desirable. Our results have shown that this principle coexists with a tendency to prioritise processing in the LH. The precise relationship between these two principles may be a complex one. It may be that there are critical differences in the profiles of intra-hemispheric and inter-hemispheric processing between different tasks, between different individuals, between different words, between different orthographies and between different languages. As a case in point, the shallow orthography of a language such as Spanish suggests a closer relationship between the orthographic and phonological domains as they are expressed in terms of the information available to each hemifield.

An equitable hemispheric division of labour in both the normal and the dyslexic reader may be desirable as a means of devoting more processing resources to a difficult problem, and as a means of generating intersecting sets of solutions based on different problem-solving parameters. More generally, it may reflect a strategy by which the brain minimises the necessity for inter-hemispheric transfer by exposing each hemisphere directly to the relevant information as it exists in the world, showing both hemispheres as much of the fixated word as possible as opposed to letting one hemisphere see more of the word and then relying on callosal transfer to inform the other hemisphere. Facilitating hemispheric interaction may be particularly important for the dyslexics, given that they may have atypical hemispheric transfer.

Acknowledgements

The first author was supported by ESRC fellowship R/000/27/1244. The second author was supported by Wellcome Trust grant GR064240AIA.

Notes

1. Elsewhere, we have claimed that separate populations of pre-planned refixations may be partly responsible for fixations falling further left of this optimal point (see McDonald & Shillcock, 2004).
2. We have conservatively assumed that word length is known across the hemispheric divide. The role of word length is currently controversial with an argument being made for word identification being independent of word length information (see Inhoff & Eiter, 2003; Inhoff et al., 2003). However, we have found a better fit with empirical data concerning landing position in eye movements by using uncertainty measures that incorporate word length (McDonald & Shillcock, 2005).
3. It is vital to use a normalisation technique in order to compare validly two words that vary substantially in corpus frequency, because the cosine is sensitive to vector sparseness (all else being equal, the cosine tends to be smaller the more sparse the co-occurrence vector).
4. In the top two panels of Figure 3 (i.e. word lengths of five and six) we omit the leftmost point for the LH curve because the whole word is visible to the LH and uncertainty is therefore zero. This point is not zero in the bottom panels of Figure 3 because the six-letter visual span may occlude some of the last letters of the words.
5. In Figure 4, we omit the leftmost point of the RH's curve as there is no meaningful measure of uncertainty, given that the left visual field contains no letter information.

References

Baayen, R.H., Pipenbrock, R. & Gulikers, L. (1995). *The CELEX Lexical Database (CD-ROM)*. Philadelphia, PA: Linguistic Data Consortium, University of Pennsylvania.

Beeman, M., Friedman, R.B., Grafman, E. & Perez, E. (1994). Summation priming and coarse semantic coding in the right hemisphere. *Journal of Cognitive Neuroscience*, 6, 26–45.

Brysbaert, M. (2004). The importance of interhemispheric transfer for foveal vision: A factor that has been overlooked in theories of visual word recognition and object perception. *Brain and Language*, 88, 259–267.

Bryden, M.P., Mondor, T.A., Loken, M., Ingleton, M.A. & Bergstrom, K. (1990). Locus of information in words and the right visual field effect. *Brain & Cognition*, 14, 44–58.

Cohen, L., Dehaene, S., Naccache, L., Lehéricy, S., Dehaene-Lambertz, G., Hénaff, M.A. & Michel, F. (2000). The visual word form area: Spatial and temporal characterization of an initial stage of reading in normal subjects and posterior split-brain patients. *Brain*, 123, 291–307.

Coltheart, M., Rastle, K., Perry, C., Langdon, R. & Ziegler, J. (2001). The DRC model: A model of visual word recognition and reading aloud. *Psychological Review*, 108, 204–258.

Davidson, R.J. & Saron, C.D. (1992). Evoked potential measures of interhemispheric transfer time in reading disabled and normal boys. *Developmental Neuropsychology*, 8, 261–277.

Farid, M. & Grainger, J. (1996). How initial fixation position influences visual word recognition: A comparison of French and Arabic. *Brain and Language*, 53, 351–368.

Foxe, J.J. & Simpson, G.V. (2002). Flow of activation from V1 to frontal cortex in humans: A framework for defining 'early' visual processing. *Experimental Brain Research*, 142, 139–150.

Gazzaniga, M.S. (2000). Cerebral specialization and interhemispheric communication. *Brain*, 123, 1293–1326.

Inhoff, A.W. & Eiter, B. (2003). Knowledge of word length does not constrain word identification. *Psychological Research*, 67, 1–9.

Inhoff, A.W. & Topolski, R. (1994). Use of phonological codes during eye fixations in reading and in on-line and delayed naming task. *Journal of Memory and Language*, 36, 505–529.

Inhoff, A.W., Radach, R., Eiter, B. & Juhasz, B. (2003). Parafoveal processing: Distinct sub-systems for spatial and linguistic information. *Quarterly Journal of Experimental Psychology*, 56, 803–827.

Ivry, R. & Lebby, P.C. (1998). The neurology of consonant perception: Specialized module or distributed processor? In M. Beeman & C. Chiarello (Eds.), *Right hemisphere language comprehension: Perspectives from Cognitive Neuroscience*. Mahwah, NJ: Lawrence Erlbaum Associates.

Kelly, M.L., Jones, M.W., McDonald, S.A. & Shillcock, R.C. (2004). Dyslexics' eye fixations may accommodate to hemispheric desynchronisation. *NeuroReport*, 15, 2629–2632.

Lamme, V.A.F. (2003). Why visual attention and awareness are different. *Trends in Cognitive Science*, 7, 12–18.

Lavidor, M. (2003). Cortical representation of the fovea: Implications for visual half-field research. A reply to Annukka L. Lindell and Michael E.R. Nicholls. *Cortex*, 39, 118–120.

Lavidor, M., Ellison, A. & Walsh, V. (2003). Examination of a split-processing model of visual word recognition: A magnetic stimulation study. *Visual Cognition*, 10, 341–362.

Lavidor, M. & Walsh, V. (2004). The nature of foveal representation. *Nature Reviews Neuroscience*, 5, 729–735.

Lavidor, M., Hayes, A., Shillcock, R. & Ellis, A.W. (2004). Evaluating a split processing model of visual word recognition: Effects of orthographic neighborhood size. *Brain and Language*, 88, 312–320.

Leff, A. (2004). A historical review of the representation of the visual field in primary visual cortex with special reference to the neural mechanisms underlying macular sparing. *Brain and Language*, 88, 268–278.

Lund, K. & Burgess, C. (1996). Producing high-dimensional semantic spaces from lexical co-occurrence. *Behavior Research Methods, Instruments & Computers*, 28, 203–208.

McDonald, S. (2000). *Environmental determinants of lexical processing effort*. PhD thesis, University of Edinburgh.

McDonald, S.A. & Shillcock, R.C. (2003). Low-level predictive inference in reading: The influence of transitional probabilities on eye movements. *Vision Research*, 43, 1735–1751.

McDonald, S.A. & Shillcock, R.C. (2004). The potential contribution of preplanned refixations to the preferred viewing location. *Perception & Psychophysics*, 66, 1033–1044.

McDonald, S.A. & Shillcock, R.C. (2005). The implications of foveal splitting for saccade planning in reading. *Vision Research*, 45, 801–820.

Monaghan, P. & Pollmann, S. (2003). Division of labour between the hemispheres for complex but not simple tasks: An implemented connectionist model. *Journal of Experimental Psychology: General*, 132, 379–399.

O'Regan, J.K., Lévy-Schoen, A., Pynte, J. & Brugaillère, B. (1984). Convenient fixation location within isolated words of different lengths and structure. *Journal of Experimental Psychology: Human Perception & Performance*, 10, 250–257.

Orton, S.T. (1937). *Reading, writing and speech problems in children and selected papers*. Baltimore: The International Dyslexia Association.

Pammer, K., Hansen, P.C., Kringelbach, M.L., Holliday, I., Barnes, G., Hillebrand, A., Singh, K.D. & Cornelissen, P.L. (2004). Visual word recognition: The first half second. *Neuroimage*, 22, 1819–1825.

Plaut, D.C., McClelland, J.L., Seidenberg, M.S. & Patterson, K. (1996). Understanding normal and impaired word reading: Computational principles in quasi-regular domains. *Psychological Review*, 103, 56–115.

Seidenberg, M.S. (1995). Visual word recognition: An overview. In J. Miller & P. Eimas (Eds.), *Speech, language, and communication*. New York: Academic Press.

Shillcock, R., Ellison, T.M. & Monaghan, P. (2000). Eye-fixation behaviour, lexical storage and visual word recognition in a split processing model. *Psychological Review*, 107, 824–851.

Thorpe, S., Fize, D. & Marlot, C. (1996). Speed of processing in the human visual system. *Nature*, 381, 520–522.

Underwood, G., Clews, S. & Everatt, J. (1990). How do readers know where to look next? Local information distributions influence eye fixations. *Quarterly Journal of Experimental Psychology*, 42, 39–65.

VanEssen, D.C. & Felleman, D.J. (1991). Distributed hierarchical processing in the primate cerebral cortex. *Cerebral Cortex*, 1, 1–47.

4

Dissociations between serial position and number of letters effects in lateralised visual word recognition

Michal Lavidor and Peter J. Bailey

Visual word recognition performance in skilled reading varies systematically with the location of the word in the visual field. For example, performance varies with retinal eccentricity, as visual acuity decreases on either side of the fixation point, even within the fovea (Nazir, Heller & Sussman, 1992). Word recognition performance has also been reported to vary between the two visual hemifields, with a typical right visual field (RVF) advantage with right-handed subjects (Ellis, Young & Anderson, 1988; Iacoboni & Zaidel, 1996).

Several studies of visual word recognition have reported an interaction between visual hemifield (VHF) and word length, such that the number of letters in a word has a stronger effect on performance for words presented in the left visual field (LVF) than for words presented in the right visual field (RVF) (Bouma, 1973; Gill & McKeever, 1974). This result has been reported for measures of lexical decision latency (Bub & Lewine, 1988; Chiarello, 1988; Ellis, Young & Anderson, 1988; Iacoboni & Zaidel, 1996; Weekes et al., 1999), word identification accuracy (Young & Ellis, 1985) and semantic decision latency (Ellis, Young & Anderson, 1988). However, the smaller effect of length in the RVF only occurred when words were presented in a standard, horizontal format. Distorting the format, for example by rotating the letters (Babkoff, Faust & Lavidor, 1997), using mixed case (Lavidor & Ellis, 2001) or presenting words vertically (Bub & Lewine, 1988; Ellis, Young & Anderson, 1988), led to equivalent word-length effects in both hemifields. Similarly, measures based on report of nonwords also showed equivalent length effects in both hemifields (Bub & Lewine, 1988; Ellis, Young & Anderson, 1988; Weekes et al., 1999).

A model of visual word recognition consistent with this pattern of results has been proposed (Bub & Lewine, 1988; Ellis, Young & Anderson, 1988; Iacoboni & Zaidel, 1996; Young & Ellis, 1985), involving two modes. One mode operates independent of string length and is seen only in the left hemisphere (LH/RVF) analysis of familiar words in familiar formats, while a second mode is length dependent, is the only mode possessed by the right hemisphere (RH/LVF) and is employed by the LH when processing nonwords and familiar words in unusual formats. In this model, length effects are not primarily the result of serial, left-to-right processing, but rather reflect increasingly poor performance on letters in the middle of strings as length increases (Ellis, Young &

Anderson, 1988). This could result from 'ends-in scanning' (Bradshaw et al., 1977) or increasing lateral inhibition with increasing number of letters (Estes, 1972).

As with right visual-field presentation, word length also has little influence on performance when words are fixated at their centre, despite the fact that every additional letter in the word moves the extreme letters of the word further out into retinal regions of lower resolution. The absence of word-length effects in RVF and central position found with skilled readers contrasts with the findings of studies with beginning readers, which have shown that a word-length effect is present in children in the early stages of reading acquisition, but diminishes slowly over the first five years of reading practice (Aghababian & Nazir, 2000). Hence, something about words is acquired between first grade and skilled reading which overcomes (some) limits of acuity, and equalises performance for short and longer words.

The possibility that perceptual learning processes are involved in the acquisition of reading skills may offer another possible explanation for the observed visual field effects in the perception of print. Reading-specific visual pattern memories may develop even at very early stages of processing (Gilbert, 1994), and may explain some of the variation in observed visual field effects. According to Nazir (2000), perceptual learning occurs during processing of print, hence reading practice leads to improvement in performance. However, this improvement appears to depend on the precise configuration of the stimulus, including its orientation and location in the visual field (Ahissar & Hochstein, 1996, 1997; Dill & Fahle, 1998; Nazir & O'Regan, 1990). Thus, participants who learned to recognise an unfamiliar visual pattern displayed at one location on the retina may be better at recognising this pattern when displayed at the trained location than when displayed at other locations in the visual field (Ahissar & Hochstein, 1996; Nazir & O'Regan, 1990). Nazir (2000) suggested that similar preferences for the trained location may also influence reading processes. Statistics of where readers locate their initial fixations in words during natural reading indicate that the distribution of the position of the landing site of the eye in words is asymmetric. Thus, independent of word length, there is a tendency for the eye to land slightly before the centre of a word, and the probability of fixating the beginning of a word is higher than the probability of fixating the last half of the word (e.g. Rayner, 1979). Although ongoing linguistic processing modulates eye-movement behaviour during text reading (Rayner, Sereno & Raney, 1996), most authors agree that the location in a word where the eye lands initially is mainly determined by low-level or visuo-motor factors (Vitu et al., 1995). That is, the tendency for the eye to land slightly before the centre of words is essentially a consequence of moving the eye rapidly through the stimulus array by using coarse visual information such as the spaces between words to guide saccades (Rayner, 1998). Given that during natural reading the majority of words are fixated only once (Rayner & Pollatsek, 1989), these landing-site distributions provide a rough estimation of the frequency with which words are displayed at a given location on the retina. When word recognition performance is considered, it turns out that accuracy varies with fixation location in the same way as the frequency of initial fixation. Performance is best when the word is fixated slightly before the centre (this point of fixation was termed the 'optimal viewing position' by O'Regan and Levy-Schoen, 1987), and scores are higher for fixations at the beginning compared to the end of words. The relationship between the pattern of retinal exposure and recognition performance suggests that some kind of early perceptual learning may develop with reading experience (Nazir, 2000; Nazir, Jacobs & O'Regan, 1998).

The probability of landing at the beginning of a word is similar for words of different lengths, but the frequency of landing at the end of a word decreases significantly as words become longer. Note that when words are fixated at the beginning, all letters apart from the fixated letter are in the RVF. When words are fixated at the end, most letters are in the LVF. Thus Nazir (2000) argued that the length effects found in the LVF, but not in the RVF, might depend on the frequency of having read printed words of various lengths displayed at different retinal locations. Since the preference to fixate on the first letters (leading to RVF presentation) is not sensitive to word length, word recognition performance is insensitive to word length in the RVF, but performance decreases as word length increases in the LVF.

Another account for the hemifields and word-length interaction, by Brysbaert (1994), suggested that differences in processing times between the two visual fields reflect inter-hemispheric transmission times. By this account the word-length effect in the LVF arises because when longer words are presented to the LVF more letters must be transferred from the RH to the language-expert LH, leading to longer reaction times for longer words presented to the left, but not right visual fields. However, this account requires that word recognition is done exclusively by the LH, a position that is currently less widely accepted than the notion that there are distinct processing modes in the two hemispheres (Ellis, 2004).

Recently Jordan, Patching and Milner (2000) challenged the basis for the proposal of two processing modes with data from an experiment concerned with serial position effects in both hemifields, using the Reicher-Wheeler task for four-letter words (Reicher, 1969; Wheeler, 1970). In this procedure, each presentation of a (lateralised) word stimulus is immediately followed by a forced choice between two alternative letters, each of which forms a legal word at a specific position in the context of the other letters in the target word; the participant's task is to choose the letter that was presented in the original target word. For example, recognition of the letter in word-final position following presentation of *king* may be tested by asking participants to choose between the letters *g* and *d*. The pattern of results reported by Jordan, Patching and Milner (2000) showed performance in the Reicher-Wheeler paradigm to follow an inverted U-shaped function with letter position and, critically for the present purposes, to be similar in both visual fields. The authors argued that this was inconsistent with the two-mode model, which they interpreted as predicting that the LVF length-sensitive mode should show a monotonic drop in performance from first to last position, whereas the parallel orthographic analysis characteristic of LH processing for RVF words in a standard format should give identical levels of performance across all letter positions. In defence of the two-mode model, one may note that this prediction depends on a particular interpretation of the serial nature of the process which, as noted above, Ellis, Young and Anderson (1988) argued does not necessarily imply 'serial left-to-right'.

A distinctive feature of the Jordan, Patching and Milner (2000) approach was their task, which has not previously been used in studies of word-length and visual field interactions. They argued that the letter search task is well suited to test hemispheric differences in orthographic analysis, but it remains unclear why length and hemifield interactions have been such a common finding in previous studies that have used other tasks.

The experiments reported here were designed to test the hypothesis that this difference in outcome may be attributable in part to the different experimental tasks employed. We also investigated the assumption that the effects of number of letters (the traditional operational measure for effects of word length) in the two visual fields are similar to the effects of serial position.

   To test this hypothesis, two experiments were conducted, both of which used the same set of words. In the first experiment participants were given a letter-search task (Maxfield, 1997) and in the second experiment the task was lexical decision. In both experiments words (and nonwords for Experiment 2) of different lengths (four and seven letters) were presented to the left and right visual fields. It was predicted that serial position effects would be similar in the two hemifields when the task was letter search (Experiment 1), in accordance with Jordan, Patching and Milner (2000), and that the typical word length by hemifield interaction would be obtained when the task was lexical decision (Experiment 2) in line with previous findings (Bub & Lewine, 1988; Ellis, Young & Anderson, 1988; Lavidor & Ellis, 2001, 2002). Crucially, the use of two different word lengths in the letter-search task (Experiment 1) enabled a critical examination of the effects in the two hemifields of serial position and the number of letters: if they are the result of the same mental processes, then both hemispheres should show the predicted inverted-U shape performance with serial position to the same extent for both word lengths (four- and seven-letter words). However, if effects of serial position and number of letters reflect separate underlying processes, they should differ in their pattern in the two visual hemifields; specifically, effects of serial position should be similar in the two hemifields, consistent with Jordan, Patching and Milner (2000), but for word length an interaction should be expected with hemifields, consistent with the two-mode model. The novelty of the current research was to use a letter-search task to explore a potential dissociation between effects of serial position and number of letters by manipulating both in the same experiment.

Experiment 1

Experiment 1 was designed to explore the effects of number of letters and the serial position of letters in the right and left visual fields. Since the intent was to assess these effects for words of substantially different lengths, the Reicher-Wheeler procedure was not optimal, because there are relatively few seven-letter words that differ in only one position (like *consent*-content), compared with four-letter words, where this requirement is more easily met. Accordingly the experiment involved a different letter-search task, slightly less demanding than the Reicher-Wheeler paradigm in that it did not require the participant to remember both the target word and the test letters at the same time, and having the further advantage that stimulus presentation within a trial was fully lateralised (unlike Jordan, Patching and Milner, 2000). In this task participants searched the word for the presence or absence of a particular letter, which was presented vertically above the target. The stimulus array on a typical (positive) trial, presented either in RVF or LVF, had the following general form:

LLLL

SALT

Participants were instructed that the letter string ('LLLL' in the example) indicated which letter they should search for in the target word ('SALT' in the example). This particular letter-search task was reported to rely more on processing involving letter level than on whole-word processing, since it was demonstrated that the letter-search task does not give rise to semantic priming (for instance, priming from SALT to PEPPER), whereas silent reading of the prime ('SALT') does (see Maxfield, 1997, for a review). The letter-search task is analogous to the Reicher-Wheeler task in its emphasis on letter-level processes, but having the virtue of allowing comparison of performance for words of substantially different lengths, and avoiding the possible consequences of mixing foveal and parafoveal stimulus presentation (for a review of the dependencies between foveal and parafoveal displays see Lavidor & Walsh, 2004).

Method

Participants

Thirty-two native English speakers from the University of York served as participants. All had normal or corrected to normal vision and were aged 18–27 (mean age 19.5, *sd* 1.6). Each participant received either course credit or £3 for his/her participation. All the participants were right-handed and scored at least 80 on the Edinburgh handedness inventory (Oldfield, 1971). There were 14 males and 18 females.

Stimuli

The experiment used 120 four-letter English words and 120 seven-letter words as stimuli (Appendix 1). Half of the words were assigned to the 'negative match' trials, where the letter-search decision was negative (i.e. none of the letters of the word appeared in the search string). The rest of the words were assigned to the 'positive match' group. These words were divided into eight sets, created from the combinations of four different letter positions (all the positions for the four-letter words and positions 1, 3, 5 and 7 in the seven-letter words) and two word lengths, with 15 words in each set. The eight sets were matched for written word frequency, imageability and orthographic neighbourhood size (see Table 1).

In order to equate acuity conditions for the letter-search task between the four- and seven-letter stimuli, the letters in four-letter words were spaced such that the physical length of four-letter and seven-letter words was the same, and the four letter-search positions were identical, as illustrated in Figure 1. Bruyer and Janlin (1989) have tested lateralised spaced four-letter words and seven-letter words, and reported that the critical

Table 1. Mean frequency, imageability and orthographic neighbourhood (N) as a function of set and word length of the experimental stimuli (Experiments 1 and 2).

	Mean frequency	Mean imageability	Mean N
Four-letter words			
Set 1 (1st letter)	29	488	4
Set 2 (2nd letter)	29	469	4
Set 3 (3rd letter)	31	450	3
Set 4 (4th letter)	31	500	4
Seven-letter words			
Set 1 (1st letter)	31	444	2
Set 2 (3rd letter)	32	470	2
Set 3 (5th letter)	33	463	2
Set 4 (7th letter)	33	458	2

Figure 1. Demonstration of the spaced four-letter stimuli and seven-letter stimuli (Experiments 1 and 2).

factor in the length and in the hemifields' interaction is number of letters rather than the physical length.

Each stimulus contained a string of four identical letters presented vertically above a four- or seven-letter word, presented such that the test letters were above positions 1, 2, 3, 4 for the spaced four-letter words, or above positions 1, 3, 5 and 7 for normally-spaced seven-letter words (see Figure 1). In half the cases – positive trials – the letter in the test string appeared in the word (in any position from the four in equal proportions) and in the other half – negative trials – the letter in the test string did not appear in the word. The stimuli were presented as white lower-case letters on a blue background in a system-fixed font (14 point). Stimuli were presented for 150 ms, at a displacement of 2.5° from the fixation point to the centre of the word. The displacement was to the left or to the right of a central fixation point (LVF and RVF, respectively). The final letters in the LVF words and the first letters in the RVF words were presented 1.18° to the left or right of fixation, respectively, and the furthest letters (from fixation) were presented at a distance of 3.18° away from fixation.

Design

Each participant was assigned to one of the eight versions of the experiment. The different versions rotated the eight word sets across the experimental conditions. Each session began with ten practice trials to introduce the task of letter search, followed by an additional thirty-six practice trials using lateralised stimuli. Every stimulus was presented twice – once to each visual field. Half of the stimuli were first presented to the left visual field, and half to the right, and vice versa. Each combination of variables – number of letters (2), visual field (2) and letter position (4) – was repeated 15 times, to give a total of 240 positive and 240 negative trials for each participant. The stimuli were presented in a random order with the restriction that the same combination did not appear within three successive trials.

Procedure

The participant sat at a viewing distance of 50 cm from a 17″ SVGA display, with the head positioned in a chin rest. The experiment was designed using Super-Lab version 2. Trials began with a fixation cross (+) in the centre of the screen for 400 ms (2000 ms on the first trial), which disappeared for 150 ms while the target word was presented, either to the left or to the right of the fixation point. The fixation cross reappeared immediately after the end of the stimulus presentation and remained for 1800 ms until the next trial. The participant's task was to decide, as quickly and as accurately as possible, whether the word contained the letter appearing in the test string. Participants responded by pressing one of two available response keys, labelled 'yes' and 'no' on a standard 'QWERTY' keyboard. For half of the participants the response 'yes' was made by pressing the 'N' key, and 'no' by pressing the 'V' key. For half of the participants the response keys were reversed. The duration of inter-trial interval was 1800 ms, independent of the response. The participants were randomly assigned to one of the two response options. Instructions to participants emphasised the importance of maintaining fixation on the position of the central fixation cross.

Results

Two repeated-measures analyses of variance for the positive trials were performed, one with RT for correct positive decisions as the dependent variable and one with percentage of incorrect positive decisions as the dependent variable. The within-subject factors were word length (four- and seven-letter words), visual field (LVF, RVF) and position of the matched letter (four possible positions).

Reaction time

A main effect of visual field, $F(1,31) = 12.6$, $p<0.01$, was found. Performance to RVF stimuli ($M = 670$ ms) was faster than to LVF stimuli ($M = 704$ ms). Word length significantly affected latency, $F(1,31) = 13.4$, $p<0.01$, with faster responses to four-letter words ($M = 670$ ms) than to seven-letter words ($M = 704$ ms). Letter position had a significant effect on latency, $F(3,29) = 31.3$, $p<0.01$. RTs when the letter was at the first position were the fastest ($M = 618$ ms). RTs when the letter was at the last position ($M = 693$ ms) were significantly slower than the first position, and faster than the two inner positions, which did not differ significantly (second position: 722 ms and 714 ms for the third position). All post hoc differences mentioned in the results section were obtained using Bonferroni corrected ($p<0.05$) post hoc comparisons.

The only significant interaction was for word length and visual field, $F(1,30) = 8.9$, $p<0.01$. RTs for four-letter words ($M = 664$ ms in RVF, $M = 676$ in LVF) did not differ significantly from seven-letter words presented to RVF ($M = 676$ ms), but RTs to the seven-letter words in the LVF ($M = 732$ ms) were the slowest (as indicated by Bonferroni corrected post hoc comparisons, $p<0.05$). In other words, word length had a significant effect only in LVF. The interactions with letter positions were not significant (see Figure 2).

Error rates

A main effect of visual field, $F(1,31) = 7.4$, $p<0.05$, was found. Error rates to RVF stimuli ($M = 12.3\%$ errors) was lower than to LVF stimuli ($M = 19.7\%$ errors). Word length significantly affected error rates, $F(1,31) = 5.2$, $p<0.05$, with lower rates to four-letter words ($M = 14.2\%$ errors) than to seven-letter words ($M = 17.5\%$ errors). Letter position had a significant effect on error rates, $F(3,29) = 6.7$, $p<0.05$. Error rates when the letter was at the first position were the lowest ($M = 7.7\%$ errors). Error rate when the letter was in the last position ($M = 16.2\%$ errors) was significantly higher than the first position, and lower than the two inner positions which did not differ significantly (second position: 19.7% errors; third position: 20.5% errors). These post hoc differences were obtained using Bonferroni corrected ($p<0.05$) post hoc comparisons. The interactions were not significant.

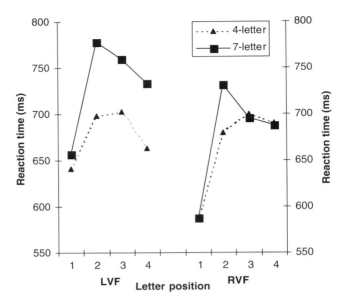

Figure 2. Mean reaction times to words as a function of number of letters, position of searched letter and visual field (Experiment 1).

Discussion

The results of a lateralised letter-search task had shown that the letter position had a U-shaped effect on performance in both visual fields: performance for the first and last letters was better than when the to-be-searched letters occupied the inner positions in the target words. In general, these findings are in accordance with Jordan, Patching and Milner (2000), who reported U-shaped functions in both hemifields (with a general RVF advantage) when using a different letter-search task. In addition, the first letter position was better than the last letter so that the functions were asymmetrical. This asymmetry was significant, consistent with Bradshaw et al. (1977).

Since number of letters was manipulated as well, it was possible to dissociate the effects of serial position and the number of letters in a letter-search task. The analysis shows that number of letters did not interact with the serial position. However, there was a significant interaction between number of letters and hemifield, such that performance in RVF was not affected by number of letters, but larger number of letters decreased performance when stimuli were presented to LVF. This replicates a common finding in other studies that the RVF advantage increases for longer words.

The findings of Experiment 1 suggest that while letter-search tasks may use the same orthographic analysis in both hemispheres, this similarity is limited to a certain level of processing only. The interaction between number of letters and visual hemifields clearly demonstrates a qualitative difference in the way words are processed in the two cerebral hemispheres. Both hemispheres showed U-shape serial letter position functions, indicating similar letter representation processes. However, for longer words these processes were more efficient in the RVF (left hemisphere) than in the LVF (right hemisphere), resulting in similar effects of number of letters in the right visual field but weaker performance in the left visual field for longer words. We interpret this by assuming some reliance on whole-word processing even in the letter-level oriented letter-search task: although it has been argued that letter search is mainly performed via letter-level processing (Maxfield, 1997), it has also been shown that letter search is better for words than nonwords (Reicher, 1969; Wheeler, 1970), so even in letter-level task some word-level boosting of performance may be expected. The contribution of word-level processing in the letter-search task employed caused the RVF advantage, and this advantage was larger for longer words. This pattern is in line with the prediction of the two-mode model (Ellis, Young & Anderson, 1988).

Experiment 2

In Experiment 2 we used the same words as in Experiment 1 in a lateralised lexical decision task, rather than a letter-search task. Experiment 2 therefore manipulated visual field and number of letters to confirm that the typical word length and hemifield interaction would be found in a task that encouraged whole-word processing.

Method

Participants

Twenty-four native English speakers from the University of York served as participants. All of the participants had normal or corrected to normal vision and were aged 18–25 (mean age 18.9, sd 1.3). Each participant received either a course credit or £2 for his/her participation. All the participants were right-handed and scored at least 80 on the Edinburgh test (Oldfield, 1971). There were 12 males and 12 females. None of them participated in Experiment 1.

Stimuli

The 60 four-letter and 60 seven-letter words that served as the positive trials in Experiment 1 were the words group in Experiment 2 (see Appendix 1). The remaining 120 words were changed to produce pronounceable nonwords. Every two sets from the matched sets (see the stimuli section of Experiment 1) were grouped together, such that the two matched word lists in each length were rotated across the two presentation conditions (LVF and RVF).

In order to equate acuity conditions between the four- and seven-letter stimuli, the four-letter words were spaced such that their physical length was equal to the seven-letter words (see Figure 1). The stimuli were presented in system-fixed font, size 14 point, in lower case. The letters appeared white on a blue background to minimise flicker. The stimuli were presented for 150 ms, at a displacement of 2.5° from the fixation point to the centre of the word. The displacement was to the left or to the right of a central focus point (LVF and RVF, respectively).

Design

Each participant was assigned to one of the two versions of the experiment. The different versions rotated the two word sets across the visual fields. Each session began with ten practice trials to introduce the lexical decision task, followed by additional twenty-four practice trials that presented lateralised lexical decision. Each within-participants variables combination was repeated 30 times (number of letters (2), visual field (2)), so there were 120 words (and 120 nonwords) for each participant. The stimuli were presented in a random order with the restriction that the same combination did not appear within three successive trials.

Procedure

The apparatus was the same as used in Experiment 1. Each trial began with a + appearing in the centre of the screen for 400 ms. For the first trial, the + remained for 2000 ms, and disappeared when the target word was presented. The + would again reappear to allow projection of the next stimuli. Stimuli were briefly presented for 150 ms (either a word or a nonword trial), to the left or to the right of the focus point, and then replaced immediately by the fixation + for 1800 ms. The participants' task was to decide, as quickly and as accurately as possible, whether the letter string was a legal English word or a nonword. Participants responded by pressing one of two available response keys, labelled 'word' and 'nonword' on a standard 'QWERTY' keyboard. For half of the participants the response 'word' was made by pressing the 'N' key, and 'nonword' by pressing the 'V' key. For half of the participants the response keys were reversed. The next sequence of fixation-stimulus-fixation started every 1800 ms, no matter what was the response. The participants were randomly assigned to one of the two response options. Instructions to participants emphasised the importance of maintaining fixation on the position of the central fixation cross.

Results

Two repeated-measures analyses of variance were performed, one with RT for correct responses to words as the dependent variable and one with percentage of incorrect responses for word stimuli as the dependent variable. The within-subject factors for the words stimuli were number of letters and visual field. The results are shown in Table 2 and Figure 3.

Reaction time

A main effect for visual field was found, $F(1,23) = 9.3$, $p<0.01$. RTs to RVF words ($M = 575$ ms) was significantly faster than to LVF stimuli ($M = 625$ ms). Number of letters did not affect lexical decision latency, $F(1,23) = 1.24$, ns. Visual field and number of letters interacted significantly, $F(1,22) = 7.8$, $p<0.01$. Number of letters affected performance only for LVF words, with significantly longer latencies to seven-letter LVF words ($M = 649$ ms) than to four-letter LVF words ($M = 600$ ms). When presented to

Table 2. Mean reaction times (RT) and standard deviation (*sd*) in ms and percentage of correct responses to words as a function of word length and visual field (Experiment 2).

		LVF	RVF
Four-letter words	Mean RT	600	571
	(*SD*)	(93)	(85)
	% correct	90	92
Seven-letter words	Mean RT	649	580
	(*SD*)	(79)	(86)
	% correct	91	90

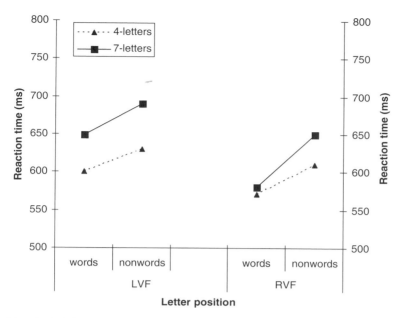

Figure 3. Mean lexical decision latencies (RT) in ms to words and nonwords as a function of number of letters and visual field (Experiment 2).

RVF, the four-letter ($M = 571$ ms) and the seven-letter words ($M = 580$ ms) did not differ, as indicated using the Bonferroni corrected post hoc comparisons, $p < 0.05$.

Error rates

Error rates for words were not significantly affected by visual field or number of letters (see Table 2).

Discussion

Experiment 2 replicated the previously reported interaction between number of letters and visual field when the four- and seven-letter words were matched for frequency, imageability, orthographic neighbourhood size, and had the same physical length. Response times to RVF words were not affected by number of letters, but number of letters had a significant effect on LVF performance. This finding is well in accordance with the many previous lateralisation studies that formed the basis for the two-modes processing theory (e.g. Bub & Lewine, 1988; Ellis, Young & Anderson, 1988; Young & Ellis, 1985).

The lack of effects in the accuracy measure may be due to ceiling effects resulting from high accuracy (90–92% correct) in all the experimental conditions.

General discussion

The experiments reported here aimed to test the hypotheses that previously reported contrasting findings regarding word-length effects in the hemifields may be attributable in part to the different experimental tasks employed and to different operational definitions of word length. In particular we investigated whether the similarity between hemifields found for serial position effects by Jordan, Patching and Milner (2000) would also be seen in the effects of number of letters (the traditional operational measure for the word length effect). In Experiment 1, we employed a lateralised letter-search task with four- and seven-letter words, and found that letter position had a U-shaped effect on performance in both visual fields: performance for the first and last letters was better than when the to-be-searched letters occupied the inner positions in the target words, in accordance with Jordan, Patching and Milner (2000) and Bradshaw et al. (1977), who reported U-shaped functions in both hemifields when using different letter-search tasks. However, when comparing performance for the four- and seven-letter words in the letter-search task, a significant interaction was found between hemifield and number of letters, replicating the pattern predicted by the two-modes model (Ellis, Young & Anderson, 1988): the effect of number of letters was larger in the left than in the right visual field.

In Experiment 2, the same target words from Experiment 1 were used in a lexical decision task. There was an interaction between number of letters and hemifield, such that performance for four- and seven-letter words did not differ significantly when presented to RVF, but the number of letters affected performance for LVF stimuli. This finding is in line with numerous previous studies (Bub & Lewine, 1988; Ellis, Young & Anderson, 1988; Weekes et al., 1999; Iacoboni & Zaidel, 1996; Young & Ellis, 1985) that have inspired the two processing modes theory.

As in all divided visual fields experiments (including the original studies that investigated the visual hemifields and word-length interaction), the initial letters in words presented to the RVF were closer to fixation than the initial letters in LVF words. As visual acuity decreases on either side of the fixation point, even within the fovea (Nazir, Heller & Sussman, 1992), the initial letters in the RVF enjoyed better acuity than the LVF initial letters. Since the initial letters of words may be more informative than their endings (Pynte, 1996), and as the stimuli are not symmetrical, the important initial letters are closer to fixation in the RVF, so that there is an inevitable imbalance between LVF and RVF trials. However, the uncontrolled differences between LVF and RVF in the present experiments were also uncontrolled in all previous divided visual field studies, implying a general need for caution in interpreting the data from this type of experiment. Future research might explore this limitation by either increasing stimulus size in the LVF to compensate for the lower acuity, or employing mirror writing; both solutions have advantages and disadvantages.

Taken together, the two experiments are consistent with the notion that the different language processing modes in the two hemispheres that have been suggested to account for the word-length and hemifields interaction are more evident in word-level processing rather than in earlier, letter-level processing. The letter-search task resulted in a similar pattern of serial position effects for both word lengths in both hemispheres. Thus the letter-level processing may be similar in both hemifields, and be performed in an outside-in manner, resulting in the external letters being more accessible (Estes, 1972). The lexical decision task with the same stimuli revealed hemispheric differences in whole-word processing: when comparing the two word lengths, the well-established interaction between number of letters and hemifield was found, indicating that there are qualitative differences between the hemispheres in processing of words, in accordance with the two-modes model. The different processing modes are evident when processing relies on whole-word analysis, where the left hemisphere is capable of more efficient processing than the right hemisphere.

If both hemispheres decode letters in the same way, as is suggested by the similar serial position effects in the two hemifields, why was there a word-length by hemifield interaction in the letter-search task, such that for longer words, the mean RVF advantage over the LVF increased for every letter position? We suggest this is because letter search reflects interactions between letter and word levels of representation. Letters are better searched in words than in nonwords (Reicher, 1969; Wheeler, 1970), implying that word-level processing can boost letter-search performance. The more efficient word-level processing in the LH resulted in better letter search in the RVF, an advantage that became larger for the longer words. This explanation has additional support from earlier studies that showed a greater word superiority effect in the RVF than in the LVF (Krueger, 1975).

In summary, we have shown hemispheric differences in the processing of letter strings. The novel finding of the current research is that effects of number of letters and of serial position are separable in a letter-search task. Number of letters and visual field interacted significantly when four- and seven-letter words were compared in both experimental tasks, in line with previous findings that employed lexical decision or naming (Ellis, Young & Anderson, 1988; Young & Ellis, 1985). Letter strings can be processed in a length-sensitive pattern, where more letters in the string affect performance, or in a length-insensitive pattern, where the number of letters in the string does not alter performance. We take this to be consistent with previous studies showing that the length-sensitive processing mode is found in the LVF for familiar words in any format and for familiar words in RVF in non-standard formats. This distinction between the two processing modes becomes particularly evident when word-level processing is dominant, as in reading, naming, semantic categorisation and lexical decision. When the task involved explicit letter search, the serial position of the letters affected performance in both visual fields, since letters are processed in outside-in manner in both hemispheres. The different hemispheric asymmetries revealed for effects of number of letters and of serial position suggest they reflect different cognitive structures.

Acknowledgement

This study was supported by the European Commission, with a Marie Curie fellowship grant, contract no. HPMF-CT-1999-00205 and by a BBSRC research grant (ML). We wish to thank Andy Ellis for helpful discussions and comments on earlier versions of this manuscript.

References

Aghababian, V. & Nazir, T.A. (2000). Developing normal reading skills: Aspects of the visual processes underlying word recognition. *Journal of Experimental Child Psychology*, 76, 123–150.

Ahissar, M. & Hochstein, S. (1996). Learning pop-out detection: Specificities to stimulus characteristics. *Vision Research*, 36, 3487–3500.

Ahissar, M. & Hochstein, S. (1997). Task difficulty and the specificity of perceptual learning. *Nature*, 387, 401–406.

Babkoff, H., Faust, M. & Lavidor, M. (1997). Lexical decision, visual hemifield and angle of orientation. *Neuropsychologia*, 35, 487–495.

Bouma, H. (1973). Visual interference in the parafoveal recognition of initial and final letters of words. *Vision Research*, 13, 767–782.

Bradshaw, J.L., Bradley, D., Gates, A. & Patterson, K. (1977). Serial, parallel, or holistic identification of single words in the two visual fields. *Perception and Psychophysics*, 21, 431–438.

Bruyer, R. & Janlin, D. (1989). Lateral differences in lexical access: Word length vs. stimulus length. *Brain and Language*, 37, 258–265.

Brysbaert, M. (1994). Interhemispheric transfer and the processing of foveally presented stimuli. *Behavioural Brain Research*, 64, 151–161.

Bub, D.N. & Lewine, J. (1988). Different modes of word recognition in the left and right visual fields. *Brain and Language*, 33, 161–188.

Chiarello, C. (1988). Lateralization of lexical processes in the normal brain: A review of visual half-field research. In H.A. Whitaker (Ed.), *Contemporary reviews in neuropsychology*. New York: Springer-Verlag.

Dill, M. & Fahle, M. (1998). Limited translation invariance of human visual pattern recognition. *Perception & Psychophysic*, 60, 65–81.

Ellis, A.W. (2004). Length, formats, neighbours, hemispheres, and the processing of words presented laterally or at fixation. *Brain and Language*, 88, 355–366.

Ellis, A.W., Young, A.W. & Anderson, C. (1988). Modes of word recognition in the left and right cerebral hemispheres. *Brain and Language*, 35, 254–273.

Estes, W.K. (1972). Interactions of signal and background variables in visual processing. *Perception and Psychophysics*, 12, 278–286.

Gill, K.M. & McKeever, W.F. (1974). Word length and exposure time effects on the recognition of bilaterally presented words. *Bulletin of the Psychonomic Society*, 4, 173–175.

Gilbert, C.D. (1994). Early perceptual learning. *Proceedings of the National Academy of Sciences of the United States of America*, 91, 1195–1197.

Iacoboni, M. & Zaidel, E. (1996). Hemispheric independence in word recognition: Evidence from unilateral and bilateral presentations. *Brain and Language*, 53, 121–140.

Jordan, R.T., Patching, G.R. & Milner, A.D. (2000). Lateralized word recognition: Assessing the role of hemispheric specialization, modes of lexical access, and perceptual asymmetry. *Journal of Experimental Psychology: Human Perception and Performance*, 26, 1192–1208.

Krueger, L.E. (1975). The word-superiority effect: Is its locus visual-spatial or verbal? *Bulletin of the Psychonomic Society*, 6, 465–468.

Lavidor, M. & Ellis, A.W. (2001). MiXeD CaSe effects in lateralized word recognition. *Brain and Cognition*, 46, 192–195.

Lavidor, M. & Ellis, A.W. (2002). Word length and orthographic neighborhood size effects in the left and right cerebral hemispheres. *Brain and Language*, 80, 45–62.

Lavidor, M. & Walsh, V. (2004). The nature of foveal representation. *Nature Reviews Neuroscience*, 5, 729–735.

Maxfield, L. (1997). Attention and semantic priming: A review of prime task effects. *Consciousness and Cognition*, 6, 204–218.

Nazir, T.A. (2000). Traces of print along the visual pathway. In A. Kennedy, R. Radach, D. Heller & J. Pynte (Eds.), *Reading as a perceptual process*. North Holland: Elsevier Science Ltd.

Nazir, T.A. & O'Regan, K. (1990). Some results on translation invariance in the human visual system. *Spatial Vision*, 5, 81–100.

Nazir, T.A., Heller, D. & Sussmann, C. (1992). Letter visibility and word recognition: The optimal viewing position in printed words. *Perception and Psychophysics*, 52, 315–328.

Nazir, T.A., Jacobs, A.M. & O'Regan, J.K. (1998). Letter legibility and visual word recognition. *Memory and Cognition*, 26, 810–821.

O'Regan, J.K. & Lévy-Schoen, A. (1987). Eye movement strategy and tactics in word recognition and reading. In M. Coltheart (Ed.), *Attention and performance XII: The psychology of reading*. (pp. 363–383). Hillsdale, NJ: Lawrence Erlbaum Associates.

Oldfield, R.C. (1971). The assessment and analysis of handedness. The Edinburgh inventory. *Neuropsychologia*, 9, 93–113.

Pynte, J. (1996). Lexical control of within-word eye movements. *Journal of Experimental Psychology: Human Perception and Performance*, 22, 958–969.

Rayner, K. & Pollatsek, A. (1989). *The psychology of reading*. Englewood Cliffs, NJ: Prentice-Hall, Inc.

Rayner, K. (1979). Eye guidance in reading: Fixation location within words. *Perception*, 8, 21–30.

Rayner, K. (1998). Eye movements in reading and information processing: 20 years of research. *Psychological Bulletin*, 124, 372–422.

Rayner, K., Sereno, S.C. & Raney, G.E. (1996). Eye movement control in reading: A comparison of two types of models. *Journal of Experimental Psychology: Human Perception and Performance*, 22, 1188–1200.

Reicher, G.M. (1969). Perceptual recognition as a function of meaningfulness of stimulus material. *Journal of Experimental Psychology*, 81, 275–280.

Vitu, F., O'Regan, J.K., Inhoff, A.W. & Topolski, R. (1995). Mindless reading: Eye-movement characteristics are similar in scanning letter strings and reading texts. *Perception & Psychophysics*, 57, 352–364.

Weekes, N.Y., Capetillo-Cunliffe, L., Rayman, J., Iacoboni, M. & Zaidel, E. (1999). Individual differences in the hemispheric specialization of dual route variables. *Brain and Language*, 67, 110–133.

Wheeler, D.D. (1970). Processes in the visual recognition of words. *Cognitive Psychology*, 1, 59–85.

Young, A.W. & Ellis, A.W. (1985). Different methods of lexical access for words presented in the left and right visual hemifields. *Brain and Language*, 24, 326–358.

Appendix 1

Stimuli for Experiments 1 and 2.

	1st letter	2nd letter	3rd letter	4th letter
Four-letter words	PLUG	SIGN	DUSK	FORK
	EARL	ARMY	AUNT	GORE
	GRIP	VETO	CULT	FURY
	OVEN	DELL	EXIT	NEWT
	PITY	DUTY	HAUL	HALF
	GASP	ACRE	FIRM	PALM
	SOIL	LEWD	HERO	EVIL
	PREY	BEAM	EASE	ITEM
	STEW	LENS	FILM	OBEY
	VICE	RIOT	ENVY	MENU
	TOMB	SAND	LION	SHED
	VERB	SWIM	RUNG	SOAP
	OATH	THAW	DISC	UNIT
	ECHO	TINY	RELY	WALK
	WHOM	DUEL	STIR	HOWL

	1st letter	3rd letter	5th letter	7th letter
Seven-letter words	BREADTH	AUCTION	ABSENCE	ANXIETY
	CARAMEL	CHARMER	ADVANCE	BENEATH
	CONSENT	COMFORT	BREATHE	CULTURE
	DEVOTED	CONDUCT	CONCISE	DESTROY
	DISPLAY	CURIOUS	CONTENT	EVIDENT
	DRAUGHT	FALSIFY	DECEIVE	FORMULA
	FLAVOUR	FICTION	EXPENSE	INSTEAD
	PAYMENT	LATERAL	FLICKER	LIGHTER
	PERFECT	PROVIDE	HEAVILY	PRICKLY
	REQUEST	REMOVAL	ORGANIC	PROMISE
	SIGNIFY	SERVICE	PYRAMID	PUMPKIN
	TRAINED	TOUCHED	STORAGE	READILY
	UNKNOWN	TRAGEDY	THICKEN	SENATOR
	VITAMIN	UNIFORM	WELCOME	STEPSON
	WARFARE	VERANDA	WELFARE	VERSION

5

Letter-position encoding and dyslexia

Carol Whitney and Piers Cornelissen

Following the pioneering work of Liberman and colleagues (1974), research into dyslexia has focused on phonological deficits. As discussed by Castles and Colheart (2004), there is a wide range of evidence that dyslexics are impaired in phonological awareness tasks, such as phoneme deletion, phoneme counting and phoneme lending. This correlation has largely been taken to reflect causality. That is, impaired phonological awareness is thought to reflect abnormal phonological representations, which are thought to be the fundamental cause of dyslexia. However, a causal relationship between phonological awareness and reading ability has not directly been established (Castles & Coltheart, 2004). It may instead be the case that poor performance on phonological tasks is a result of poor reading ability. Indeed, several studies have shown that phoneme awareness tasks are influenced by properties of the corresponding orthographic representations (Castles et al., 2003; Stuart, 1990; Treiman & Cassar, 1997), indicating that performance on phonological tasks may tap into letter-based, rather than purely phonemic, representations.

Thus, deficits of phonological awareness may be a symptom, rather than a direct cause, of dyslexia; it may be more accurate to say that dyslexia results from the failure to form normal grapheme-phoneme associations (Castles & Coltheart, 2004). Thus such a failure could potentially arise from the grapheme (visual) side, or from problems in forming the relevant visual-auditory associations. A deficit in any aspect of processing could then have repercussions throughout the entire network that is normally recruited to sub-serve reading.

To study dyslexia, it is useful to determine when and where processing first diverges from that of normal readers. MEG technology has revealed that this divergence occurs quite early, at the visual level. In normal subjects, a left-hemisphere (LH) infero-temporal area was preferentially activated by letter strings (as opposed to symbols or faces) at about 150 ms post-stimulus (Tarkiainen, Cornelissen & Salmelin, 2002; Tarkiainen et al., 1999), while 80% of the dyslexic subjects did not show this activation (Helenius et al., 1999). Thus it seems that normal readers have learned some type of string-specific visual processing, while most abnormal readers have not.

What is the cause of this difference in visual processing? What can this difference tell us about the root cause(s) of dyslexia? To understand what goes wrong in visual processing in dyslexics, it is necessary to understand the nature of this processing in normal readers. What is the source of the early string-specific LH activation? What form do normal orthographic codes take? One approach to answering these questions is via computational modelling of how the early, retinotopic representation of a letter string is progressively converted into an abstract encoding of letter order. A recent model of letter-position encoding, dubbed the SERIOL model (Whitney, 2001; Whitney & Berndt, 1999), fits this bill. The SERIOL model was formulated via consideration of neurobiological constraints and behavioural data, and has yielded new insights into hemifield asymmetries in visual word recognition (Whitney, 2004a, 2004b; Whitney & Lavidor, 2004, 2005 forthcoming).

The purpose of this article is to provide an account of abnormal visual/orthographic processing in dyslexics, based on the SERIOL model. We consider how auditory and/or visual deficits could lead to a failure to learn normal string-specific visual processing, and how such a failure could contribute to difficulties in learning grapheme-phoneme correspondences. This discussion is a first step in applying the SERIOL model to dyslexia; it is admittedly quite sketchy and highly speculative. It is hoped that such consideration of the visual aspect of visual word recognition may inspire fruitful avenues of research in dyslexia.

This article is organised as follows. In the next section, the SERIOL model is presented. Then experimental evidence is presented supporting some key proposals of the model relevant to the issues at hand. These preliminary sections review previously completed work. We then extend the model to include a phonological route, and to address reading acquisition. After reviewing auditory and visual deficits in dyslexia, we are then in a position to apply the model to dyslexia. We discuss how visual/orthographic processing may break down during reading acquisition, and how this process may interact with phonological encoding.

Review of SERIOL model

The SERIOL (Sequential Encoding Regulated by Inputs to Oscillations within Letter units) model is a theory of processing in the proficient reader. It specifies how an abstract letter position encoding is generated from a retinotopic representation, and how that encoding activates the lexical level. Note that SERIOL is not a full model of visual word recognition, as it does not address phonological processing. Rather, the model has focused on the orthographic route to the lexicon. However, this focus is not meant to imply a lesser role for phonological processing. A phonological route is assumed, but heretofore has not been elaborated. We will address the phonological route at a fairly high level later in this article.

We first give a brief overview of the existing model, and then discuss the processing in each layer in more depth. The model consists of five layers: edge, feature, letter, bigram and word. Each layer is comprised of nodes, which represent neural assemblies. Within each layer, the activation of a letter is taken to be the total amount of activity across nodes representing that letter. To illustrate the representations and activation patterns at each layer, we will consider the stimulus CART, for fixation between the A and R.

The lowest layer of the model, the edge layer, corresponds to the early visual cortical areas, which are retinotopically mapped. At this level, there is an activation pattern arising from visual acuity. In our example, A and R would have the highest activation, and C and T would have lower activations (because there are more edge nodes representing A and R than C and T). At the feature layer, this acuity pattern is transformed into an activation gradient, dubbed the locational gradient, where activation decreases from left to right. That is, C would attain the highest activation, A the next highest, R the next and T the lowest activation. At the letter layer, the locational gradient interacts with oscillatory letter nodes to induce a serial encoding of order. That is, the C node fires, then A, then R, then T. At the next layer, temporally ordered pairs of letters activate bigram nodes. That is, a bigram node XY is activated when letter X fires before letter Y. In our example, bigram nodes *C, CA, CR, AR, CT, AT, RT and T* (where *

denotes a word boundary) become activated. The bigrams then activate lexical representations at the word layer. In our example, the word node CART would become more highly activated than any other word node.

Thus the retinotopic representation is converted into an abstract, location-invariant encoding of letter order via the creation of a serial representation. This serial encoding activates lexical representations via bigram nodes, which encode relationships between letters. See Figure 1 for a schematic of the letter through word layers. The choice of these representations and the transformations between representations are best illustrated in a top-down manner, as presented next.

Bigram layer to word layer

First we consider what type of orthographic representation contacts the lexical layer. The results of priming experiments in which the order of letters from the target word is manipulated in the prime (Humphreys, Evett & Quinlan, 1990; Peressotti & Grainger, 1999) place strong constraints on the nature of the highest pre-lexical representation (Grainger & Whitney, 2004). These experiments indicate that order is important, not absolute position within the string. For example, GRDN primes GARDEN while GDRN

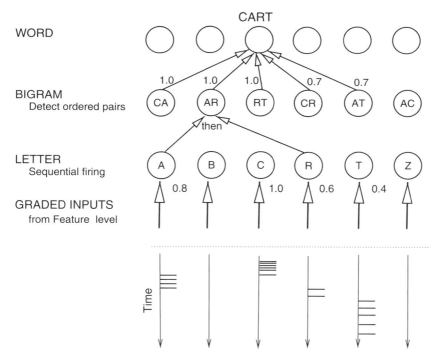

Figure 1. Architecture of the letter, bigram and word levels of the SERIOL model, with example of encoding the word CART.

Notes: At the letter level, simultaneous graded inputs are converted into serial firing, as indicated by the timing of firing displayed under the letter nodes. Bigram nodes recognise temporally ordered pairs of letters (connections shown for a single bigram). Bigram activations (shown above the nodes) decrease with increasing temporal separation of the constituent letters. Activation of word nodes is based on the conventional dot-product model.

does not, and the prime G_RD_N does not provide any more facilitation than GRDN. Thus, it is relative position that matters. These results can best be accommodated by units encoding the information that letter X preceded letter Y, where X and Y are not necessarily contiguous in the string.

The activation level of a bigram node is sensitive to the separation between the constituent letters. Activation decreases as the amount of time between the firing of the two letters increases. In our example, the RT node would have a higher activation than AT, which would have a higher activation than CT. Bigram nodes connect to word nodes via standard weighted connections, where the weights on the connections into each word node are proportional to the bigram activation pattern for that word.

Letter layer to bigram layer

How are such bigram nodes activated? Priming studies of letter trigrams indicate that priming can occur across letter positions (Peressotti & Grainger, 1995). This indicates that a letter detector can be activated by the corresponding letter in any string position. Therefore, we assume that such position-independent letter nodes comprise the next lower layer of the model. Because these nodes only encode letter identity, positional information must be dynamically associated with such nodes. Two possibilities are that position is represented by activation level, or by firing order. Representation via activation level would require a monotonically decreasing activation gradient (e.g., in the CART example, the letter node C would have the highest activation, A the next highest, R the next and T the lowest). However, such an activation pattern at the letter layer is inconsistent with the well-known final-letter advantage; the final letter is perceived better than the internal letters, indicating a higher activation level than the internal letters. Therefore, in line with evidence for left-to-right string processing (Harcum & Nice, 1975; Nice & Harcum, 1976), letter order is taken to be represented serially. A bigram node is activated when its constituent letters fire in the correct order. For example, bigram node CA is activated when C fires before A, but not vice versa.

Feature layer to letter layer

How is this serial firing induced at the letter layer? Hopfield (1995) and Lisman and Idiart (1995) have proposed related mechanisms for precisely controlling timing of firing, in which nodes undergo synchronous, sub-threshold oscillations of excitability. For convenience, we designate the trough of this oscillatory cycle to be the 'start' of the cycle. Input level then determines how early in the cycle such a node can cross threshold and fire (see Figure 2). Near the beginning of the cycle, excitability is low, so only a node receiving a high level of input can cross threshold and fire. Excitability increases over time, allowing nodes receiving less and less input progressively to fire. Thus serial firing at the letter level can be accomplished via letter nodes that oscillate in synchrony and take input in the form of an activation gradient. In our example, the C node would receive the most input, A the next, R the next and T the least, allowing C to fire the earliest, A next, R next and finally T. Thus all nodes fire within a single oscillatory cycle, which is taken to be on the time scale of 200 ms (Lisman & Idiart, 1995).

An activated letter node inhibits other letter nodes. In our example, once C starts firing, how then does A ever start firing? As a letter node continues to fire, its firing rate slows, reducing lateral inhibition to the other nodes. This allows a new letter node to start firing. When an active letter node receives lateral inhibition, it then becomes strongly inhibited,

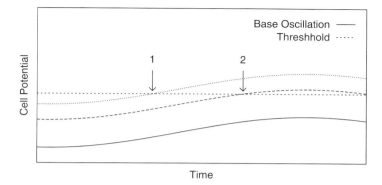

Figure 2. Interaction of input level and timing of firing for a cell undergoing a sub-threshold oscillation of excitability.

Notes: When a relatively high level of input (top curving line) is added to the base oscillation, the cell crosses threshold at time 1 (action potential not illustrated). If less input were received, the cell would cross threshold later in the cycle, such as at time 2.

so that it will not refire for the remainder of the oscillatory cycle.[1] Thus graded input levels and lateral inhibition create strictly sequential firing at the letter layer.

This process also creates varying activation levels. The activation of a letter node depends on both the rate and duration of firing. Under the assumptions that a higher input level leads to faster firing and that firing duration is fairly constant across letters, there is a decreasing activation gradient at the letter level. However, the node representing the final letter is not inhibited by a subsequent letter. It can continue to fire until the end (down-phase) of the oscillatory cycle.[2] Therefore, the final letter could potentially fire longer than the other letters, and reach a higher level of activation than the internal letters even though it receives less input. This is consistent with the well-known final-letter advantage. As discussed below, this proposal also explains some counter-intuitive experimental results on letter perceptibility.

Thus there must be a monotonically decreasing activation gradient across the next lower layer of the model, to provide input to the letter layer. Because this gradient decreases from left to right (i.e. by spatial location), these lower-level units must be tuned to retinal location. Thus, a retinotopic representation is converted into a serial representation, creating a location-invariant encoding; location invariance is achieved by mapping space on to time. This location-invariant encoding is resumed to occur in the LH.

Edge layer to feature layer

Based on the architecture of the visual system, there are several important characteristics of the edge layer that determine the nature of the transformations from the edge to the feature layer. The fibres from each retina divide, such that information reaching V1 is split by visual field, not by eye. The left visual field (LVF) projects to the right hemisphere (RH), while the right visual field (RVF) projects to the left hemisphere (LH). Available evidence indicates that there is little or no overlap in the cortical representation of the visual fields along the vertical meridian (Brysbaert, 1994; Lavidor & Walsh, 2004; Leff, 2004). That is, letters immediately to the left of fixation are only projected to the RH, while letters immediately to the right of fixation are only projected to the LH. It is well known that the number of cortical cells representing a fixed area of space decreases as distance from fixation increases. Thus, activation decreases as eccentricity increases, giving a different activation pattern at the edge level from at the feature level (where activation decreases from left to right).

Therefore, the acuity pattern must be converted to the locational gradient as the edge layer activates the feature layer. Note that for a fixated word, the acuity pattern across the letters in the RVF/LH is the same as the locational gradient (i.e. decreasing from left to right). Thus the acuity gradient can serve as the locational gradient for those letters. However, in the LVF/RH, the acuity gradient increases from left to right; its slope is in the opposite direction as required for the locational gradient. Therefore, when the edge level activates the feature level, the acuity gradient must be inverted in the LVF/RH, while it can be maintained for the RVF/LH. Next we consider the details of this processing.

Obviously, activation levels cannot be increased by increasing the number of cells representing a letter. Rather, the locational gradient is created via modification of firing rates. In the LVF/RH, the acuity gradient is inverted via a combination of strong excitation and direction-specific lateral inhibition. This process is displayed in Figure 3. We propose that letter features in the LVF/RH become more highly activated by edge-layer inputs than those in the RVF/LH. This allows the first letter to reach a high level of activation. This could occur either via higher bottom-up connection weights from the edge layer, or by stronger self-excitatory connections within the feature layer. Within the RH feature layer, we propose that there is strong left-to-right lateral inhibition. That is, a feature node inhibits nodes to its right. As a result, letter features corresponding to the first letter receive no lateral inhibition, and inhibition increases as letter position increases. (Actually, there would be a gradient within each letter, but for simplicity we consider the mean activation level of a letter's features.) Thus, the features comprising the first letter attain the highest activation level (as a result of strong excitation and lack of lateral inhibition), and activation decreases towards fixation (due to sharply increasing lateral inhibition).

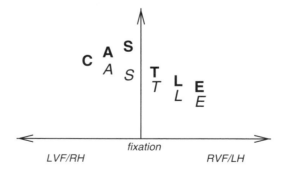

Figure 3. Formation of the locational gradient at the feature layer, for the centrally fixated stimulus CASTLE.

Notes: The horizontal axis represents retinal location, while the vertical axis represents activation level. The bold-face letters represent bottom-up input levels, which are higher in the RH than the LH. In each hemisphere, activation decreases as eccentricity increases, due to the acuity gradient. The italicised letters represent the effect left-to-right inhibition within the RH, and RH-to-LH inhibition in the LH. In the RH, C inhibits A, and C and A inhibition S, creating a decreasing gradient. The RH inhibits each letter in the LH by the same amount, bringing the activation of T lower than that of S. As a result, activation monotonically decreases from left to right.

In the RVF/LH, the acuity gradient serves as the locational gradient. Overall excitation is weaker than to the LVF/RH. Left-to-right inhibition is not necessary, although some weak such inhibition may steepen the slope of the gradient. The two hemispheric gradients are 'spliced' together via cross-hemispheric inhibition. The RH features inhibit the LH features, bringing the activation of the LH features lower than the activation of the least activated RH features. As a result, an activation gradient that is strictly decreasing from left to right is created.

Summary

The following are the important assumptions about processing at each layer.

Edge layer

- Retinotopic;
- representation of central vision split across hemispheres;
- activation levels based on acuity gradient.

Feature layer (for a left-to-right language)

- Retinotopic;
- representation still split across hemispheres;
- activation decreases from left to right (locational gradient);
- locational gradient formed by hemisphere-specific processing:
  - stronger excitation to RH than LH;
  - strong left-to-right lateral inhibition within RH;
  - RH inhibits LH.

Letter layer

- Position-independent letter nodes, located in LH;
- letter nodes undergo synchronous, sub-threshold oscillations in excitability;
- lateral inhibition between letter nodes;
- interaction of oscillations, lateral inhibition and locational-gradient input give a serial firing;
- letter-node activation level depends on:
  - firing rate – determined by input level (from locational gradient);
  - firing duration – determined by when next letter starts to fire, which is determined by the input level to that letter.

Bigram layer

- Bigram XY activated when letter X fires and then letter Y fires;
- activation of bigram XY decreases with the amount of time between the firing of letter X and letter Y.

Word layer

- Receives weighted connections from bigram layer.

Evidence for SERIOL model

Having discussed the details of and motivations for the model, we now review some experimental support for the particulars of the model, based on novel experiments and new analyses of previous studies.

Letter perceptibility

It is well known that the external letters of a string (first and last letters) are the best perceived under central fixation. However, for unilateral presentation of short strings (three or four letters) at large eccentricities, a counter-intuitive pattern arises. In the LVF/ RH, the first letter is the best perceived of all the letters; in the RVF/LH, the last letter is the best perceived (Bouma, 1973; Estes, Allemeyer & Reder, 1976; Legge, Mansfield & Chung, 2001). Thus, in each visual field, the letter farthest from fixation (where acuity is the lowest) is the most likely to be correctly reported. This pattern is present even at long exposure durations. For example, see Figure 4.

As discussed above, the induction of the serial encoding leads to differing activations at the letter level. These activation patterns depend on the interaction of the locational gradient and the oscillatory cycle. Such dynamics explain these patterns of letter perceptibility, as follows.

For a centrally fixated string, the initial-letter advantage and final-letter advantage arise for different reasons. The initial letter has an advantage because it receives the highest level of bottom-up input, allowing it to fire the fastest. It receives the most input because it is not inhibited from the left at the feature level. The final letter has an advantage because it is not inhibited by a subsequent letter during the induction of serial firing. That is, it is not inhibited from the right at the letter level. Thus, like others, we also attribute the advantage for the external letters to a lack of lateral inhibition. However, this reduced lateral inhibition does not arise from a lack of masking at a very low level (as is generally

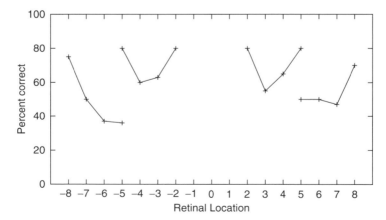

Figure 4. Experimental results from Estes and colleagues (1974) for four-letter strings, occurring at two different retinal locations in each visual field.

Notes: Exposure duration was 2400 ms. Subjects were trained to maintain central fixation, and their gaze was monitored.

assumed). Rather it arises from string-specific processing, consistent with the finding that non-letter, non-digit symbols do not display an outer symbol advantage. That is, the outer symbol is the least well perceived, as would be expected on the basis of acuity (Mason, 1982).

This analysis of the external letter advantage implies that it should be possible to affect differentially the initial- and final-letter advantages. The initial-letter advantage should disappear if the amount of bottom-up input to the initial letter node is not significantly higher than to the other letters. The final-letter advantage should disappear if the final letter node starts firing late in the oscillatory cycle, and so is unable to fire for a longer time than the other letters. As we shall see, these proposals explain the counter-intuitive perceptibility patterns for lateralised presentation of short strings. First however, a more in-depth consideration of activation patterns at the feature level is required.

Recall that locational gradient formation requires different processing across the hemispheres. In the RVF/LH, the acuity gradient serves as the locational gradient. In the LVF/RH, the acuity gradient is inverted via strong bottom-up excitation and left-to-right lateral inhibition. Because the locational gradient is formed by different mechanisms in each hemisphere, the shape of the resulting gradient may vary with hemisphere, especially at large eccentricities. The acuity gradient is known to fall off less quickly as distance from fixation increases. That is, the slope of the acuity gradient is steepest near fixation, and becomes shallower as eccentricity increases. Because the RVF/LH locational gradient is based on the acuity gradient, this implies that the RVF/LH locational gradient becomes more shallow as eccentricity increases. (See right half of Figure 5.)

In the LVF/RH, formation of the locational gradient depends on left-to-right lateral inhibition. For strings at large eccentricities, inhibition may be too strong at early string positions, because of their relatively low level of activation (but, as discussed below, inhibition may become too weak at later string positions, because of the increasing acuity). (See left half of Figure 5.) Thus the prediction is that the locational gradient should vary with visual field. The proposal of a steeper LVF locational gradient (across string positions 1 to 4) explains an observed interaction between string position, eccentricity and visual field (Wolford & Hollingsworth, 1974), as discussed in Whitney (2001).

Now we are in a position to explain the unilateral perceptibility patterns. In particular, we will consider the results of Estes, Allemeyer and Reder (1976), given in Figure 4. In the following, primacy will signify that a letter is perceived better than all other letters, whereas advantage will mean that an external letter is perceived better than the internal letters.

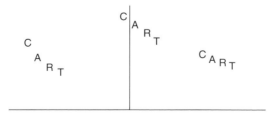

Figure 5. Schematic of locational gradients for the stimulus CART at three different presentation locations.

Notes: The vertical axis represents activation, while the horizontal axis represents retinal location. For central presentation, the gradient is smoothly and rapidly decreasing. For RVF presentation, the gradient is shallower because the acuity gradient is shallower. For LVF presentation, the initial letter strongly inhibits nearby letters, but the gradient flattens out as acuity increases.

First we consider LVF presentation. At the feature layer, there is strong left-right inhibition, causing a steep locational gradient. Therefore, at the letter level, the first letter can fire for a (relatively) long time, as it is not quickly cut off by the next letter. Thus there is an initial-letter primacy. As a result of its low input level, the firing of the final letter is pushed late into the oscillatory cycle. Therefore, it cannot fire longer than the other letters, and no final-letter advantage emerges. This explains the perceptibility pattern for locations − 8 to − 5.

For RVF presentation, there is weak left-to-right inhibition, while the acuity/locational gradient is quite shallow. Therefore the activation of the second letter's features is quite close to that of the first letter. As a result, at the letter level, the firing of the first letter is rapidly cut off by the second letter, giving no initial-letter advantage. Each successive letter quickly inhibits the preceding letter, allowing the final letter to start firing early in the oscillatory cycle. Therefore the final letter can fire longer than the other letters, creating a final-letter primacy. This explains the perceptibility patterns for locations 5 to 8. The proposed activation patterns for both visual fields are displayed in Figure 6.

This account explains the initial/final difference within a single retinal location (at − 5 and 5 in Figure 4). In the LVF/RH, the left-to-right, feature-level inhibition creates a disadvantage for a final letter, whereas an initial letter does not receive this inhibition. In the RVF/LH, the shallow locational gradient creates a disadvantage for an initial letter because its firing at the letter layer is rapidly inhibited by the second letter. For a final letter, firing at the letter layer can continue until the end of the oscillatory cycle instead.

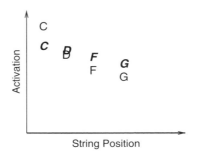

Figure 6. Locational gradients and resulting firing patterns for LVF/RH presentation (normal font) and RVF/LH presentation (bold italics).

Notes: Top: Comparison of locational gradient for string CDFG under RVF/LH presentation and LVF/RH presentation. Bottom: Cartoon of resulting firing pattern at the letter level. The point in the oscillatory cycle at which the down phase prevents further firing is marked *. In the LVF/RH, the first letter fires faster and longer than the other letters, because it receives a much higher level of input. The variations in the amount of bottom-up input create decreasing activation across the string. The final letter starts firing late in the cycle, and is soon cut off by the end of the oscillatory cycle, giving no final-letter advantage. In the RVF/LH, each letter rapidly cuts off the previous letter, allowing the final letter to fire a long time. As a result, activation is flat across the string and rises for the final letter. These firing patterns account for the perceptibility patterns at the larger eccentricities in Figure 4.

In contrast to the patterns at the larger eccentricity, the perceptibility function is U-shaped for both − 5 to − 2 and 2 to 5. As a result of higher acuity, bottom-up input is higher overall. In the LVF/RH, this allows the final letter to start firing earlier in the cycle, creating a final-letter advantage. Along with the usual initial-letter advantage, this gives the U-shaped pattern. In the RVF/LH, the acuity/locational gradient is steeper than for the larger eccentricity, so the difference in input to the first and second letters is larger, creating an initial-letter advantage and giving an overall U-shape.

Next we consider the implications of this account for differing exposure durations. Under the assumption that a longer exposure duration increases the overall level of bottom-up input, the above analysis suggests that the RVF final-letter primacy and the LVF initial-letter primacy should be differentially affected by variations in durations. In the RVF, we would not expect to see a final-letter primacy at very brief exposures, because the very low level of input pushes the firing of the final letter late into the oscillatory cycle. As exposure duration increases, the firing of all the letters is shifted earlier and earlier into the cycle, allowing the final letter to fire longer and longer. In contrast, the activation of a non-final letter should not change much, because its firing is still quickly cut off by the subsequent letter. Thus, in the RVF, a final-letter primacy should emerge as exposure duration increases.

However, in the LVF, the initial-letter primacy should be present at very brief durations, because strong left-to-right inhibition at the feature level does not depend on temporality. As exposure duration increases, the initial letter should be the primary beneficiary because, at the feature level, the increased bottom-up input to non-initial letters is cancelled by increased lateral inhibition from the first letter.

To summarise, in the RVF, the final-letter primacy should not be present at very brief exposures. Increasing exposure duration should primarily benefit the final letter, creating a final-letter primacy. In the LVF, the initial-letter primacy should be present at very brief exposures. Increasing exposure duration should primarily benefit the initial letter, increasing its primacy.

A search of the literature revealed that a relevant experiment had already been performed, in which retinal location and exposure duration were systematically varied in a trigram identification task (Legge, Mansfield & Chung, 2001). However, the published data were not presented in a way that would allow evaluation of the above predictions. So the first author requested the raw data from the authors, who kindly provided it. The data were analysed for the largest two eccentricities (− 11 to − 9 and − 10 to − 8 versus 8 to 10 and 9 to 11, in units of letter widths) for very brief exposures (50 ms and 80 ms) versus longer exposures (125 ms and 200 ms). This analysis did indeed reveal the predicted patterns, as shown in Figure 7 (Whitney, forthcoming).

Lexical asymmetries

Different patterns for the left and right visual fields have also been observed for lexical properties, such as length. For the lexical-decision task, length has no effect on reaction times (RTs) for RVF/LH presentation, while each additional letter increases RT by 20–30 ms for LVF/RH presentation (Ellis, Young & Anderson, 1988). This asymmetry has generally been taken to reflect dual modes of lexical access, with inefficient, letter-by-letter activation of the lexicon for the LVF/RH, and efficient, parallel activation for the RVF/LH (Ellis, Young & Anderson, 1988), although the source of the asymmetry has remained a subject of debate (Jordan, Patching & Thomas, 2003; Nazir, 2003).

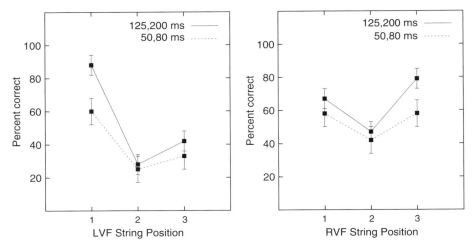

Figure 7. Results from Experiment 2 (Legge et al., 2001) for the two largest eccentricities, grouped by exposure duration, with 95% confidence intervals.

Indeed, the dual-modes account is inconsistent with brain-imaging evidence indicating that lexical access is routed through the LH, independently of presentation location (Cohen et al., 2002). Instead, this asymmetry may reflect the asymmetric activation patterns discussed above. For a long word in the LVF/RH, the resulting locational gradient would not be smoothly decreasing. Strong inhibition to the second and third letters would make their activations quite low, while inhibition may be insufficient at letters close to fixation. As a result, the locational gradient is initially steeply decreasing, and then flattens out. Such an activation pattern would provide a non-optimal encoding of letter order, which could increase settling time at the word level, thereby increasing reaction time. Thus a length effect may occur in the LVF/RH because the locational gradient becomes more and more degraded as string length increases.

This analysis suggests that it should be possible to abolish the LVF length effect by making the locational gradient smoother. Activation level can be experimental-ly manipulated by changing contrast level. Thus, for a six-letter word, increasing the contrast of the second and third letters, while decreasing the contrast of the final letter should result in a smoother gradient, thereby abolishing the length effect. That is, reaction times to LVF six-letter words under such a contrast adjustment should be equal to four-letter words under normal presentation. However, in the RVF, such a contrast adjustment should degrade a previously smooth gradient, creating a length effect. We performed such a study (Whitney & Lavidor, 2004), and these predictions were confirmed, as shown in Figure 8. These results demonstrate that a length effect is not an inherent feature of RH processing, suggesting that the dual-modes theory is incorrect. Rather, the asymmetry of the length effect is due to activation patterns, as predicted and explained by the SERIOL model. Whitney and Lavidor (forthcoming) have also shown that activation patterns are the source of a hemifield asymmetry related to the effect of orthographic neighbourhood size (Lavidor & Ellis, 2002).

However, if letter-level activations occur serially, as proposed, it should take more time for all the letters of a long word to fire than of a short word. Why then is there no effect of string length for RVF (and central) presentation? It may be the case that settling

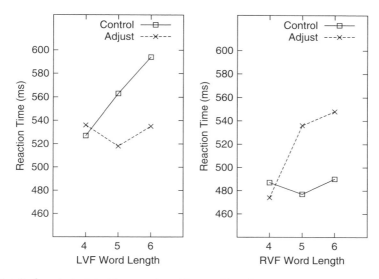

Figure 8. Results from lexical decision experiment for word targets.

Notes: Under the Adjust condition, contrast levels were manipulated as described in the text.

time is increased for a short word (as compared to a long word). That is, the reduced amount of bottom-up input to the word layer (from fewer letters) could potentially increase the amount of time required to reach response criterion after the final letter fires. If this increased settling time for a shorter word were to offset exactly the earlier firing of its final letter, there would no effect of length. Thus reaction times are not necessarily a reliable indicator of serial versus parallel processing.

A recent study demonstrates the need for these more complex scenarios. New and colleagues (New, Ferrand, Pallier & Brysbaert, forthcoming) undertook an investigation of the effect of word length based on the English Lexicon Project, which is an online database of lexical-decision RTs for over 40,000 words (Balota, Cortese, Sergent-Marshall & Spieler, 2004). Once the effects of frequency, number of syllables and orthographic-neighbourhood size were factored out, they found that RTs actually decrease with increasing string length for words of three to five letters,[3] are constant with length for words of five to eight letters, and increase with length for words of eight or more letters. Thus string length has differing effects over different lengths. It is highly unlikely that these effects reflect differences in the method of lexical access. Rather, these results most likely indicate that the effect of length is the sum of multiple influences, where the relative strength of opposing components varies with length. For example, the data are explained by assuming a facilitatory component which decreases in strength as word length increases, coupled with a steady linearly increasing cost of string length due to a serial encoding. Such a facilitatory effect may arise from decreased settling time at the word level as a result of more bottom-up activation, and this effect may be strongest for short words and then taper off, reaching a ceiling level. Thus for short words, the facilitatory effect dominates; for medium-length words, the two components cancel each other out, as discussed above; for long words, the cost of seriality dominates.

Serial processing

The most controversial aspect of the SERIOL model is the proposed serial representation of letter order. How could the proposal of seriality be investigated if reaction times do not provide a reliable index? In order to investigate a temporal phenomenon, time should be used directly. Harcum and Nice (1975) used this approach in a clever experiment in which pairs of eight-letter compound words were very briefly presented in sequence. The pairs were selected to allow meaningful blends. For example, the stimuli 'headache' and 'backrest' could be recombined to give 'headrest' or 'backache'. When fixating on the centre of the stimuli, subjects tended to report the first half of the first word, and the second half of the second word (e.g. 'headache' then 'backrest' yielded 'headrest'). This result unambiguously shows sequential readout. The first half of the first word was processed first. By the time that the second half of the stimulus was reached, the stimulus had changed and the second half of the second word was processed.

   They also included trials where fixation fell within the first or second half of the stimuli. Fixation within the second half yielded the same response pattern as central fixation. However, for fixation within the first half of the stimuli, the pattern reversed (e.g. 'backache' tended to be reported instead of 'headrest'). The authors took these results as evidence for left-to-right processing for central fixation, and peripheral-to-central processing for non-central presentation. However, we propose a more parsimonious explanation, based entirely on left-to-right processing. It has been shown that fixation within the first half of a word provides the Optimal Viewing Position (OVP) and the fastest processing (O'Regan, LevySchoen, Pynte & Brugaillere, 1984). Therefore, when fixation fell at the OVP, there may have been time to process the first word in its entirety. Then the second word would have been processed starting at the beginning, overwriting the representation of the first word. The second word was presented more quickly than the first, so there may only have been enough time to process its first half. Therefore, the response was comprised of the first half of the second word, and the second half of the first word.

Summary

These accounts provide explanations of letter perceptibility patterns and hemifield asymmetries that are otherwise difficult to explain. Thus they provide strong support for the theory of locational gradient formation at the feature level, and for the proposed interaction of the locational gradient and the oscillatory cycle at the letter level. As discussed below, learning to form such a locational gradient would be a crucial aspect of reading acquisition. First, however, we discuss the proposed nature of the phonological route in visual word recognition. (In some dual-route terminologies this would be referred to as the sub-lexical as opposed to the lexical route).

Phonological route

The reading system must exploit the visual and phonological processing used in object recognition and language. Therefore, we consider how the phonological route in visual word recognition may form on top of the phonological processing system. Of course, this first requires understanding the phonological processing system. Based on models proposed by Hickok and Poeppel (2004), and Levelt (2001), we propose the following architecture.

In the middle superior temporal gyrus, the auditory input is encoded into acoustic features suitable for speech recognition. This representation is then transformed into a phonological encoding in posterior superior temporal gyrus. This phonological representation contacts lexico-semantic representations in middle temporal gyrus.

What is the nature of this phonological representation? Experiments have indicated that the granularity of auditory word recognition is likely sub-phonemic. As a vowel's spectrum shifts due to the place of articulation of the upcoming consonant, this information about place of articulation is used to restrict possible lexical candidates even before the identity of the consonant is known (Warren & Marslen-Wilson, 1988). Further studies have indicated that this information is likely not relayed via partial activation of a phonemic level, but rather via direct contact with the lexical level. Thus lexical activation depends on abstract phonetic features (Marslen-Wilson & Warren, 1994).

How are the phonetic features matched to phonological word forms? Phonetic features are activated serially by the incoming auditory input. However, the long-term representation of word forms cannot be based on (serial) firing patterns, but rather must be static (i.e., based on connection weights). It is difficult to see how to compare directly a serial representation with a stored representation. Rather, it is more straightforward to assume that activated phonological representation depends on a parallel encoding of the phonetic relationships, allowing comparison of an activation pattern (vector) with a weight vector. This is not to say that the entire phonetic encoding must be present for such a comparison to be made. For example, recall that in the SERIOL model, bigrams are activated sequentially and lexical activations occur incrementally, yet the bigram encoding itself does not depend on serial firing. That is, all bigrams could be activated at the same time and they would still encode the same information; the encoding of the information itself does not directly depend on serial bigram activations, as is evident from a simulation in which bigrams were activated in parallel (Whitney & Berndt, 1999).

Thus we assume that there is a mechanism for converting serial, phonetic input into a parallel encoding of that sequence. We propose a similar solution as to the bigram case. That is, the parallel phonetic representation is based on open biphones, which encode that phonetic feature A occurred before phonetic feature B. Thus, the biphone encoding would activate lexical items via the same type of mechanism as the bigram encoding.

For output, this biphone representation is read out via areas near the temporo-parietal junction (Hickok & Poeppel, 2004), to be mapped to an articulatory representation in inferior frontal cortex. As discussed by Levelt (2001), output is likely to be based on syllabic units, which are constructed on the fly. That is, the biphone representation is read out serially, and converted into a sequence of syllables.

We propose that preliterate phonological encodings do not include a level of representation corresponding to phonemes. (The appearance of phoneme-like units in categorical perception and in speech errors may arise from representation at a lower, biphone level.) Rather, reading acquisition itself creates a phonemic representation, via linkages of graphemes to groups of phonetic features. We will use the term 'graphoneme' to refer to such phonemes, highlighting the proposal that the phonemic encoding depends on a linkage to orthography. Thus the phonological route in reading activates graphonemes, then phonetic features and then biphones, allowing recognition along the auditory word-recognition pathway. Graphonemic representations would likely reside in the angular gyrus, a multi-modal association area at the occipital/temporal/parietal boundary. It is well known that lesions near this region cause alexia.

During reading, interactions between the orthographic and phonological routes would occur at both the word and biphone levels, as the phonological route activates lexical representations (via an assembled biphonic representation), and the orthographic route activates stored biphonic representations (via lexical items). The resulting biphonic representation would specify the ultimate output of reading the string. See Figure 9 for an overview of the proposed system.

We propose that phonological awareness tasks are performed over the graphonemic representation, consistent with evidence for orthographic influences in such tasks. Thus the inability of dyslexics to perform phonological-awareness tasks would indicate the absence of graphonemic representations. This proposal is consistent with the results of brain imaging studies of phonological tasks (Grunling et al., 2004). In normal readers, such tasks activate posterior brain areas; in dyslexics, such tasks activate more anterior, pre-frontal regions, likely indicating an attempt to perform such tasks over a syllabic representation.

This proposal is also consistent with the double dissociation in lexical/sub-lexical abilities observed across patients with focal lesions, as discussed in Hickok & Poeppel (2004). Some patients are unimpaired in auditory word recognition, yet cannot perform sub-lexical tasks involving syllable identification and/or phoneme manipulation, while some patients show the opposite pattern (ability to do sub-lexical tasks, but impairments in auditory word recognition). The former pattern would result from damage to graphonemic representations and/or syllabification procedures, while leaving the

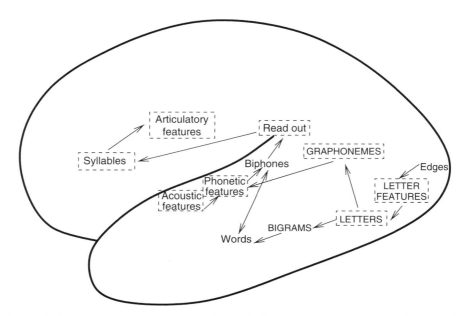

Figure 9. Schematic of proposed reading and phonological system, where representations are shown approximately at their anatomical locations.

Notes: Dashed boxes indicate representations that depend directly on serial firing to encode order information. Capital letters indicate novel representations created by reading acquisition. Arrows show primary direction of processing, but are not meant to rule out processing in the other direction, or other pathways.

phonetic-feature/biphone/lexical pathway intact. Indeed, such a pattern results from lesions near the temporoparietal junction. The latter pattern would result from a dis-connection between biphone and lexical representations. Indeed, such a pattern results from lesions to inferior temporal cortex. Overall, these patterns indicate that the sub-lexical representations used in meta-linguistic tasks are a super-set of those used in auditory word recognition, as we suggest.

For the present purposes, the specification of the phonological route at this high level is sufficient. We leave for future work the further (non-trivial) details of the neural encoding of the phonological representations.

Reading acquisition

Thus far we have discussed the principles of the SERIOL model of orthographic processing, experimental evidence for those principles, and conjectures about the phonological route in visual word recognition. Next we consider which aspects of the proposed orthographic processing must be innate, and which are learned. The learned aspects then have implications for what goes wrong when visual and phonological processing of letter strings is impaired for dyslexics.

What is innate and what is learned?

The edge layer of the SERIOL model is based on known properties of the primary visual areas, and these properties are therefore innate.

At the feature layer, the left-to-right nature of the locational gradient is learned, as it depends on reading direction. (In a language read from right to left, the locational gradient would decrease from right to left.) Furthermore, distinguishing objects by horizontal relationships is unnatural. The identity of a natural object does not change as it is rotated around the vertical axis; a lion is still a lion regardless of whether it is facing to the left or to the right. Thus the visual system must learn to distinguish horizontal order for the purpose of processing words, and it must learn to impose a monotonically decreasing activation gradient.

At the letter layer, the serial encoding depends on the oscillatory nature of letter nodes. Obviously, the brain does not learn to use oscillations to encode information. Rather, the general mechanism of using oscillatory nodes to create a location-invariant representation via the conversion of spatial representation (with varying activation levels) into a temporal representation is taken to be innate. For convenience in the remainder of this article, we will refer to the serial firing resulting from such an interaction as a scan. Such low-level scans do not rely directly on visual attention, but rather arise from the interaction of activation gradients and oscillatory cells. (However, visual attention could affect such a scan by modulating the way in which low-level activation patterns are filtered.) We assume that an innate oscillatory mechanism operates in the visual system during normal object recognition. For present purposes, this would take the form of a radial scan from fixation towards the periphery. Such an outward scan would depend directly on the acuity gradient. Thus the proposal is that formation of the locational gradient modifies the normal, symmetrical, outward processing to produce an asymmetrical left-to-right scan for string processing (in left-to-right language, of course). Indeed, Efron, Yund & Nichols (1990) have presented evidence for an outward visual scan, which seems to be perceptual and not attention based, and the pattern of the scan is influenced by the literacy of the subject (Ostrosky-Solis, Efron & Yund, 1991).

At the next layer of the model, bigram nodes represent the ordering between two letters. Thus, relationships between the sub-elements (letters) of the stimulus are encoded as a set of pairs. The general capacity to represent relationships in this way is taken to be innate. Thus in the case of strings, the visual system learns to form bigram nodes to represent relationships between pairs of letters.

The word level of the model corresponds to the lexicon. Obviously, people must learn to associate an orthographic representation with the corresponding lexical/semantic representations. Such learning would be based on general mechanisms of Hebbian/ associationist learning.

Thus these general representational mechanisms are taken to be innate: the pairwise representation of relationships, the existence of oscillatory cells, and the capacity to use these oscillatory cells to convert space into time via differences in activation levels.

Processing that is highly specific to visual word recognition occurs primarily at the feature level. Recall that, in normal readers, there was early, string-specific, LH inferotemporal activation (Tarkiainen et al., 1999). This activation may be associated with the detection of a letter string, and the triggering of string-specific processing (i.e. induction of the locational gradient). It may be the case that dyslexics fail to learn this string-specific processing. Next we consider how normal readers may learn to form the locational gradient, and then we are in a position to discuss what can go wrong in dyslexic readers.

Learning to read

Most early readers have been taught the sounds that letters make. Such conscious knowledge of letter sounds is likely to be based on lexico-semantic encodings. That is, knowledge that 'a B makes the /b uh/ sound' may be encoded similarly to the knowledge that 'a dog says /w uh f/', where /w uh f/ and /b uh/ are stored as phonological word forms associated with lexical items.

For simplicity in the following discussion, we will equate a letter and a grapheme. At the earliest stage of reading acquisition, we assume that the reader fixates each letter sequentially, focusing visual attention onto the fixated letter; this focused attention allows only that letter to become activated. If the reader is explicitly sounding out the word, each letter activates the lexical sound representation. The early reader may blend these sounds together via the same mechanism that blends morphemes' phonological representations together to make a word.

Once a pronunciation of the word is available, the reader can fixate each letter in sequence, while slowly saying or rehearsing the word. Alternatively, a teacher may slowly say the word while pointing to the corresponding letter(s). Thus, the sequence of letters and the sequence of phonetic features are temporally aligned; each letter fires in close proximity to a corresponding phonetic representation. This temporal synchrony then provides the basis for the formation of intermediate representations that link the orthographic and phonetic representations (i.e. for the formation of graphonemes). Over time, as graphoneme units become more stable, the phonological representation can be directly formed via activation of a sequence of phonetic features, rather than by blending a sequence of lexical sound representations.

If the reader fixates on the first letter but fails to restrict attention to that letter, all letters will automatically rapidly fire in order, under the above assumption of an automatic outward visual scan. If graphonemes have been learned, this will allow the rapid generation of the corresponding phonetic representation. However, if graphonemes are not present, there will be insufficient time to consciously activate the lexical sound representation for each letter, and thus the reading system will not be able to take advantage of such rapid visual processing. Thus the formation of graphonemes also allows faster visual processing; sequential fixations are no longer necessary, as a word can be rapidly processed by fixating on the first letter.

However, fixation on the first letter limits the visibility of letters near the end of the word. The reader then learns to process a word with fixation falling nearer the centre. Consider a four-letter word. Assume that the reader fixates between the first and second letters, evenly distributing visual attention across all the letters. This strategy will lead to an incorrect graphonemic representation, because the outward visual scan would cause letters one and two to fire at the same time (then three, then four, because of the RVF/LH acuity gradient). Thus the generated graphonemic representation would not be serial and would be erroneous, and therefore the phonetic features and biphones would not be activated correctly.

However, if the reader happens to pay more attention to the letter on the left (the first letter) than the letters on the right, the first letter would fire before the second letter. (Think of a top-down attentional gradient, rather than a bottom-up locational gradient, across the feature level.) Then letters in positions three and four will fire. This would cause the corresponding graphonemes to be activated sequentially, providing a suitable phonetic representation. Therefore, the reader learns to invoke an attentional gradient across the letters to produce left-to-right, serial processing. As a result, the graphonemes learned during the first stage then reinforce sequential processing of letters during subsequent stages of learning.

So, initially there is a serial letter-based representation as a result of sequential fixations. When this serial representation is temporally aligned with the blended phonological representation, graphonemes are formed. Graphonemes then allow processing of multiple letters in a single fixation. As such a shift occurs, there is pressure to maintain a serial letter-based representation, in order to generate a serial phonetic representation via the graphonemes. The generated phonetic representation (or the phonetic representation of a correction provided by a teacher) can be internally replayed in synchrony with the rapid, serial letter-based representation. This temporal correspondence then further reinforces the formation of graphoneme units and automatic processing.

Over time, the top-down attentional gradient would drive learning of automatic, bottom-up formation of an activation gradient (i.e. the locational gradient). Indeed, a simulation utilising weight adjustments on both excitatory and inhibitory connections demonstrated the feasibility of such learning. The system was able to learn to convert a symmetrical activation gradient (corresponding to the acuity gradient) into a monotonically decreasing activation gradient for strings at varying 'retinal locations' (Whitney, 2004b, p. 95).

In summary, the key proposals are as follows.

(1) The initial formation of graphoneme units is driven by the synchronous activation of a single letter and the corresponding phonetic features.
(2) The graphoneme units and the serial nature of phonology drive serial processing of letters within a single fixation, which in turn reinforces the formation of graphoneme units.
(3) The serial processing of letters within a single fixation is initially driven by a top-down attentional gradient. Over time, the visual system learns to form an activation

gradient in a bottom-up manner (i.e. learns the proposed edge-to-feature level processing in the SERIOL model).

Consistent with the proposed importance of serial processing in learning to read, young readers show a strong length effect, which slowly diminishes in magnitude until adult competence is reached, at which point a length effect is absent (Aghababian & Nazir, 2000). Because the length effect steadily decreases, its disappearance is likely a result of increasing efficiency, rather than a shift from serial to parallel processing. That is, the per-letter processing time steadily decreases as readers become more proficient. At pre-adult competence levels, the per-letter processing time dominates, giving a length effect. At the adult level of proficiency, the per-letter processing time is short enough that the time cost of an additional letter is offset by speeded settling at the lexical level (due to increased bottom-up input from the additional letter), giving no length effect.

As above, we leave the details of this proposal for future research. In particular, mechanisms for the formation of graphoneme units are non-trivial. In a language like English, where there is no simple one-to-one correspondence between graphemes and phonemes, learning to create graphoneme units would be particularly challenging, consistent with the increased prevalence of dyslexia in English compared to languages with shallow orthographies (Spencer, 2000). However, any account of the learning of grapheme-phoneme correspondences must solve alignment/segmentation problems; a key proposal here is that temporality contributes to the solution of these problems.

What can go wrong?

Next we review sensory/cognitive deficits observed in dyslexics in tasks not directly related to reading or phonological awareness. Based on the present account of reading acquisition, we discuss how such deficits could lead to abnormal processing of letter strings.

Auditory deficits

It is well known that dyslexics show deficits in phonological awareness tasks. But do they show differences from normal readers in more basic aspects of the processing of spoken language? Behavioural and ERP studies have given evidence for categorical problems in phoneme detection (Mody, Studdert-Kennedy & Brady, 1977; Schulte-Korne, Deimel, Bartling & Remschmidt, 1998; Tallal, 1980). However, most such studies have used synthetic speech sounds; a recent study using both natural and synthetic speech showed categorical perception deficits in dyslexics for the synthetic speech only (Blomert & Mitterer, 2004), suggesting that perceptual auditory deficits do not interfere with the processing of ecologically valid speech input. An ERP study of auditory lexical decision, where the target was preceded by a prime, showed differences in the N1 and N2 time windows for normal versus dyslexic children (Bonte & Blomert, 2004). In particular, N1 amplitude was reduced in dyslexics, and was insensitive to alliteration between prime/target onsets, while normals' N1 amplitude was modulated by alliteration. In contrast, normals and dyslexics did not differ in the N400 time window. The authors conclude that the dyslexics have a deficit of early phonetic/phonological processing, but not of phonological/lexical processing.

But do such differences directly cause dyslexics' reading disability? By the definition of dyslexia, dyslexics have normal spoken language ability. Thus, such differences were not severe enough to cause difficulty with the automatic acquisition of spoken language. If auditory/phonological deficits did not interfere with such a complex, implicit learning task, how could they interfere with reading, which is explicitly and systematically taught?

We suggest that the observed deficits are not causal per se, but rather are concomitant symptoms of anatomical anomalies, where the root problem is abnormal left-hemisphere connectivity from auditory cortex into other cortical areas (Paulesu et al., 1996), such as the angular gyrus in particular. Indeed, diffusion tensor MRI has revealed micro-structural abnormalities in white matter of dyslexics' temporo-parietal region (Klingberg et al., 2000). PET studies have shown strong functional connectivity (activation covariance) between Wernicke's area, left angular gyrus and left extrastriate cortex in normals during pseudoword reading, but no functional connectivity between those areas in dyslexics (Horwitz, Rumsey & Donahue, 1998; Pugh et al., 2000). This lack of functional connectivity may well be a consequence of weakened anatomical connectivity.

Therefore, we propose that reading acquisition breaks down as follows. During the first stage (single-letter processing under sequential fixations), the formation of graphonemic representations is not as robust as usual. That is, the visual and phonological repre-sentations are essentially normal, but there is a failure adequately to form associations between them to create graphonemes.

As discussed above, a lack of graphonemes would limit the speed with which letters could be visually processed, preventing employment of the automatic visual scan. The continued co-activation of a letter and a lexically-based sound representation would reinforce this style of processing, further precluding the development of graphonemes. So some readers may remain at the stage of slow, explicit blending (yielding the so-called surface or dyseidetic subtype). Thus, letter processing is serial (but induced via sequential within-word fixations) and grapheme-phoneme correspondences are encoded via lexical sound representations. Sub-lexical processing occurs via successive loops through the lexical/orthographic route, where lexical access occurs at the letter level, rather than for the word as a whole.

Other readers may instead forgo serial processing. Under an absence of graphonemes, an outward visual scan would not create an erroneous phonetic representation; conversely, a left-to-right scan would not give a suitable phonetic representation. Therefore, there is no pressure to create an attentional gradient to support rapid, left-to-right processing of letters. Rather the reader processes letter strings like other visual objects. This lack of a serial representation then further precludes the formation of graphonemic units. As a result, the reader adopts a holistic word-recognition strategy, with no sub-lexical processing (yielding the so-called phonological or dysphonetic sub-type). However, without a left-to-right scan, the encoding of letter order is not robust, so orthographic lexical access is not as reliable as in normal readers. The lack of a robust encoding of letter order would also contribute to spelling problems.

In both cases, there is a failure to learn the mechanisms for string-specific visual processing, which further contributes to abnormal phonological processing. Next we consider how a similar breakdown could occur from the visual side.

Visual deficits

Recent research has revealed a magnocellular deficit in some dyslexics (Demb, Boynton & Heeger, 1998; Livingstone, Rosen, Drislane & Galaburda, 1991; Stein & Walsh, 1997). The dorsal stream of the visual system, which specialises in motion processing, spatial localisation and attention, primarily receives inputs from the magnocellular system (Maunsell, Nealey & DePriest, 1990). Interestingly, it has been shown that magnocellular function (as indexed by coherent-motion detection threshold) is correlated with letter-position encoding ability (as indexed by the ability, in lexical decision, to reject non-words that are anagrams of words) (Cornelissen, Hansen, Gilchrist, Cormack, Essex & Frankish, 1998). Thus it is has been proposed that magnocellular dysfunction may lead to visual attentional difficulties which result in reduced ability to localise the position of letters in a string (Cornelissen et al., 1998; Vidyasagar, 2001, 2004).

Indeed, dyslexics exhibit abnormalities in visual-attention tasks. Some studies have shown LVF mini-neglect and RVF over-distractibility (Facoetti & Molteni, 2001; Hari, Renvall & Tanskanen, 2001). Others have shown deficits in serial (but not parallel) search (Iles, Walsh & Richardson, 2000), and a lack of a benefit for pre-cueing the location of a target (Roach & Hogben, 2004).

Thus there is evidence that some dyslexics are unable to focus visual attention normally. Recall that the proposed initial stage of reading acquisition depends on the ability to activate a single letter (per fixation) in tandem with hearing the corresponding phonetic features. If the early reader is unable to localise visual attention to the fixated letter, all letters will fire in each fixation, within the time span of each phoneme. Thus it will not be possible to form reliable graphoneme representations, because graphemes are temporally associated with non-corresponding phonetic features.

Without reliable graphoneme units, there is no pressure to invoke rapid, left-to-right processing of letters. Furthermore, attentional difficulties may preclude the formation of the top-down attentional gradient necessary to generate such processing via the low-level visual scan (unless fixation always falls on the initial letter).

The end result is the same as in the auditory-deficit case of non-serial processing. String-specific processing is not learned, and graphoneme representations are not formed. Words are processed like other visual objects, leading to a whole-word recognition strategy.

Vidyasagar (2001, 2004) has made a somewhat similar proposal, suggesting that proficient readers sequentially deploy attention across the string in a rapid, top-down manner, and that dyslexics are unable to do so. In contrast, we propose that proficient readers have learned to form an activation gradient in a bottom-up manner; this locational gradient automatically yields serial processing. Learning to form this locational gradient depends on the ability to form a top-down attentional gradient; the impetus for forming this top-down attentional gradient depends on learned associations between letters and phonetic features; the formation of these learned associations initially depends on the ability to focus visual attention onto a single letter.

Discussion

We have proposed that there are two important aspects to reading acquisition:

(1) The creation of a serial phonemic representation that is not present for spoken language.
(2) The induction of string-specific visual processing that operates from left to right.

These two novel types of serial representations mutually reinforce each other, allowing proficient reading. When the graphoneme representation does not develop normally, because of an inability to focus visual attention or to abnormal connectivity between the auditory and visual areas, the string-specific visual processing does not develop normally either. When string-specific visual processing does not develop normally, rapid phonetic processing is not possible.

In layman's terms, dyslexia is associated with inability to distinguish reversible letters, and with mis-ordering of letters. These symptoms are indeed present in dyslexic children at much higher rates than normal readers (Kaufman, 1980; Terepocki, Kruk & Willows, 2002), but they have been largely ignored of late in the scientific literature. A purely phonological approach to dyslexia does not explain the prevalence of such errors.

In contrast, consideration of the proposed visual aspect of processing does. Both types of reversals may be symptoms of the absence of the locational gradient to induce rapid, left-to-right processing. Note that for an outward visual scan (where feature activation levels depend directly on acuity in both VFs), the relative activation levels of the features of 'd' vary with fixation. When a 'd' is in the LVF, the straight vertical segment has a higher activation level than the curved segment. When a 'd' is in the RVF, the curved segment has a higher activation level than the straight segment. Thus it is not possible to form an invariant recognition procedure of 'd' (versus 'b') based on the activation levels of the constituent features. However, under the locational gradient, the curved segment of 'd' always has a higher activation level than the straight segment (and vice versa for 'b'), allowing such an invariant recognition procedure. Thus we suggest that reliable identification of reversible letters depends on the presence of left-to-right processing. If the normal encoding of letter order depends on such an automatic left-to-right scan, the absence of such a scan will impair the encoding of letter order, explaining the concurrence of the two types of reversal errors. Furthermore, if the encoding of letter order is impaired, the normal procedures for mapping grapheme sequences to phoneme sequences will be disrupted.

How could aspects of the present proposals be tested? As discussed above, we have proposed that counter-intuitive letter perceptibility patterns (particularly for short strings at large eccentricities) arise from the formation of the locational gradient and the conversion of this activation gradient into serial firing. If this processing is absent in dyslexics, they should show a different letter perceptibility pattern – one that is more dependent on acuity.

What are the implications for treatment of dyslexia? Continuing with the speculative nature of this work, we offer some suggestions. We propose that phonological training is successful insofar as it promotes formation of non-lexically based phonemic units. For example, the task 'remove the N sound from /l a n d/' would promote processing of phonetic sequences on the single phoneme level, without requiring the use of lexicalised phonemic representations (and so should be beneficial). In contrast, the task 'divide /l a n d/ into its phonemes' would require that the output be given in lexicalised phonemic representations (and so would not be as beneficial).

The association between letters and phonemes should be reinforced implicitly via temporal synchrony between visual and phonological representations. For example, a word could be displayed on a computer monitor, and, as the pronunciation of the word is provided, the corresponding letters are sequentially brightened. (There should then be some task related to the word or to the letters, in order to promote vigilance during the sound/letter display). This strategy should promote the formation of direct linkages between letters and phoneme units that have been established by phonological training, cementing the creation of graphonemes.

Then further visual training would be important, in order to promote rapid serial processing. This could be provided by flashing a fixation point on the screen, and then flashing a short word, where the task is to read the word. The location of the fixation point would be varied across trials, as would the position of the word relative to the fixation point. This would provide training in the allocation of visual attention, and in multi-letter processing within a single fixation. Moreover, there should be a contrast gradient across the letters. This would mimic a top-down attentional gradient and promote left-to-right processing via the automatic visual scan. Hopefully, such a contrast gradient would foster learning of bottom-up formation of the locational gradient. Over time, the contrast gradient could be phased out.

A previous study has shown that treatment utilising brief presentation (100 to 300 ms) of words, either centrally or randomly lateralised, improved spelling ability in dyslexics, whereas longer central presentation (1500 ms) or presentation to a single visual field did not (Lorusso, Facoetti & Molteni, 2004). This increased spelling ability may reflect a more reliable orthographic lexicon, stemming from more robust letter-position encoding. Perhaps brief presentation alone forced formation of the locational gradient, because overt scanning was not an option. It would be interesting to see if imposition of a contrast gradient would generate a greater improvement in reading/spelling ability than standard stimuli.

The suggested treatments would be appropriate for any root cause(s) of dyslexia. The hope is that such training would result in the formation of graphonemes and string-specific visual processing. Once such representations were firmly established, reading acquisition might then occur normally.

In conclusion, letter strings are unique visual objects because they are comprised of symbols representing sounds. This induces a left/right asymmetry that is not present for other objects. Because of these factors, letter strings require specialised visual processing. The SERIOL model provides a theory of this processing, indicating that learning to form a rapid, serial encoding of letter order may be an indispensable aspect of becoming a proficient reader. This proposal of a serial encoding was originally motivated by the necessity of providing a mechanism to create a location-invariant representation of letter order. Moreover, such a serial encoding meshes well with the serial nature of phonology. To fully understand what goes wrong in dyslexia, it would seem necessary to understand normal visual processing in reading, and how it interacts with phonological processing. The present work is an initial step in this direction.

Acknowledgements

The final form of this paper derives from an extensive and detailed e-mail dialogue between the two authors during the course of Summer and Autumn 2004. Piers Cornelissen would like to acknowledge that a considerable part of his contribution to this dialogue stems from his long-standing collaboration with Dr Peter Hansen at the University Laboratory of Physiology, Oxford. We would also like to thank the two anonymous reviewers for their inspiring comments.

Notes

1. This raises the question of how repeated letters are handled. We assume that there are multiple copies of each letter mode, and a different mode becomes activated for each instance.

2. This assumes that a single word is being processed, as in experimental studies. Under natural reading conditions, multiple short words could be represented in a single oscillatory cycle.

3. It is likely that the reason that this facilitatory effect of word length has not been previously observed is that the effect of orthographic-neighbourhood size (N) was not controlled. N is the number of words that can be formed by changing one letter of the target to another letter (Coltheart, Davelaar, Jonasson & Besner, 1977). High N is actually facilitatory for words in lexical decision (Andrews, 1997). Because N generally decreases with word length, reduced N facilitation for longer words may have cancelled out the facilitatory effect of more letters.

References

Aghababian, V. & Nazir, T.A. (2000). Developing normal reading skills: Aspects of the visual processes underlying word recognition. *Journal of Experimental Child Psychology*, 76, 123–150.

Andrews, S. (1997). The effect of orthographic similarity on lexical retrieval: Resolving neighborhood conflicts. *Psychonomic Bulletin and Review*, 4, 439–461.

Balota, D., Cortese, M., Sergent-Marshall, S., Spieler, D.H. & Yap, M. (2004). The English Lexicon Project: A web-based repository of descriptive and behavioral measures for 40,481 English words and nonwords. Available at http://elexicon.wustl.edu. Washington University.

Blomert, L. & Mitterer, H. (2004). The fragile nature of the speech-perception deficit in dyslexia: Natural vs synthetic speech. *Brain and Language*, 98, 21–26.

Bonte, M.L. & Blomert, L. (2004). Developmental dyslexia: ERP correlates of anomalous phonological processing during spoken word recognition. *Cognitive Brain Research*, 21, 360–376.

Bouma, H. (1973). Visual interference in the parafoveal recognition of initial and final letters of words. *Vision Research*, 13, 767–782.

Brysbaert, M. (1994). Interhemispheric transfer and the processing of foveally presented stimuli. *Behavioral Brain Research*, 64, 151–161.

Castles, A. & Coltheart, M. (2004). Is there a causal link from phonological awareness to success in learning to read? *Cognition*, 91, 77–111.

Castles, A., Holmes, V.M., Neath, J. & Kinoshita, S. (2003). How does orthographic knowledge influence performance on phonological awareness tasks? *Quarterly Journal of Experimental Psychology A.*, 56, 445–467.

Cohen, L., Lehericy, S., Chochon, F., Lemer, C., Rivaud, S. & Dehaene, S. (2002). Language-specific tuning of visual cortex? Functional properties of the Visual Word Form Area. *Brain*, 125, 1054–1069.

Coltheart, M., Davelaar, E., Jonasson, J. & Besner, D. (1977). Access to the internal lexicon. In S. Dornic (Ed.), *Attention and Performance VI.* (pp. 535–555). Hillsdale, NJ: Lawrence Erlbaum Associates.

Cornelissen, P.L., Hansen, P.C., Gilchrist, I., Cormack, F., Essex, J. & Frankish, C. (1998). Coherent motion detection and letter position encoding. *Vision Research*, 38, 2181–2191.

Demb, J.B., Boynton, G.M. & Heeger, D.J. (1998). Functional magnetic resonance imaging of early visual pathways in dyslexia. *Journal of Neuroscience*, 18, 6939–6951.

Efron, R., Yund, E.W. & Nichols, D.R. (1990). Detectability as a function of target location: Effects of spatial configuration. *Brain and Cognition*, 12, 102–116.

Ellis, A.W., Young, A.W. & Anderson, C. (1988). Modes of word recognition in the left and right cerebral hemispheres. *Brain and Language*, 35, 254–273.

Estes, W., Allemeyer, D. & Reder, S. (1976). Serial position functions for letter identification at brief and extended exposure durations. *Perception and Psychophysics*, 19, 1–15.

Facoetti, A. & Molteni, M. (2001). The gradient of visual attention in developmental dyslexia. *Neuropsychologia*, 39, 352–357.

Grainger, J. & Whitney, C. (2004). Does the huamn mind raed wrods as a wlohe? *Trends in Cognitive Science*, 8, 58–59.

Grunling, C., Ligges, M., Huonker, R., Klingert, M., Mentzel, H.J., Rzanny, R., Kaiser, W.A., Witte, H. & Blanz, B. (2004). Dyslexia: The possible benefit of multimodal integration of fMRI- and EEG-data. *Journal of Neural Transmission*, 111, 951–969.

Harcum, E.R. & Nice, D.S. (1975). Serial processing shown by mutual masking of icons. *Perception and Motor Skills*, 40, 399–408.

Hari, R., Renvall, H. & Tanskanen, T. (2001). Left minineglect in dyslexic adults. *Brain*, 124, 1373–1380.

Helenius, P., Tarkiainen, A., Cornelissen, P., Hansen, P.C. & Salmelin, R. (1999). Dissociation of normal feature analysis and deficient processing of letter-strings in dyslexic adults. *Cerebral Cortex*, 9, 476–483.

Hickok, G. & Poeppel, D. (2004). Dorsal and ventral streams: A framework for understanding aspects of the functional anatomy of language. *Cognition*, 92, 67–99.

Hopfield, J.J. (1995). Pattern recognition computation using action potential timing for stimulus representation. *Nature*, 376, 33–36.

Horwitz, B., Rumsey, J.M. & Donahue, B.C. (1998). Functional connectivity of the angular gyrus in normal reading and dyslexia. *Proceedings of the National Academy of Sciences*, 95, 8939–8944.

Humphreys, G.W., Evett, L.J. & Quinlan, P.T. (1990). Orthographic processing in visual word identification. *Cognitive Psychology*, 22, 517–560.

Iles, J., Walsh, V. & Richardson, A. (2000). Visual search performance in dyslexia. *Dyslexia*, 6, 163–177.

Jordan, T.R., Patching, G.R. & Thomas, S.M. (2003). Assessing the role of hemispheric specilisation, serial-position processing, and retinal eccentricity in lateralised word recognition. *Cognitive Neuropsychology*, 20, 49–71.

Kaufman, N.L. (1980). Review of research on reversal errors. *Perceptual Motor Skills*, 51, 55–79.

Klingberg, T., Hedehus, M., Temple, E., Salz, T., Gabrieli, J.D., Moseley, M.E. & Poldrack, R.A. (2000). Microstructure of temporo-parietal white matter as a basis for reading ability: Evidence from diffusion tensor magnetic resonance imaging. *Neuron*, 25, 493–500.

Lavidor, M. & Ellis, A.W. (2002). Orthographic neighborhood effects in the right but not in the left cerebral hemisphere. *Brain and Language*, 80, 63–76.

Lavidor, M. & Walsh, V. (2004). Magnetic stimulation studies of foveal representation. *Brain and Language*, 88, 331–338.

Leff, A. (2004). A historical review of the representation of the visual field in primary visual cortex with special reference to the neural mechanisms underlying macular sparing. *Brain and Language*, 88, 268–278.

Legge, G.E., Mansfield, J.S. & Chung, S.T. (2001). Psychophysics of reading. XX. Linking letter recognition to reading speed in central and peripheral vision. *Vision Research*, 41, 725–743.

Levelt, W.J. (2001). Spoken word production: A theory of lexical access. *Proceedings of the National Academy of Sciences*, 98, 13464–13471.

Liberman, I.Y., Shankweiler, D., Fischer, F.W. & Carter, B. (1974). Explicit syllable and phoneme segmentation in the young child. *Journal of Experimental Child Psychology*, 18, 201–212.

Lisman, J.E. & Idiart, M.A. (1995). Storage of $7 +/- 2$ short-term memories in oscillatory subcycles. *Science*, 267, 1512–1515.

Livingstone, M.S., Rosen, G.D., Drislane, F.W. & Galaburda, A.M. (1991). Physiological and anatomical evidence for a magnocellular defect in developmental dyslexia. *Proceedings of the National Academy of Sciences*, 88, 7943–7947.

Lorusso, M.L., Facoetti, A. & Molteni, M. (2004). Hemispheric, attentional, and processing speed factors in the treatment of developmental dyslexia. *Brain and Cognition*, 55, 341–348.

Marslen-Wilson, W. & Warren, P. (1994). Levels of perceptual representation and process in lexical access: Words, phonemes, and features. *Psychological Review*, 101, 653–675.

Mason, M. (1982). Recognition time for letters and non-letters: Effects of serial position, array size, and processing order. *Journal of Experimental Psychology*, 8, 724–738.

Maunsell, J.H., Nealey, T.A. & DePriest, D.D. (1990). Magnocellular and parvocellular contributions to responses in the middle temporal visual area (MT) of the macaque monkey. *Journal of Neuroscience*, 10, 3323–3334.

Mody, M., Studdert-Kennedy, M. & Brady, S. (1977). Speech perception deficits in poor readers: Auditory processing or phonological coding? *Journal of Experimental Child Psychology*, 64, 199–231.

Nazir, T. (2003). On hemispheric specialization and visual field effects in the perception of print: A comment on Jordan, Patching, and Thomas. *Cognitive Neuropsychology*, 20, 73–80.

New, B., Ferrand, L., Pallier, C. & Brysbaert, M. (forthcoming). Re-examining word length effects in visual word recognition: New evidence from the English Lexicon Project.

Nice, D.S. & Harcum, E.R. (1976). Evidence from mutual masking for serial processing of tachistoscopic letter patterns. *Perception and Motor Skills*, 42, 991–1003.

O'Regan, J.K., Levy-Schoen, A., Pynte, J. & Brugaillere, B. (1984). Convenient fixation location within isolated words of different length and structure. *Journal of Experimental Psychology: Human Perception and Performance*, 10, 250–257.

Ostrosky-Solis, F., Efron, R. & Yund, E.W. (1991). Visual detectability gradients: Effect of illiteracy. *Brain and Cognition*, 17, 42–51.

Paulesu, E., Frith, U., Snowling, M., Gallagher, A., Morton, J., Frackowiak, R.S. & Frith, C.D. (1996). Is developmental dyslexia a disconnection syndrome? Evidence from PET scanning. *Brain*, 119, 143–157.

Peressotti, F. & Grainger, J. (1995). Letter-position coding in random constant arrays. *Perception and Psychophysics*, 57, 875–890.

Peressotti, F. & Grainger, J. (1999). The role of letter identity and letter position in orthographic priming. *Perception and Psychophysics*, 61, 691–706.

Pugh, K.R., Mencl, W.E., Shaywitz, B.A., Shaywitz, S.E., Fulbright, R.K., Constable, R.T., Skudlarski, P., Marchione, K.E., Jenner, A.R., Fletcher, J.M., Liberman, A.M., Shankweiler, D.P., Katz, L., Lacadie, C. & Gore, J.C. (2000). The angular gyrus in developmental dyslexia: Task-specific differences in functional connectivity within posterior cortex. *Psychological Science*, 11, 51–56.

Roach, N.W. & Hogben, J.H. (2004). Attentional modulation of visual processing in adult dyslexia: A spatial-cuing deficit. *Psychological Science*, 15, 650–654.

Schulte-Korne, G., Deimel, W., Bartling, J. & Remschmidt, H. (1998). Auditory processing and dyslexia: Evidence for a specific speech processing deficit. *Neuroreport*, 9, 337–340.

Spencer, K. (2000). Is English a dyslexic language? *Dyslexia*, 6, 152–262.

Stein, J. & Walsh, V. (1997). To see but not to read; the magnocellular theory of dyslexia. *Trends in Neuroscience*, 20, 147–152.

Stuart, M. (1990). Processing strategies in a phoneme deletion task. *Quarterly Journal of Experimental Psychology A*, 42, 305–327.

Tallal, P. (1980). Auditory temporal perception, phonics, and reading disabilities in children. *Brain and Language*, 9, 182–198.

Tarkiainen, A., Cornelissen, P.L. & Salmelin, R. (2002). Dynamics of visual feature analysis and object-level processing in face versus letter-string perception. *Brain*, 125, 1125–1136.

Tarkiainen, A., Helenius, P., Hansen, P.C., Cornelissen, P.L. & Salmelin, R. (1999). Dynamics of letter string perception in the human occipitotemporal cortex. *Brain*, 122, 2119–2132.

Terepocki, M., Kruk, R.S. & Willows, D.M. (2002). The incidence and nature of letter orientation errors in reading disability. *Journal of Learning Disabilities*, 35, 214–233.

Treiman, R. & Cassar, M. (1997). Can children and adults focus on sound as opposed to spelling in a phoneme counting task? *Developmental Psychology*, 33, 771–780.

Vidyasagar, T.R. (2001). From attentional gating in macaque primary visual cortex to dyslexia in humans. *Progress in Brain Research*, 134, 297–312.

Vidyasagar, T.R. (2004). Neural underpinnings of dyslexia as a disorder of visuo-spatial attention. *Clinical and Experimental Optometry*, 87, 4–10.

Warren, P. & Marslen-Wilson, W.D. (1988). Cues to lexical choice: Discriminating place and voice. *Perception and Psychophysics*, 43, 21–30.

Whitney, C. (2001). How the brain encodes the order of letters in a printed word: The SERIOL model and selective literature review. *Psychonomic Bulletin and Review*, 8, 221–243.

Whitney, C. (2004a). Hemisphere-specific effects in word recognition do not require hemisphere-specific modes of access. *Brain and Language*, 88, 279–293.

Whitney, C. (2004b). The Neural Basis of Structured Representations. PhD thesis, University of Maryland, College Park, MD.

Whitney, C. (forthcoming). Supporting the serial in the SERIOL model.

Whitney, C. & Berndt, R.S. (1999). A new model of letter string encoding: Simulating right neglect dyslexia. *Progress in Brain Research*, 121, 143–163.

Whitney, C. & Lavidor, M. (2004). Why word length only matters in the left visual field. *Neuropsychologia*, 42, 1680–1688.

Whitney, C. & Lavidor, M. (forthcoming). Facilitatory orthographic neighborhood effects: The SERIOL model account. *Congnitive Psychology*.

Wolford, G. & Hollingsworth, S. (1974). Retinal location and string position as important variables in visual information processing. *Perception and Psychophysics*, 16, 437–442.

6

The word shape hypothesis re-examined: evidence for an external feature advantage in visual word recognition

John R. Beech and Kate A. Mayall

An enduring and unresolved issue in visual word recognition research has been the role of a word's outline shape in lexical access (e.g. Cattell, 1886; Haber, Haber & Furlin, 1983). An efficient and rapidly operating word recognition system might be expected to develop simplifying procedures that initially identify letter features on the outer edges of words, as the ascending, descending and neutral letters of words often produce unique configurations of salient features. One issue is whether it is the envelope (or the external contour) surrounding a word or the features on the periphery (e.g. the dot in the letter *i*) that are important. As will be seen, current evidence appears to be against the word envelope hypothesis, but not necessarily against the notion that the salient external features are important.

Previous studies that have examined the role of word shape in lexical access have had mixed results. Haber, Haber and Furlin (1983) used a cloze paradigm, in which students read a passage that ended mid-sentence. In one condition the clue to what followed was a symbolic representation of the ascenders, descenders and neutral letters in the word. This provided only crude information on the word envelope and length, and yet improved the chances of guessing the word correctly. But these guesses were not timed and errors were high, so this result cannot be generalised to assume that word shape has a role in normal reading.

In contrast to Haber, Haber and Furlin, Paap, Newsome and Noel (1984) examined the effects of word shape over four experiments and found no word shape effect. In the first experiment a proofreading task was used, which manipulated letters to examine the effect of changing the shape of words. They found that changing word shape tended not to be detected, whereas changes in letter distinctiveness were. Thus changing *than* to *tban*, which substitutes a confusable letter while maintaining shape was difficult to detect compared to substituting *tdan*, which also purportedly maintains shape but contains a distinctively different letter. An example of word shape alteration but with a confusable letter was changing *than* to *tnan*. However, it could be argued that there is a confound between these manipulations, such that distinctive letter substitutions also make subtle but nevertheless salient distortions to the word's outer features. The outer features of *than* are more similar to *tban* than *tdan*. Contrary to Paap, Newsome and Noel's (1984) result, in a similar proofreading task Monk and Hulme (1983) deleted or replaced a letter with an ascender and found that changing the shape of the word was detected (see also Healy & Cunningham, 1992).

More negative evidence for the word shape hypothesis comes from Paap, Newsome and Noel's (1984) second experiment, in which a letter followed presentation of a masked word or masked nonword. The task was to decide if the letter was contained in the previously presented stimulus. They found the usual 'word superiority effect' in which nonwords produced less accurate responses than words (e.g. Reicher, 1969; Wheeler, 1970). Paap, Newsome and Noel also compared rare word shapes with common shapes for both words and nonwords by classifying sequences of ascenders, descenders and neutral letters (e.g. *cellar* has a rare shape, so the nonword *cullar* was produced as a nonword with a rare shape). But no effect of shape frequency was found, thus the shape of the word appeared not to contribute to the word superiority effect.

One problem here is that Paap, Newsome and Noel proposed that word shape can be defined just by classifying letters into ascenders, descenders and neutrals. However, this ignores much of the featural information available from letters. For example, taking just the ascenders: they can occur to the right, middle or left of the centre of the letter, come out at different heights and they can be straight, curly or have a dot. These outer visual features on the upper part of a word alone could all be potentially useful in distinguishing one word from another.

Walker (1987) tested Paap, Newsome and Noel's assumptions on the Kučera and Francis (1967) word corpus and concluded, not unexpectedly, that this kind of exercise would rarely identify just one word from the corpus. However, if this shape information is combined with prior sentence context (e.g. Faust, Babkoff & Avidor-Reiss, 2000) performance is improved considerably. A second problem is that even if manipulating ascenders and descenders does produce a difference, as in the case of Monk and Hulme, this would not be conclusive support for the word shape hypothesis. It could mean instead that ascenders and descenders are more important for recognising the constituent letters of words (Oden, 1984).

Another approach to investigating the word shape hypothesis had been by means of case mixing. This approach challenges the word shape hypothesis, in both the word envelope and outer feature versions, because studies such as those by Besner and Johnston (1989) and Mayall and Humphreys (1996) have shown that case mixing has a greater effect for nonwords than real words. A word shape hypothesis would have predicted the reverse: if word shape is important for recognition, disruption by case mixing ought to have much more impact on real words than nonwords. However, there could be several reasons for the finding of greater disruption in nonword reading without necessarily rejecting the word shape hypothesis. For instance, case alternation disrupts the appearance of graphemic patterns (e.g. 'cH'), which would disrupt the phonemic generation on which nonword pronunciation might rely (see Pring, 1981). An explanation forwarded by both Besner and Johnston, and Mayall and Humphreys, is that nonwords are more difficult to pronounce because their pronunciation cannot be cross-checked with known words in the naming task. Similarly, they cannot be checked for familiarity in naming and in lexical decision tasks. Mayall and Humphrey's argument was that transletter features are disrupted by case mixing in both words and nonwords. Words recover quicker, however, as they receive top-down lexical information.

Comparing the processing of words in lower case and upper case is a similar approach to testing the word shape hypothesis as converting to the upper-case form alters the word shape normally available in lower case while retaining the same letter identities. Both Mayall and Humphries (1996, Experiment 1) and Perea and Rosa (2002) found that high frequency words were unaffected by case, in contrast to low frequency words. The word shape hypothesis might have predicted the contrary outcome whereby high frequency words would be more disrupted by the change from lower to upper case. In the instance of Mayall and Humphries, their main focus was a comparison with mixed case in the same experiment, which may have affected their participants' processing of the stimuli. Perea and Rosa (2002) undertook this experiment in Spanish, which has a much more transparent orthography than English, so wholistic word processing may be less likely here, with more emphasis on parallel letter processing. Two other aspects might also be noted: (1) the pace of their lexical decision task was fast, with an inter-trial interval of only 400 ms followed by 250 ms of warning before the next stimulus, and (2) the extent of the inclusion of ascenders and descenders in the stimuli is not reported. In contrast to these two experiments Paap, Newsome and Noel (1984) failed to find a differential frequency effect in similar circumstances. Nevertheless, a word shape hypothesis would predict superiority in processing lower-case words compared to upper-case ones, and if there were an effect in these experiments it would appear to be quite small in size.

There has been only a limited amount of work on the processing of the external features of words such as that by Johnston, Anderson and Duncan (1991). They examined the effect of manipulating the number of ascenders and descenders in words on children's naming performance. They found that children with a reading age of eight years named words with ascenders and descenders more accurately than words made up of neutral letters. Children with a reading age of ten years showed no effect in terms of errors in reading; however their reaction times were not tested. Johnston, Anderson and Duncan concluded that those children with a younger reading age were using a logographic process to read words. This is a coarse type of analysis hypothesised to rely on holistic visual features such as word shape alone. However, there is an implicit assumption that skilled readers do not recognise words in this way, and that therefore these effects would not carry through to adulthood. Lété and Pynte (2003) found in experimental work with French adults an interaction with frequency such that for high frequency words there was no difference between words with neutral letters and words with ascenders and descenders; by contrast less frequent words with ascenders and descenders were responded to 57 ms faster than words with neutral letters. These authors argued on the basis of this and other findings that shape information has a role in word recognition.

From the work reviewed, the weight of evidence does not support the 'crude envelope' form of the word shape hypothesis. Despite this, the visual features on the periphery of words may have an important function. There has been no direct experimentation on the featural analysis of ascender and descender information in skilled reading. Given that the external features of a word may be more important for word recognition, the approach in the present study is to compare the effects of presenting words that have had their inner features removed with words that have had their outer features removed.

The first experiment examined whether readers appear to have a bias towards peripheral analysis of a word's features. This was tested by means of a forward priming paradigm in which word fragments appeared briefly followed by the rest of the word. The effect of priming with a word with its inner features removed is to isolate the effects of the pattern of external (or outer) visual features that are produced by the ascenders and descenders. Conversely, stripping a word of its outer features enables examination of the effects of its inner features. A masked priming procedure, similar to one first used by Forster and Davis (1984), was used here and involved presenting a visual noise mask, briefly followed by a prime, and then the target, which remained present until a naming response was made. In Experiment 1 the prime was either the inner or outer part of a word and the target that followed was the intact word. This design enabled a brief masked exposure to the prime. Despite the observer generally being unaware of such primes, these exposures can produce effects on the target words (e.g. Evett & Humphreys, 1981).

In Experiment 1 the word frequency of the stimuli was manipulated to examine potential additive or interactive effects with the inner and outer word fragments. An implicit assumption of a word shape hypothesis is that word shape would have more of an effect on highly frequent words. Frequent exposure to particular words with unique contours may mean that outer configurations of these are much better learned than lower frequency contours. Although an interaction with word frequency is not a necessary condition for the word shape hypothesis, it would certainly strengthen the case. High frequency words may be more likely to be recognised as a whole, whereas low frequency words may require more detailed analysis of all features.

Alternatively, a main effect of frequency without an interaction could be explained in connectionist or logographic terms. Primes activate several words with similar features and as high frequency words have developed stronger connections they would be more highly activated (e.g. Seidenberg & McClelland, 1989). Similarly, featural information bombarding the logogens would trigger more easily those representing high frequency words due to their lower thresholds. (e.g. Morton, 1969, 1980). Thus, in these two forms word shape information may enhance processing, but not interactively with frequency.

In the present paradigm, prime type could potentially affect the reaction time to name the subsequently exposed target word. This will enable investigation into whether the outer features of a word contain enough information alone to initiate lexical access compared to the inner features. In addition, the duration of the prime was varied in a between-subjects design here in order to examine temporal development on the processing of both internal and external features.

Experiment 1: primed word recognition

Method

Participants

The participants were 128 psychology undergraduates from the University of Leicester. They were all native English speakers and had either normal or corrected vision. They volunteered in order to earn credits for their first-year laboratory class.

Stimuli and design

In order to partition words into inner and outer segments, the horizontal bars of the lower case letter *z* in Arial font were used to define our criterion for the two boundaries on all letter stimuli. The upper cut-off was such that the upper horizontal bar of the letter *z* is present within the 'outers' segment, but absent within the 'inners' segment. Similarly, the lower bar is shown in the 'outers' segment, but not within the 'inners'. When words are divided in this manner certain letters share common inner or outer features; for instance, the inner part of *b* and *p* is identical in Arial font. An example of one of the words ('bring') is shown in Figure 1.

The corpus of 4,187 five-letter words from Kučera and Francis (1967) was searched and categorised using a Visual Basic program as follows. Words were inspected for all letters sharing internal or external features. (The letter sets sharing common inner or outer features were: *c-e-o-s; b-p; d-g-q; f-i-j-l-t; h-n*; and *v-y*.) Checking across the whole set of words, only words that had unique patterns of inner and outer features were selected. The words chosen as stimuli were balanced so that there was the same number of words in each frequency set with one or two neutral letters (e.g. *think* has one neutral letter, which is 'n'). Any irregularly spelled words and any plurals were excluded. As a result of these selections 64 low frequency (<20 per million) and 64 high frequency stimuli (frequencies between 20 to 433 per million) were chosen.

A further analysis of the word stimuli involved calculating the print surface area exposed by their inner and outer features, respectively. The raw data were expressed as area (mm^2) of print exposed for each letter divided into three segments by the two cut-off boundaries (based on the letter *z* as already described) printed in 36-point Arial font. The top and bottom segments were added together to calculate outer print area and the middle segment constituted the inner print area. This showed that for the high frequency words the average area occupied by the inners was 54.9% compared with 45.1% for the outers. For the low frequency words the ratio was very similar at 54.8% to 45.2%.

Procedure

Participants sat in front of a Powerpaq computer and the individual words were presented in the centre of the screen in black (36-point Arial font) on a white background. A computer program written in Borland C++ controlled the presentation.

A trial was initiated by the appearance of a + that served as both a fixation point and a warning. After 500 ms this was replaced by a mask of non-alphanumeric symbols (&$@%£) for a further 500 ms. Then a prime appeared for 50, 100, 150 or 250 ms. There were four prime types: blank, masking, inner and outer. A blank prime was a blank white field and the masking prime was a set of neutral characters (#####). This masking prime was included to examine the possibility that the inner and outer primes, instead of facilitating performance, acted as forward pattern masks. Following the prime, the whole word was presented and remained on the screen until a vocal response was made, which triggered a voice key and signalled the end of the reaction time measurement. Participants were instructed to look at the word appearing at the location of the cross and name it as quickly and as accurately as possible.

The words were divided into four blocks of 16 stimuli for each level of word frequency. These blocks were counterbalanced across the four types of priming condition. Furthermore, within each block each participant received a different random order of

Figure 1. An outer fragment of 'bring'.

stimulus presentation. There were 12 practice trials followed by the experimental stimuli across 128 trials (16 in each frequency × prime condition). Thirty-two participants were run in each of the 4-prime duration conditions.

Results and discussion

Table 1 shows the means and standard deviations of the reaction times and error data on high and low frequency words for the four types of prime as a function of prime duration. Table 2 shows the tables of within-subject analyses of variance for each prime duration for each group with a final analysis of variance, between-subjects across duration. A second similar set of analyses was performed across items. The main focus of interest is the relative performance on words following inner and outer primes (part of 'prime type' variable in the analysis of variance) as a function of word frequency and prime duration.

The ANOVAs show significant main effects for prime type in all durations in all analyses and significant interactions with word frequency for the two longest durations for the subjects analysis and for the 150 ms duration for the items analysis. The 250 ms duration interaction marginally failed to reach significance, $p = 0.07$, in the items analysis.

The final column in Table 1 showing the absolute difference between outer and inner primes illustrates the advantage of the outer prime over the inner prime. It shows that the effect is negligible at 50 ms, then at 100 ms there is a greater effect for high frequency words and for the 150 and 250 ms durations, the outer advantage is strongest, with little difference between the frequency conditions. This indicates that within 100 ms outer features are impacting on word recognition of high frequency words and by 150 ms (and at least up to 250 ms) both high and low frequency words are identified significantly faster if primed by outer features, compared with inner features.

Post hoc tests on the subject analyses (Newman-Keuls) showed that at 100 ms, priming of the outer part of the word significantly speeded-up reaction times relative to priming with the inner part. Inspection suggests that much of this effect was for the high frequency words, although the frequency × prime-type interaction did not reach statistical significance (see Table 1). Newman-Keuls tests for the high and low frequency words separately for the longer durations (150 and 250 ms) confirmed that the outers were significantly faster than the inners for both high and low frequencies and for both these durations ($p < 0.01$).

Newman-Keuls analyses also showed that at 50 and 100 ms, pooling for frequency, the masking prime produced significantly slower latencies than the other prime conditions ($p < 0.01$). At 100 ms, the outer prime reaction times were significantly faster than the inner primes ($p < 0.05$). Thus the masking prime had the effect of significantly prolonging the forward masking effect relative to the other primes. The interfering effect of the masking prime persisted up to the maximum duration of 250 ms and this was confirmed by post hoc testing (set at $p < 0.01$) in which the masking prime produced significantly slower RTs than all other primes.

A further analysis involved taking each subject's four mean reaction times for word frequency versus prime type (inner-LF; inner-HF; outer-LF; and outer HF) and deducting from these their corresponding RTs in either the blank inner or the blank outer conditions. This method was used so that each participant was their own control in terms of their relative performance against their performance on the blank primes. Figure 2 shows how

Table 1. Mean reaction times (RTs; in ms) and errors in the word naming task as a function of prime duration, frequency and type of prime in Experiment 1.

			Type of prime		
Stimulus type	Blank	Masking	Inner (I)	Outer (O)	I − O
50 ms prime					
High frequency					
RT mean	512	539	510	505	5
RT SD	66	61	60	67	
% error	1.4	1.0	2.0	2.2	
% spoiled	1.6	2.2	2.7	1.4	
Low frequency					
RT mean	514	545	516	514	2
RT SD	62	80	60	69	
% error	1.6	2.2	2.0	2.8	
% spoiled	1.8	1.6	2.5	1.2	
100 ms prime					
High frequency					
RT	498	536	501	487	14
RT SD	64	66	56	60	
% error	1.2	0.8	1.6	1.0	
% spoiled	0.8	2.0	1.4	0.6	
Low frequency					
RT mean	504	550	510	506	4
RT SD	68	68	72	98	
% error	0.6	1.2	1.2	0.6	
% spoiled	1.4	1.0	1.0	1.2	
150 ms prime					
High frequency					
RT mean	462	490	460	418	42
RT SD	50	43	46	49	
% error	2.6	0.4	1.4	1.4	
% spoiled	1.6	2.0	1.4	0.4	
Low frequency					
RT mean	458	496	471	434	37
RT SD	44	46	45	46	
% error	1.0	1.8	2.6	1.4	
% spoiled	1.4	1.0	1.6	0.8	
250 ms prime					
High frequency					
RT mean	495	516	478	424	54
RT SD	51	54	58	63	
% error	0.8	1.4	1.0	0.4	
% spoiled	1.6	3.1	2.9	1.2	
Low frequency					
RT mean	499	522	499	446	53
RT SD	55	55	59	67	
% error	1.0	0.4	1.4	1.2	
% spoiled	2.5	1.8	2.2	2.3	

Note: RT = reaction time. Spoiled trials were trials in which the voice key was activated inadvertently or failed to be activated.

Table 2. Analyses of variance for Experiment 1.

By subject analysis Source	df	F_1	By item analysis Source	df	F_2
50 ms prime					
Frequency (F)	1	10.77**	F	1	3.17
F X S within group error	31	(205.75)	F X I within group error	126	(3034.74)
Prime Type (PT)	3	38.38***	PT	3	33.26***
PT X S within group error	93	(370.75)	F X PT	3	0.69
F X PT	3	0.51	PT X I within group error	378	(899.36)
F X PT X S within group error	93	(316.34)			
100 ms prime					
F	1	9.26**	F	1	5.16*
F X S within group error	31	(978.10)	F X I within group error	126	(3185.48)
PT	3	56.53***	PT	3	43.92***
PT X S within group error	93	(510.83)	F X PT	3	0.88
F X PT	3	1.00	PT X I within group error	378	(1326.66)
F X PT X S within group error	93	(476.95)			
150 ms prime					
F	1	17.59**	F	1	3.65
F X S within group error	31	(187.51)	F X I within group error	126	(2197.07)
PT	3	38.38***	PT	3	150.93***
PT X S within group error	93	(474.61)	F X PT	3	2.64*
F X PT	3	5.45**	PT X I within group error	378	(627.70)
F X PT X S within group error	93	(222.62)			
250 ms prime					
F	1	25.79***	F	1	9.93**
F X S within group error	31	(407.96)	F X I within group error	126	(2515.60)
PT	3	148.35***	PT	3	182.86***
PT X S within group error	93	(549.36)	F X PT	3	2.44
F X PT	3	4.46**	PT X I within group error	378	(889.65)
F X PT X S within group error	93	(345.32)			
Overall					
Between subjects			Between items		
Prime Duration (PD)	3	6.77***	F	1	6.05*
S within group error	124	(26634.33)	I within group error	126	(9282.10)
Within subjects			Within items		
F	1	51.33***	PD	3	669.27***
F X PD	3	1.69	PD X F	3	1.77
F X S within group error	124	(444.83)	PD X S within group error	378	(550.26)
PT	3	294.95***	PT	3	277.12***
PT X PD	9	22.29***	F X PT	3	3.61*

Table 2. (Continued)

| By subject analysis | | | By item analysis | | |
Source	df	F_1	Source	df	F_2
PT X S within group error	372	(476.39)	PT X S within group error	378	(1013.32)
F X PT	3	7.44***	PD X PT	9	23.73***
F X PT X PD	9	0.84	PD X PT X F	9	0.72
F X PT X S within group error	372	(340.31)	PD X PT X S within group error	1134	(910.02)

Note: Mean square errors are in parentheses. S = subjects and I = items. In the items analysis frequency is between items and the rest are within items.
**$p<0.01$; ***$p<0.001$.

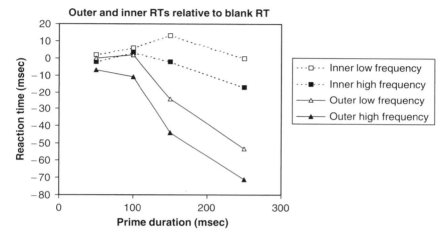

Figure 2. Outer and inner RTs relative to blank RT.

Notes: Each blank reaction time is deducted from its corresponding outer or inner reaction time and plotted as a function of prime duration and word frequency. (The more negative the resulting reaction time, the faster it is relative to the blank condition.)

the two outer prime conditions (solid lines) are substantially affected by prime duration compared with the inner conditions (dotted lines). To explain further, the solid triangle in the figure for the outer HF condition at a prime duration is -71 ms. This means that subjects were 71 ms faster when primed with an outer prime compared with when there was no prime (the blank condition). By contrast, as the RTs were uniformly above zero for the inner low frequency condition, this indicates no facilitation for any prime duration for the inner-LF primes. A $4 \times 2 \times 2$ ANOVA with prime duration between subjects and prime type and word frequency as within subjects was computed on the by-subject data. All the main effects were highly significant, $(p<0.001)$: $F_1(1,124) = 158.5$, $F_1(1,124) = 18.4$ and $F_1(3,124) = 24.4$, respectively, for prime type, word frequency and prime duration for subjects. Similarly for a by-items ANOVA the main effects in the same order were: $F_2(3,126) = 102.45$, $p<0.001$; $F_2(1,126) = 133.02$, $p<0.001$ and $F_2(1,124) = 6.20$, $p<0.05$. There was one major interaction that was significant for both the by-subject and the by-item ANOVAs and that was between prime type and prime duration, $F_1(3,124) = 32.67$, $F_2(3,126) = 99.88$ (both $p<0.001$). This interaction reflects the substantial effect of prime duration on outer primes compared with inner primes. There was a further minor interaction in the by-items ANOVA between word frequency and prime duration, $F_2(1,126) = 4.61$, $p < 0.05$ that did not occur in the by-subjects ANOVA.

In summary, outer primes induced significantly faster responses to words compared to inner primes from 100 ms; in the case of high frequency words and for the longer durations both high and low frequency words were primed better by outer primes, compared with inner primes. Thus after 100 ms the advantage of outer primes over inner primes is strong and consistent. The masking prime significantly slowed responses relative to other primes discounting the hypothesis that the primes with word fragments might have an interfering effect on word recognition.

One hypothesis to account for the results of Experiment 1 is that the outer parts of words contain more salient visual features. This implies that the outer fragments of words (that have had their inner features removed) enable better prediction of a word's identity than the inner fragments (that have had their outer features removed). The next experiment is designed as a controlling experiment to test the possibility that the outer parts of words lead more easily to identification. If this is the case, it will allow a further examination of the data in Experiment 1 to see whether, controlling for this factor of ease of guessing a word's identification, there would still be an advantage of being primed by the outer part of a word.

Experiment 2: guessing word identities from fragments

Method

Participants

The participants were 188 undergraduates from the University of Leicester. They were all native speakers of English. They volunteered in order to earn credits for their first-year laboratory class. None of these participants had been tested in Experiment 1.

Stimuli and design

All the priming stimuli (in other words all the word fragments) used in the first experiment were presented to participants in Experiment 2. The stimuli were organised into four different questionnaires within four booklets. Each booklet consisted of 64 stimuli, half of which were the inner parts of words and the other half were outer parts. The inner and outer stimuli alternated within each booklet. The first two booklets each consisted of half the stimuli, but each stimulus word had its inner version in one booklet and its outer in the other. The other two booklets had the other half of the stimuli organised in the same manner. There were four groups, with 47 participants in each group who completed each booklet.

Procedure

Participants were asked to attempt to write down the correct word for all the stimuli and were asked to guess if they were unsure. They were informed that all the items had five letters and were real words. They were covertly timed (in minutes) and this showed that they took a mean time of 16 min ($SD = 7$) with a range between 5 and 40 minutes to read the instructions and then write down the responses in their booklets.

Table 3. Means (and standard deviations in parentheses) of percentages correct as a function of inner versus outer word parts and word frequency in Experiment 2.

| | Experimental Condition | |
Stimulus Type	Inner	Outer
High Frequency	52.19 (26.06)	97.07 (8.10)
Low Frequency	50.83 (28.43)	95.18 (10.10)

Results and discussion

The main result was that the percentage correct for the outer prime stimuli was much greater than for the inner stimuli for both the high and low frequency stimuli. The mean percentages correct are shown in Table 3 and the individual data are available in the Appendix. Mixed analyses of variance on the subjects (F_1) and the stimulus items (F_2) with word frequency and inners versus outers revealed a main effect for inners versus outers, $F_1(1,187) = 802.99$, $p<0.001$, $MSE = 37.40$ and $F_2(1,126) = 281.40$, $p<0.001$, $MSE = 452.66$. A main effect for frequency was found in the subjects analysis, $F_1(1,187) = 6.6$, $p<0.05$, $MSE = 0.05$, but not for the items analysis $(F_2<0.1)$. There was no interaction $(F_1$ & $F_2<1)$. The lack of interaction between frequency and inners versus outers, whereby the prediction of a greater difference in performance on frequency for the outer stimuli was not properly tested due to the substantial ceiling effect for the outer stimuli. There were more subjects than stimuli; therefore the subjects analysis represented a more powerful test of the word frequency effect. Thus there is a frequency effect, but the effect size is small. The main result suggests that the inner features, in the case of many of the stimuli, do not provide sufficient featural information to enable an identification of the complete word and further confirms the importance of peripheral features in identifying words.

In order to obtain a more complete picture stepwise multiple regressions were computed on the primed reaction times in Experiment 1. This investigated whether the strong effects of priming by outer features found in Experiment 1 was just a result of the outer primes enabling an earlier guess at the word identity. Alternatively there could still be an effect of outer primes as a result of a bias towards attending to the outer features of word stimuli. Regressions were computed for each prime duration. Reaction time was the dependent variable and the following were the independent variables: the accuracy in guessing each word in Experiment 2; whether it was the RT for the inner or outer part of the word; word frequency; and the proportion of the print area of the primed region relative to total print area. Table 4 shows the results for prime durations 100–250 ms, with the 50 ms prime duration missing because of insignificant results. In all three cases the most important association is between accuracy in guessing the word and reaction time to the prime. Thus a word fragment that more easily evokes identification when in its primed form serves as a more potent prime than a word fragment of lower guessability. This relationship is strongest for the 250 ms prime duration and reduces in strength, as the prime duration gets shorter. At 250 ms word frequency is next in importance followed by whether the inner or outer part of the word is primed. This influence of the part of the word was more important at the 150 ms duration, followed by print area and word frequency. Overall these results indicate that the outer features of words are more important than their internal features in the naming

Table 4. Multiple regression analyses of 100–250 ms inner and outer prime RTs and accuracy in guessing word identities.

Dependent variable	Beta	R^2 change	p
250 ms prime			
Accuracy in guessing word	− 0.478	0.381	<0.001
Word frequency	− 0.129	0.015	<0.01
Inner versus outer	− 0.181	0.015	<0.05
150 ms prime			
Accuracy in guessing word	− 0.197	0.255	<0.001
Inner v. outer	− 0.609	0.036	<0.001
Print area	0.288	0.014	<0.05
Word frequency	− 0.119	0.014	<0.05
100 ms prime			
Accuracy in guessing word	− 0.137	0.019	<0.05

task, within a particular range of prime durations, even when the extent to which an actual word is triggered by the prime's guessability is controlled for. In other words, the superiority of the outers does not simply reflect participants guessing the words from the primes.

There is also a print area effect at the 150 ms duration, in which there is a positive relationship showing that reaction time is faster for primes that are smaller in print area. This adds support to the hypothesis that the outer region contains more featural information per unit of print area. Thus although there is less print area in the periphery, guessability is high; conversely, when there is more print area in the middle region guessability is lower. These outer primes cover a smaller print area and although they are in the periphery of the word, they are more potent.

In summary, the second experiment involved showing participants the partial word for an unlimited time to see if they could guess the identities of the completed words and demonstrated that words have structural characteristics that enabled much better predictability on the basis of external features. It is interesting to speculate whether these structural characteristics in turn mean that mature readers have learned to process information on the periphery of words before featural information in the centre, given that there is much more information per unit of area in the periphery.

General discussion

Previously reviewed evidence (e.g. Paap, Newsome & Noel, 1984; Walker, 1987) suggested that the crude word envelope hypothesis, entailing classifying words in terms of their ascenders, descenders and neutral letters, does not appear to be supported by empirical evidence. As a variation on this, the current experiments explored whether it was external visual letter features rather than the nature of a crude word envelope that aided word recognition. Taking the two current experiments together, there is strong support for the external features hypothesis that proposes that the outer features of a word have more influence than inner features on recognition.

In Experiment 1 the sequence was a visual mask, followed by an outer prime, then the actual word. If the duration of the prime were longer than 100 ms, it was found that RTs significantly improved compared to a prime consisting of the inner part of the word. Word frequency was also an important factor whereby outer primes of higher frequency words produced the greatest priming effect at 100 ms, about the time when primes are becoming effective.

The second experiment was a controlling experiment examining the efficacy of the information provided by these inner and outer word fragments. It was demonstrated that outer fragments evoked words much better than inner fragments, despite having a reduced print area. This has implications for any form of word shape hypothesis in that it appears that the potency of word shape or outer contour to evoke identification could be confounded by the potency of the outer features of the letters. It is perhaps still an open question whether the density of potent outer letter features (relative to inner features) is more important in determining a word's identification than 'shape' alone, if these two aspects can be separated.

Another consideration for the superiority of external features in Experiment 2 is that it is easier to extrapolate word identity from outer features, compared with extrapolation in the reversed direction. The Gestalt law of closure states that gaps in stimuli are perceptually closed by extrapolating simple features (e.g. Donnelly, Humphreys & Riddoch, 1991; Wertheimer, 1950). It might be argued that such a process could help the processing of the outer stimuli by helping the automatic mental extension of the connections between the two segments. By contrast, this would not assist the inner primes. However there are a couple of aspects to consider. First, such mental extrapolation in several cases would need to be based on letter and lexical knowledge, rather than a simple perceptual continuation of lines and curves. For example, the letters 'c', 'e', 'o' and 's' in Arial font with their inner features removed are identical as outer primes (which is why they were grouped together as part of the search for unique word shapes). The Gestalt law of closure would be more likely to predict erroneously that the representation for this prime would always be the letter 'o', or at best random, rather than the alternative letters. Extrapolating on the basis of letter knowledge alone would also be insufficient for identification in such cases, as there would have to be an interaction with lexical knowledge. Another Gestalt law, the law of 'good continuation', may be able to finish truncated curves in some cases of the inner primes, but would be even less reliable than using closure for the outer features. It might be noted anecdotally that for some participants viewing our outer primes there was an impression (or illusion) of the word being mentally completed; however, this process is not likely to be a simple perceptual operation. The second aspect concerning the closure hypothesis, if we were to suppose this hypothesis were viable, is as follows. The saliency of the information (or guessability) determined in Experiment 2, in terms of the ease with which people identified the words from the fragments, was an influential factor on RT. Multiple regression controlling for this saliency still showed a significant effect for outer word features for the longest prime durations. The participants' superiority in the external features part was because of the richness of the external letter features and (possibly) the added advantage of making a Gestalt-type of closure. When these effects were removed, what was left was an advantage for outer versus inner features for primes of 150 and 250 ms, and as such this advantage was unlikely to be connected with closure effects. Instead, these findings suggest that there could be an obligatory process that involves the prior access of the word's peripheral features.

The current findings have implications for modelling word recognition. One view is that word recognition is a pattern recognition process in which there is simultaneous analysis at several levels. There is broad agreement that at the very least component letters are analysed in parallel (e.g. McClelland & Rumelhart, 1981). More controversially, a more flexible view of word recognition is that there are other types of analysis that are also feasible that are not necessarily alternatives; instead these processes could operate in conjunction with this parallel processing of letters. For example, supra-letter features could also be processed ranging from features incorporating at least two letters to word shape information (e.g. Lété & Pynte, 2003). Processing word shape information is unlikely to account for word recognition per se. Featural information within letters has a crucial role in word identification, and as McClelland (1977) suggests, word shape information is derived from letter information. So rather than being a candidate for being the only way words are processed, word shape information may have a contribution to make to word recognition, as part of other parallel analyses. The present findings show that processing occurs more intensely within the narrow region where word shape information is most potent in two important respects. First, letter feature information is the most potent in the outer reaches of the top-to-bottom direction in the same way that Jordan, Patching and Thomas (2003) and others have studied the most potent areas in the left-right direction (in terms of letter position). Second, there is an inclination to process in this outer area, controlling for the first aspect.

Support for the efficacy of outer features in word recognition could mean that as a result of an accident of history those designing our calligraphy and typography conferred more noticeable features to letters' outer parts. It suggests that there are more salient letter features in the outer boundaries of words that enable identification. Priming these outer features, where such stimulus information is more concentrated, would be much more potent than priming inner features. The inner part of a word, by contrast, is more impoverished and so it is usually much more difficult to use this information, even though each prime was unique to only one word in the corpus.

These results may have indirect implications on the role of phonology in visual word recognition. Berent and Perfetti (1995) have proposed a two-cycle model of word identification in which first, consonants and vowels are represented separately and second, as part of assembled phonology consonants are rapidly and automatically processed followed by a second cycle in which vowels are also processed. The relevance of the current results is that most ascenders and descenders are consonants and apart from the letter 'i' and more rarely 'y', the vowels are neutral in size. The function of a first phase of processing peripheral visual features could be to process consonant information before a slower second phase that concentrates more on other aspects, including the inner parts.

In conclusion, Experiment 1 provides evidence that during a particular time-frame within word recognition the visual features on the outer edges of words are much more potent than features within the inner parts. Experiment 2 provides strong support for a hypothesis proposing that salient letter features within words are concentrated more in their outer regions, rather than being more evenly distributed or concentrated within their internal regions. The salience of these outer visual features is important for subsequent word recognition. Controlling for the potent effects of the much higher predictability inherent in letter features on the periphery, there is a more minor, but nevertheless significant effect of bias towards processing outer features.

References

Berent, I. & Perfetti, C.A. (1995). A rose is a reez: The two cycles model of phonology assembly in reading English. *Psychological Review*, 102, 146–184.

Besner, D. & Johnston, J.C. (1989). Reading and the mental lexicon: On the interaction of visual, orthographic, phonological, and lexical information. In W. Marslen-Wilson (Ed.), *Lexical processes and representation*. (pp. 291–316). Cambridge, MA: MIT Press.

Cattell, J.M. (1886). The time taken up by cerebral operations. *Mind*, 11, 277–282, 524–538.

Donnelly, N., Humphreys, G.W. & Riddoch, M.J. (1991). Parallel computation of primitive shape descriptions. *Journal of Experimental Psychology: Human Perception and Performance*, 17, 561–570.

Evett, L.J. & Humphreys, G.W. (1981). The use of graphemic information in lexical access. *Quarterly Journal of Experimental Psychology*, 33A, 325–350.

Faust, M., Babkoff, H. & Avidor-Reiss, I. (2000). Sentence and word outline shape as co-primes for target words presented to the visual hemifields. *Brain and Language*, 73, 50–61.

Forster, K.I. & Davis, C.W. (1984). Repetition priming and frequency attenuation in lexical access. *Journal of Experimental Psychology: Learning, Memory and Cognition*, 10, 680–698.

Haber, L.R., Haber, R.N. & Furlin, K.R. (1983). Word length and word shape as sources of information in reading. *Reading Research Quarterly*, 18, 165–189.

Healy, A.F. & Cunningham, T.F. (1992). A developmental evaluation of the role of word shape in word recognition. *Memory & Cognition*, 20, 141–150.

Johnston, R., Anderson, M. & Duncan, L. (1991). Phonological and visual segmentation problems in poor readers. In M. Snowling & M.E. Thomson (Eds.), *Dyslexia: Integrating theory and practice*. (pp. 154–164). Whurr: London.

Jordan, T.R., Patching, G.R. & Thomas, S.M. (2003). Assessing the role of hemispheric specialization, serial-position processing, and retinal eccentricity in lateralised word recognition. *Cognitive Neuropsychology*, 20, 49–71.

Kučera, H. & Francis, W.N. (1967). *Computational analysis of present-day American English*. Providence, RI: Brown University Press.

Lété, B. & Pynte, J. (2003). Word-shape and word-lexical-frequency effects in lexical-decision and naming tasks. *Visual Cognition*, 10, 913–948.

Mayall, K.A. & Humphreys, G.W. (1996). Case mixing and the task sensitive disruption of lexical processing. *Journal of Experimental Psychology: Learning, Memory and Cognition*, 22, 278–294.

McClelland, J.L. (1977). Letter and configurational information in word identification. *Journal of Verbal Learning and Behavior*, 16, 137–150.

McClelland, J.L. & Rumelhart, D.E. (1981). An interactive activation model of context effects in letter perception: Part 1. An account of basic findings. *Psychological Review*, 88, 375–407.

Monk, A.F. & Hulme, C. (1983). Errors in proofreading: Evidence for the use of word shape in word recognition. *Memory & Cognition*, 11, 16–23.

Morton, J. (1969). Interaction of information in word recognition. *Psychological Review*, 76, 165–178.

Morton, J. (1980). The logogen model and orthographic structure. In U. Frith (Ed.), *Cognitive processes in spelling*. (pp. 117–133). London: Academic Press.

Oden, G.C. (1984). Dependence, independence, and emergence of word features. *Journal of Experimental Psychology: Human Perception and Performance*, 10, 394–405.

Paap, K.R., Newsome, S.L. & Noel, R.W. (1984). Word shapes in poor shape for the race to the lexicon. *Journal of Experimental Psychology: Human Perception and Performance*, 10, 413–428.

Perea, M. & Rosa, E. (2002). Does 'whole-word shape' play a role in visual word recognition? *Perception & Psychophysics*, 64, 785–794.

Pring, L. (1981). Phonological codes and functional spelling units: Reality and implications. *Perception and Psychophysics*, 30, 573–578.

Reicher, G.M. (1969). Perceptual recognition as a function of meaningfulness of stimulus material. *Journal of Experimental Psychology*, 81, 274–280.

Seidenberg, M.S. & McClelland, J.L. (1989). A distributed developmental model of word recognition and naming. *Psychological Review*, 96, 523–568.

Walker, P. (1987). Word shape as a cue to the identity of a word: An analysis of the Kučera and Francis (1967) word list. *Quarterly Journal of Experimental Psychology*, 39A, 675–700.

Wertheimer, M. (1950). Untersuchungen zur Lehre von der Gestalt: II [Principles of perceptual organization]. In W.D. Ellis (Ed. and trans.), *A sourcebook of Gestalt psychology*. (pp. 71–81). New York: Humanities Press.

Wheeler (1970). Processes in word recognition. *Cognitive Psychology*, 1, 59–85.

Appendix A

Stimulus materials used for Experiments 1 and 2 with percentages correct (from Experiment 2) for the inner and outer word forms arranged by High Frequency (HF) and Low Frequency (LF).

HF	inner	outer	LF	inner	outer
added	80.9	100.0	abide	70.2	100.0
admit	44.7	97.9	adapt	53.2	97.9
adult	25.5	97.9	aided	80.9	100.0
apply	85.1	100.0	apple	100.0	100.0
badly	74.5	100.0	aptly	21.3	89.4
bible	85.1	97.9	badge	42.6	100.0
birth	21.3	100.0	baggy	61.7	97.9
black	97.9	97.9	baked	97.9	100.0
block	91.5	44.7	berth	10.6	91.5
brief	23.4	100.0	blade	83.0	97.9
bring	29.8	95.7	blast	61.7	91.5
chief	57.4	100.0	bleak	74.5	83.0
civil	97.9	89.4	blink	46.8	100.0
cloth	44.7	89.4	bliss	70.2	89.4
depth	34.0	100.0	blitz	21.3	100.0
dirty	19.1	100.0	bluff	8.5	97.9
dried	55.3	100.0	blunt	36.2	100.0
drink	93.6	100.0	bulky	38.3	74.5
dying	42.6	100.0	cliff	10.6	100.0
empty	70.2	100.0	dandy	63.8	100.0
field	21.3	100.0	dated	44.7	100.0
final	19.1	97.9	dimly	29.8	100.0
flash	29.8	100.0	ditch	40.4	97.9
flesh	55.3	74.5	dived	63.8	97.9
forth	12.8	97.9	dryly	27.7	100.0
forty	10.6	100.0	ethic	63.8	100.0
glory	42.6	100.0	flair	34.0	100.0
habit	42.6	100.0	flask	97.9	51.1
happy	91.5	100.0	fleet	19.1	91.5
hardy	55.3	93.6	flick	55.3	97.9
hated	44.7	100.0	flint	12.8	100.0
hills	38.3	80.9	flung	19.1	93.6
hired	57.4	100.0	flush	38.3	97.9
hoped	57.4	100.0	foggy	46.8	100.0
joint	34.0	100.0	gland	17.0	100.0
judge	17.0	95.7	globe	23.4	95.7
legal	70.2	100.0	grief	23.4	100.0
liked	83.0	100.0	gruff	14.9	100.0
limit	27.7	100.0	hairy	93.6	100.0
lobby	44.7	100.0	handy	70.2	100.0

Appendix A (Continued)

HF	inner	outer	LF	inner	outer
paint	76.6	97.9	hitch	42.6	95.7
party	48.9	100.0	hobby	17.0	97.9
pilot	25.5	100.0	jerky	53.2	93.6
plant	42.6	100.0	latch	66.0	97.9
point	66.0	91.5	links	93.6	83.0
pupil	57.4	100.0	midst	44.7	42.6
quick	97.9	97.9	oddly	31.9	93.6
sixth	95.7	97.9	orbit	36.2	100.0
smith	27.7	97.9	pinch	91.5	100.0
spite	21.3	87.2	print	38.3	100.0
stuff	17.0	100.0	rally	66.0	93.6
style	42.6	100.0	ridge	34.0	100.0
swift	19.1	100.0	sadly	83.0	87.2
thank	97.9	97.9	shyly	40.4	100.0
thick	72.3	100.0	silly	80.9	97.9
thing	44.7	100.0	spell	93.6	95.7
think	85.1	100.0	stint	10.6	97.9
third	31.9	100.0	theft	4.3	100.0
total	40.4	100.0	timed	89.4	100.0
trial	31.9	97.9	trill	17.0	95.7
valid	61.7	97.9	twist	89.4	91.5
vital	55.3	100.0	villa	95.7	97.9
vivid	83.0	97.9	width	53.2	100.0
yield	68.1	100.0	wiped	91.5	95.7

7

Integration of the visual and auditory networks in dyslexia: a theoretical perspective

Kristen Pammer and Trichur R. Vidyasagar

Dyslexia research is a bit like trying to assemble a jigsaw puzzle; over the years a large amount of knowledge about each of the individual pieces of the puzzle has been acquired, but how the pieces fit together to form the overall picture remains elusive. Few researchers have been able to provide a successful theory of dyslexia because the disorder is too heterogeneous for one theory to fit all (although refer to Stein, 2001). One way in which dyslexia researchers have dealt with heterogeneity is to describe dyslexic symptoms in terms of subgroups of reading impairment (e.g. Castles & Coltheart, 1993). This paper aims to provide a hypothesis to propose how impaired visual and auditory coding processes observed in sub-groups of individuals with dyslexia might be able to explain their phonological coding problems, and subsequent reading difficulties.

Dyslexia and phonological coding

In this paper 'dyslexia' will be used as synonymous with 'developmental dyslexia' and will be used to explain the situation in which a child fails to learn to read at the level expected for their age, despite adequate intelligence, teaching instruction, socio-economic opportunity, and with no other concomitant organic disturbances. Furthermore, the heterogeneous nature of dyslexia may be highly influential in contributing to the disparity of experimental results and conclusions (Hogben, 1996). For this reason, we will be restricting the discussion to dyslexia as representing children who have underlying difficulties in some degree of phonological processing. In doing so this necessarily neglects the many children who have reading difficulties from other causes, such as visual discomfort (e.g. Wilkins, Huang & Cao, 2004). Nevertheless, a difficulty in phonological coding is indicative of a large proportion of dyslexic readers, and is generally believed to be intrinsic in the failure to develop satisfactory reading skills (e.g. Brady & Shankweiler, 1991; Olson et al., 1992; Wagner & Torgeson, 1987).

One of the strongest and most enduring themes in dyslexia research is that dyslexic children consistently demonstrate problems in the coding, manipulation and comprehension of the sounds of spoken words (Castles & Coltheart, 2004; Goswami & Bryant, 1990; Mattingly, 1972; also see Snowling, 2000, for a full discussion). While there is some debate regarding exactly which phonological skills are most important in learning to read (e.g. Bryant, 2002; Muter et al., 2004), there is no doubt that an awareness and understanding of the constituent sounds of words is one of the most important sub-skills in reading development (e.g. Bowey, 2002; Bradley & Bryant, 1983; Goswami & Bryant, 1990; Hulme et al., 2002; McDougall et al., 1994; Muter et al., 1998, 2004). Similarly, phonemic awareness appears to be the primary persisting difficulty for compensated adult readers who have subsequently developed good reading skills (Bruck, 1992, 1993). In discussions about the fundamental deficit in dyslexia, the severe impairment in phonological awareness exhibited by most dyslexics (e.g. Liberman, 1973; Goswami & Bryant, 1990) has been taken as an argument against visual perceptual deficits. However, there is no unequivocal evidence linking competence in phonological awareness causally to acquisition of reading and spelling skills (Castles & Coltheart, 2004). The consistent finding of concomitant sensory processing difficulties in many dyslexic readers has been a thorny issue, and it is the difficulties in resolving these seemingly disparate empirical positions that proves to be such a problem in dyslexia research.

Dyslexia and visual processing

Magnocellular processing

There is a wide body of evidence to implicate early visual sensory coding difficulties in dyslexia. Differences between poor readers and normal readers have been demonstrated primarily in their sensitivity to dynamic visual stimuli, including tasks such as: coherent motion (Cornelissen et al., 1995; Hansen et al., 2001), contrast sensitivity (Evans, Drasdo & Richards, 1994; Martin & Lovegrove, 1984), uniform field flicker (Brannan & Williams, 1988), spatial frequency doubling (Buchholz & McKone, 2004; Pammer & Wheatley, 2001), visual search (Casco & Prunetti, 1996; Vidyasagar & Pammer, 1999), flicker fusion (Chase & Jenner, 1993) and temporal order judgement (Slaghuis, Twell & Kingstone, 1996). Differences between normal and dyslexic readers in the functioning of the visual pathway have been confirmed anatomically (Livingstone et al., 1991), elecrophysiologically (e.g. Lehmkuhle et al., 1993) and using functional MRI (Eden et al., 1996). The triangulation of these results is impressive, and collectively has become known as the 'magno-deficit' theory of dyslexia (see Stein, 2001). The rationale is that the visual deficits stem from deficient visual coding mechanisms in the magnocellular (magno) path of the visual system but not the parvocellular (parvo) visual pathway. However, the outstanding issue is whether such visual processing problems cause reading difficulties or whether they are epiphenomenal. This is compounded by the fact that there are few coherent theories to account for how a magno-deficit might in fact relate to reading, or a reading difficulty. Moreover, the evidence of a magnocellular deficit in dyslexia has been questioned on several grounds. Several studies have failed to demonstrate visual processing differences between dyslexic and normal readers, believed to be dependent upon magnocellular functioning (e.g. Amitay et al., 2002; Ben-Yehuda et al., 2001; Olson & Datta, 2002; Ramus et al., 2003; Stuart, McAnally & Castles, 2001) and it has been suggested (Amitay et al., 2002; Ben-Yehuda et al., 2001; Stuart, McAnally & Castles, 2001) that the visual deficits observed with dyslexic readers may in fact reflect a more generalised deficit in attention, and/or the ability to integrate visual information over time. These conflicting findings may be as a result of the possibility that only a sub-group of dyslexic readers have a magno-deficit (Borsting et al., 1996), or the possibility that the magno-deficit theory needs to be refined further to describe the exact nature of the visual deficit.

Visual coding of letters

It has been demonstrated (Pammer, Lavis & Cornelissen, 2004; Pammer, Lavis, Hansen & Cornelissen, 2004; Pammer, Lavis et al., forthcoming) that sensitivity to the position of local characters in word-like letter strings consistently predicts reading ability in children and word recognition in adults. In these tasks, subjects are presented with strings of symbols that are designed to be analogous to words without the associated top-down influence of lexical information. In measuring the sensitivity to the manipulation of the internal components of such symbol strings, we are likely to be tapping into the same mechanisms involved in the early visual coding of letters within words. These findings have demonstrated that readers are sensitive to the configuration of internal components of symbol strings and that this predicts reading ability, such that poorer readers are less sensitive to the internal configuration of the symbol strings. The assumption here is that being able to read effectively is in part dependent upon accurate early encoding of the 'bits' of words, such that the early, pre-lexical stages of word recognition are conditional upon the successful integration of the components of words and letters. Furthermore, neuro-imaging evidence supports the proposal that early structural coding of letter strings represents an intrinsic component of the progression through the word-recognition network, such that word recognition may be characterised by visual feature encoding, followed by sensitivity to word-objects (as opposed to house-objects for example) at a pre-lexical level (Tarkiainen, Cornelissen & Salmelin, 2002; Tarkiainen et al., 1999). It is noteworthy that this early coding in dyslexic readers is either absent or delayed (Salmelin et al., 1996), suggesting that this stage of visual encoding is intrinsic to effective reading.

Dorsal processing stream

A re-evaluation of the magno-deficit theory has recently emerged from the literature, prompted by investigations of the role of the magnocellular pathway in guided visual attention. The dorsal processing stream is driven primarily by the magnocellular pathway and the ventral stream is driven primarily by the parvocellular pathway. It has been suggested that the dorsal pathway has an essential role in the mediation of guided visual search mechanisms, specifically in the pre-attentive control of spatial selection (Vidyasagar, 1999, 2001). In this theory, the dorsal pathway provides a very early, and very fast selection of visual space. This information is then fed back to the visual cortex and onto the ventral stream to allow further processing and the detailed examination of a selected location in the visual field. Therefore the dorsal stream acts as the control of an attentional spotlight, and only features that are close or spatially coexistent, will gain access to further visual analysis (see Vidyasagar, 1999, 2001, 2005 (forthcoming) for a discussion of this theory and a review of the evidence). Consider then the situation in which the magno-dominated dorsal stream is not working properly and failing to provide adequate feedback to the ventral pathway. At a local level it would be more difficult to identify and assemble a target from its local features, particularly in cluttered visual scenes. In this context, Vidyasagar suggests the following:

'The large RF's [receptive fields] of the ventral stream neurones that perform the visual discrimination between the letters cannot possibly order letters of a word or the words of a sentence without the spotlighting aid of the dorsal stream. The dorsal stream may thus be necessary for the smooth flow of attentional focus that helps the identification of letters or words'. (Vidyasagar, 1999, p. 71)

Recent neuroimaging evidence from our laboratory (Pammer, Hansen et al., forthcoming) and others (Mayall et al., 2001) has supported the suggestion of a role for the dorsal stream in the early pre-lexical processing of words. A closer examination of the neural spatio-temporal response patterns in control subjects described by Salmelin et al. (1996) in response to the presentation of concrete and abstract words, reveals within the first 200 ms of viewing a word, an early occipital source, followed by a right parietal source, and a left inferior occipito-temporal source, which supports the suggestion of early dorsal stream involvement in word recognition. However, if the dorsal stream is not doing its job properly and not providing the necessary spatial selection of the local elements in the letter string, then the information being passed to the left inferior occipito-temporal source (which, given the anatomical similarities, is likely to be analogous to the ventral processing stream) will be inadequate and subsequent processing in this region would be seriously impaired. Indeed, this is exactly what Salmelin et al. (1996) found; none of the dyslexic readers activated the left inferior occipito-temporal area within the same time-frame.

If the dorsal processing stream is vital to the selection and assembly of local elements in a visual array, then this provides a plausible mechanism to explain why sensitivity to symbols strings predicts reading ability (Pammer, Lavis & Cornelissen, 2004; Pammer, Lavis, Hansen & Cornelissen, 2004; Pammer, Lavis et al., 2005); the same dorsal-mediated, pre-attentive spatial selection of local elements is necessary to order the local elements of a symbol string, and order the letters within words. Similarly, given that the dorsal stream is driven by the magno pathway, this would also explain why many poor readers are less sensitive to visual tasks that rely on magno processing (e.g. Buchholz & McKone, 2004; Cornelissen et al., 1995; Hansen et al., 2001; Pammer & Wheatley, 2001).

Therefore, one way to address the observation that only a sub-group of dyslexic readers appear to demonstrate a magno-deficit, may be to re-consider the nature of the magno-deficit as an early dorsal stream impairment. Recent studies have suggested that a dorsal stream deficit may exist in dyslexic readers in at least the retinal level of processing (Buchholz & McKone, 2004; Pammer & Kevan, forthcoming; Pammer, Lavis & Cornelissen, 2004; Pammer, Lavis, Hansen & Cornelissen, 2004). It may be the case that a 'magno-deficit' may be better conceptualised as a deficit in the functioning of the very early stages of the dorsal stream, where specific pre-attentive spatial processing takes place. This would fit better with the suggestion (Amitay et al., 2002; Ben-Yehuda et al., 2001) that a visual deficit may lie in the fast temporal integration of visual information, which is dependent upon accurate spatio-temporal, attentional sensitivity, rather than a magnocellular processing per se. Individuals with 'higher-order' magnocellular deficits demonstrated in tasks such as coherent motion or contrast sensitivity may have a more profound deficit that snowballs through the magnocellular pathway, or a neural deficit that exists higher in the neural pathway (Vidyasagar, 1999). It has also been pointed out (Vidyasagar, forthcoming) that a magnocellular sampling deficit (Pammer & Wheatley, 2001) may not be detectable as an impairment in contrast sensitivity functions, usually measured with fairly large stimuli, but may affect visual search and associated reading functions quite significantly.

How visual deficits might cause reading problems

Early spatial-jitter in the visual system might make it difficult for early readers to acquire the alphabetic code, or grapheme-to-phoneme correspondence rules. The alphabetic code is the explicit ability to integrate phonemes with graphemic representations (Byrne & Fielding-Barnsley, 1989). Acquisition of the alphabetic code is in essence learning to read and mastering phonics is necessary to master the alphabetic code (e.g. Bradley & Bryant, 1983; Shankweiler et al., 1995). Therefore, learning to read demonstrably requires associating a consistent visual symbol ('ch' for example), with a phoneme or sound (/ch/). If early visual coding is inadequate, then it will be manifestly more difficult to learn this association. This then may provide an explanation why poor readers find it so torturous to work out how the sounds that they know relate to the squiggles they see on a page. However, this explanation still fails to explain why dyslexic readers are simply so poor at processing and manipulating the sounds themselves – or phonological awareness.

One possibility may be that the development of reading skills in fact facilitates phonological awareness. Morais et al. (1986) have provided evidence to suggest that the development of phonological representations is an outcome of the acquisition of an alphabetic orthography. This implies that learning effective reading skills at a sensory (visual) level may 'fine-tune' the whole reading network, and therefore all composite reading skills, such as phonological awareness. However, this is unlikely to be the whole explanation because poor phonological skills often exist in pre-readers before explicit instruction in the alphabetic code (e.g. DeCara & Goswami, 2003; Hulme et al., 2002). Something therefore is making it difficult for some young children to hear and decode the sounds of their language. The explanation here then is likely to be not so much in the visual coding of text, but the auditory coding of sounds.

Dyslexia and auditory processing

Selective auditory coding difficulties in dyslexia have been well documented. For example, differences in auditory processing between dyslexic readers and control readers have been demonstrated using non-verbal stimuli such as clicks or tones (e.g. Kinsbourne et al., 1991; McCroskey & Kidder, 1980; Tallal, 1980), as well as sounds more consistent with natural language, such as the discrimination of consonants (Reed, 1989). The suggestion here is that dyslexic children have problems distinguishing between rapidly presented auditory stimuli, impairing their ability to process the rapid transitions of speech sounds in language (Ahissar et al., 2000; Heath & Hogben, 2004; Reed, 1989; Tallal, 1980; Watson & Miller, 1993), and became known as the temporal processing deficit theory (see Farmer & Klein, 1993, for a review). Nicholson and Fawcett (1993, 1994) have also demonstrated slower reaction times for dyslexic readers to pure tones, and as with the visual system, post-mortem studies demonstrated evidence of abnormal auditory anatomy in the left medial geniculate nucleus of dyslexic readers, compared to normal readers (Galaburda, Menard & Rosen, 1994). Once again, however, not all studies have demonstrated auditory processing difficulties between dyslexic and normal readers (e.g. Bretherton & Holmes, 2003; Heath, Hogben & Clark, 1999; Marshall, Snowling & Bailey, 2001; McArthur & Hogben, 2001; Nittruoer, 1999). Nevertheless, as with the visual system, it may be the accurate classification of the subtleties of speech discrimination that is critical, such as sound modulations at very specific amplitude and frequency changes (McAnally & Stein, 1996; Talcott et al., 2000; Witton et al., 1998, 2002), pitch sensitivity (Foxton et al., 2003), or possibly even restricted to amplitude changes only at the onset of sounds (Goswami et al., 2000).

Witton et al. (2002) suggest that the pattern of auditory sensitivity demonstrated by dyslexic readers may be the result of indistinct auditory capture at the early stages of language acquisition. Children younger than seven years are less sensitive than adults to amplitude modulation (Hall & Grose, 1994), and Witton et al. argue that any deficiency in auditory coding at this stage of language development, when the auditory system is already in a state of developmental instability, could have quite profound consequences for the acquisition of stable phonological representations. Indeed, delayed language development has been demonstrated to be characteristic of pre-readers at risk of dyslexia (Gallagher, Frith & Snowling, 2000), and more than 50% of dyslexic readers also demonstrate a specific language deficit (McArthur et al., 2000). Moreover, it has been suggested that auditory temporal processing deficits may be apparent only when dyslexia is accompanied by concomitant oral language impairment (Heath, Hogben & Clark, 1999; Tallal & Stark, 1982).

Integrating visual and auditory deficits

Reading clearly involves the complex integration of both visual and auditory information, and the evidence reviewed here suggests that difficulties in learning to read could result from low-level auditory coding problems apparent before a child learns to read, and low-level visual coding difficulties also apparent in the pre-reader, but that only become evident when the child begins the visually subtle and complex skill of synthesising squiggles and sounds (see Figure 1).

In this theory, similar to the argument put forth by Talcott et al. (2000), reading problems may be the result of both auditory and visual processing problems, each of which influence the reading network in different ways. Low-level auditory coding difficulties may hinder the acquisition of phonological skills (Witton et al., 2002) which would make it difficult for a child to hear the sound components of language at the pre-reading stage, and then persisting in a difficulty in the acquisition of the phonological code, such that poor phonological awareness makes it difficult to form stable grapheme-to-phoneme representations. This would satisfy the finding that phonological difficulties predict subsequent reading development, because the auditory coding difficulty exists before reading acquisition. Similarly, visual coding difficulties may exist at the pre-reading stage, but the fast, spatial selection conducted by the dorsal stream only becomes apparent (or problematic for the dyslexic reader) when the visual system attempts the fine temporal co-ordination of spatial selection and feature integration required in letter and word recognition. The most obvious confirmation of this latter proposal is to find that in a longitudinal study, visual processing skills that draw on the dorsal processing stream, predict subsequent reading development, and that the weighting of visual and auditory deficits in pre-readers predicts the *relative* acquisition of orthographic and phonological skills.

Common neural sources for visual and auditory processing

Sensory information from different modalities experiences considerable interaction, and responses from one modality can drastically influence the neural mapping of another

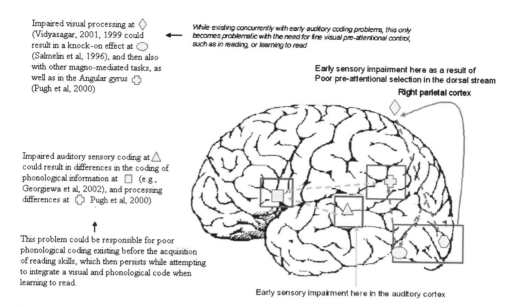

Impaired visual processing at ◇ (Vidyasagar, 2001, 1999 could result in a knock-on effect at ○ (Salmelin et al, 1996), and then also with other magno-mediated tasks, as well as in the Angular gyrus ⊡ (Pugh et al, 2000)

While existing concurrently with early auditory coding problems, this only becomes problematic with the need for fine visual pre-attentional control, such as in reading, or learning to read

Early sensory impairment here as a result of Poor pre-attentional selection in the dorsal stream
Right parietal cortex

Impaired auditory sensory coding at △ could result in differences in the coding of phonological information at □ (e.g., Georgiewa et al, 2002), and processing differences at ⊡ Pugh et al, 2000)

↑

This problem could be responsible for poor phonological coding existing before the acquisition of reading skills, which then persists while attempting to integrate a visual and phonological code when learning to read.

Early sensory impairment here in the auditory cortex

Figure 1. A neural model of the hypothesis described in the text.

Note: The schematic is highly simplified, and it is assumed that interactions between all the sites are cascaded and mediated by cortical feedback loops. Because the network is highly interactive, it is likely that network connections in the normal reader are strengthened and fine-tuned according to Hebbian-like interactions. This may occur to a lesser degree in dyslexic readers, and would support the finding that phonological awareness and reading acquisition is reciprocal (see text).

modality. Multi-sensory cells are apparent in the major visual and auditory pathways through the brain, such as in the superior colliculus (e.g. Meredith & Stein, 1986; Wurtz & Albano, 1980) and the cortex (e.g. Watanabe & Iwai, 1991). The left parietal cortex in particular appears to receive some multi-modal sensory input (Pourtois & de Gelder, 2002), and may provide a role for the integration of multi-modal synthesis of spatial information (Farah et al., 1989). Gross abnormalities, such as blinding in the neonate, can result in poor auditory spatial awareness (Spigelman, 1969), and Vidyasagar (1978, 1979) demonstrated that polymodal cells in the superior colliculus were 'taken over' by auditory and somatosensory input in dark-reared cats. Other researchers have demonstrated shifts in the auditory space map in the superior colliculus of owls (Knudsen & Brainard, 1991), and ferrets (King et al., 1988), corresponding to designed displacements of the visual field. Vidyasagar (1991, 1999) has suggested that neural sensory development provides mutual guidance and instruction, such that normal sensory development in one modality may depend on the normal development of other modalities. Interestingly, in a recent review of the extent of multi-modal plasticity, Bavelier and Neville (2002, p. 450) point out 'It is interesting to note that some of the brain functions that seem to be susceptible to early experience – such as visuo-spatial attention, global processing and episodic memory – are mediated by the dorsal pathway ...'.

Clearly reading at the cortical level is a highly dynamic system, involving the complex and subtle synthesis of auditory and visual information. It is not implausible therefore, that a subtle deficit in the neural development of one sensory modality can result in a subtle deficit in another modality. Moreover, complex neural systems are likely to be self-sustaining, such that consistent and stable interactions between different parts of the network strengthen the network interactions as a whole, and presumably then, each component of the network at an individual level. However, if for dyslexic readers the network is slightly out of sync, as a result of both visual and auditory coding problems, such that parts of the network either fail to engage, or under-engage, then this would explain why phonological skills and reading experience are reciprocally related, in that the development of reading skills (and thus the strengthening of the network) results in better phonological skills (a component of the network). Evidence for both visual and auditory processing problems in dyslexic readers is limited. Both auditory and visual sensitivity have been demonstrated to predict reading ability in an unselected sample of readers (Talcott et al., 2000), and predict subsequent reading ability in pre-readers (Hood & Conlon, 2004). However, to our knowledge no study has investigated the contribution of visual and auditory impairments in the same individuals, and how this may characterise different sub-types of dyslexia and phonological skills.

Conclusions

A large amount of research suggests that subtle sensory coding deficits exist in dyslexia in both the auditory and the visual domains. The aim of the current model is to attempt to bind these findings with the fact that dyslexia is primarily characterised by problems in phonological awareness. Anatomical evidence has provided a reasonable framework for the suggestion that multi-modal cortical maps are mutually dependent such that development in one modality guides successful development in other modalities. Given that effective reading requires the exquisite synchronicity of both auditory and visual information, it is not unreasonable then to suggest that a slight developmental impairment in one modality may result in concomitant impairment in the other modality. Such a multi-modal impairment may manifest in a reading problem with a difficulty in phonological processing on one hand, and a difficulty in visual coding on the other. Moreover, it may be the case that the different dyslexic sub-types such as Surface and Phonological dyslexia, which differ in their degree of phonological coding sensitivity, may reflect different degrees of impairment in the two modalities, with visual coding underlying problems in orthographic analysis and auditory problems underlying phonological analysis.

References

Ahissar, M., Protopapas, A., Reid, M. & Merzenich, M. (2000). Auditory processing parallels reading abilities in adults. *Proceedings of the Royal Academy of Science*, 97, 6832–6837.

Amitay, S., Ben-Yehuda, G., Banai, K. & Ahissar, M. (2002). Disabled readers suffer from visual and auditory impairments but not from a specific magnocellular deficit. *Brain*, 125, 2272–2285.

Bavelier, D. & Neville, H.J. (2002). Cross-modal plasticity: Where and how? *Nature Reviews Neuroscience*, 3(6), 443–452.

Ben-Yehuda, G., Sackett, E., Malchi-Ginzberg, L. & Ahissar, M. (2001). Impaired temporal contrast sensitivity in dyslexics is specific to retain-and-compare paradigms. *Brain*, 124, 1381–1395.

Borsting, E., Ridder, W.H., Dudeck, K., Kelley, C., Matsui, L. & Motoyama, J. (1996). The presence of a magnocellular defect depends on the type of dyslexia. *Vision Research*, 36(7), 1047–1053.

Bowey, J. (2002). Reflections on onset-rime and phoneme sensitivity as predictors of beginning word reading. *Journal of Experimental Child Psychology*, 82, 29–40.

Bradley, L. & Bryant, P. (1983). Categorising sounds and learning to read – a causal connection. *Nature*, 303, 419–421.

Brady, S. & Shankweiler, D. (1991). *Phonological processes in literacy: A tribute to Isabelle Liberman.* Hillsdale, NJ: Lawrence Erlbaum.

Brannan, J. & Williams, M. (1987). Allocation of visual attention in good and poor readers. *Perception and Psychophysics,* 41, 23–28.

Bretherton, L. & Holmes, V. (2003). The relationship between auditory temporal processing, phonemic awareness, and reading disability. *Journal of Experimental Child Psychology,* 84, 218–243.

Bruck, M. (1992). Persistence of dyslexics' phonological awareness deficits. *Developmental Psychology,* 28, 874–886.

Bruck, M. (1993). Component spelling skills of college students with childhood diagnoses of dyslexia. *Learning Disabilities Quarterly,* 16, 171–184.

Bryant, P. (2002). It doesn't matter whether onset and rime predicts reading better than phoneme awareness does or vice versa. *Journal of Experimental Child Psychology,* 82, 41–46.

Buchholz, J. & McKone, E. (2004). Adults with dyslexia show deficits on spatial frequency doubling and visual attention tasks. *Dyslexia,* 10(1), 24–43.

Byrne, B. & Fielding-Barnsley, R. (1989). Phonemic awareness and letter knowledge in the child's acquisition of the alphabetic principal. *Journal of Educational Psychology,* 81, 313–321.

Casco, C. & Prunetti, E. (1996). Visual search of good and poor readers: Effects with targets having single and combined features. *Perceptual and Motor Skills,* 82, 1155–1167.

Castles, A. & Coltheart, M. (1993). Varieties of developmental dyslexia. *Cognition,* 47, 149–180.

Castles, A. & Coltheart, M. (1996). Cognitive correlates of developmental surface dyslexia: A single case study. *Cognitive Neuropsychology,* 13(1), 25–50.

Castles, A. & Coltheart, M. (2004). Is there a causal link from phonological awareness to success in learning to read? *Cognition,* 91, 77–111.

Chase, C. & Jenner, A. (1993). Magnocellular processing deficits affect temporal processing of dyslexics. *Annals of the New York Academy of Sciences,* 682, 326–329.

Cornelissen, P., Hansen, P., Gilchrist, I., Cormack, F., Essex, J. & Frankish, C. (1998). Coherent motion detection and letter position encoding. *Vision Research,* 38, 2181–2191.

Cornelissen, P., Richardson, A., Mason, A. & Stein, J. (1995). Contrast sensitivity and coherent motion detection measured at photopic luminance levels in dyslexics and controls. *Vision Research,* 35, 1483–1494.

De Cara, B. & Goswami, U. (2003). Phonological neighbourhood density: Effects in a rhyme awareness task in five-year-old children. *Journal of Child Language,* 30, 695–710.

Eden, G., VanMeter, J., Rumsey, J., Maisog, J., Woods, R. & Zeffro, T. (1996). Abnormal processing of visual motion in dyslexia revealed by functional brain imaging. *Nature,* 382, 66–70.

Evans, B., Drasdo, N. & Richards, I. (1994). An investigation of some sensory and refractive visual factors in dyslexia. *Vision Research,* 34, 1913–1926.

Farah, M., Wong, A., Monheit, M. & Morrow, L. (1989). Parietal lobe mechanisms of spatial attention: Modality specific or supramodal? *Neuropsychologia,* 27, 461–470.

Farmer, M. & Klein, R. (1995). The evidence for a temporal processing deficit linked to dyslexia: A review. *Psychonomic Bulletin and Review,* 2, 460–493.

Foxton, J.M., Talcott, J.B., Witton, C., Brace, H., McIntyre, F. & Griffiths, T.D. (2003). Reading skills are related to global, but not local, acoustic pattern perception. *Nature Neuroscience,* 6(4), 343–344.

Galaburda, A., Menard, M. & Rosen, G. (1994). Evidence for aberrant auditory anatomy in developmental dyslexia. *Proceedings of the National Academy of Sciences, USA,* 91, 8010–8013.

Gallagher, A., Frith, U. & Snowling, M. (2000). Precursors of literacy delay among children at genetic risk of dyslexia. *Journal of Child Psychology and Psychiatry,* 41, 203–213.

Goswami, U. & Bryant, P. (1990). *Phonological skills and learning to read.* Hove: Erlbaum.

Goswami, U., Giraudo, H., Rosen, S. & Scott, S. (2000). Onset-rime awareness, perceptual centres in speech and dyslexia. *International Journal of Psychology,* 35, 317.

Hall, J. & Grose, J. (1994). Development of temporal resolution in children as measured by the temporal modulation transfer function. *Journal of the Acoustical Society of America,* 96, 150–154.

Hansen, P., Stein, J., Orde, S., Winter, J. & Talcott, J. (2001). Are dyslexics' visual deficits limited to measures of dorsal stream function? *Neuroreport,* 12, 1527–1530.

Heath, S. & Hogben, J. (2004). The reliability and validity of tasks measuring perception of rapid sequences in children with dyslexia. *Journal of Child Psychology and Psychiatry,* 45, 1275–1287.

Heath, S., Hogben, J. & Clark, C. (1999). Auditory temporal order processing in disabled readers with and without language delay. *Journal of Child Psychology and Psychiatry,* 40, 637–647.

Hogben, J.H. (1996). A plea for purity. *The Australian Journal of Psychology*, 48(3), 172–177.

Hood, M. & Conlon, E. (2004). Visual and auditory temporal processing and early reading development. *Dyslexia*, 10, 234–252.

Hulme, C., Hatcher, P., Nation, K., Brown, A., Adams, J. & Stuart, G. (2002). Phoneme awareness is a better predictor of early reading skill than onset-rime awareness. *Journal of Experimental Child Psychology*, 82, 2–28.

King, A., Hutchings, M., Moore, D. & Blakemore, C. (1988). Developmental plasticity in the visual and auditory representations in the mammalian superior colliculus. *Nature*, 332, 73–76.

Kinsbourne, M., Rufo, D., Gamzu, E., Palmer, R. & Berliner, A. (1991). Neuropsychological deficits in adults with dyslexia. *Developmental Medicine and Child Neurology*, 23, 617–625.

Knudsen, E. & Brainard, M. (1991). Visual instruction of the neural map of auditory space in the developing optic tectum. *Science*, 88, 7943–7947.

Lehmkuhle, S., Garzia, R., Turner, L., Hash, T. & Baro, J. (1993). A defective visual pathway in children with reading-disability. *New England Journal of Medicine*, 32814, 989–996.

Libermann, I. (1973). Segmentation of the spoken word and reading acquisition. *Bulletin of the Orton Society*, 23, 65–77.

Livingstone, M., Rosen, G., Drislane, F. & Galaburda, A. (1991). Physiological and anatomical evidence for a magnocellular deficit in developmental dyslexia. *Proceedings of the National Academy of Science*, 88, 7943–7947.

McAnally, K. & Stein, J. (1996). Auditory temporal coding in dyslexia. *Proceedings of the Royal Society of London*, 263, 961–965.

McArthur, G. & Hogben, J. (2001). Auditory backward recognition masking in children with specific language impairment and children with a specific reading disability. *Journal of the Acoustical Society of America*, 109, 1092–1100.

McArthur, G.M., Hogben, J.H., Edwards, V.T., Heath, S. & Mengler, E. (2000). On the 'specifics' of specific reading disability and specific language impairment. *Journal of Child Psychology and Psychiatry and Allied Disciplines*, 41, 869–874.

McCroskey, R. & Kidder, H. (1980). Auditory fusion among learning disabled, reading disabled and normal children. *Journal of Learning Disabilities*, 13(2), 69–76.

McDougall, S., Hulme, C., Ellis, A. & Monk, A. (1994). Learning to read: The role of short-term memory and phonological skills. *Journal of Experimental Child Psychology*, 58, 112–133.

Marshall, C., Snowling, M. & Bailey, P. (2001). Rapid auditory processing and phonological ability in normal readers with dyslexia. *Journal of Speech Language and Hearing Research*, 44, 925–949.

Martin, F. & Lovegrove, W. (1984). The effects of filed size and luminance control on contrast sensitivity differences between specifically reading disabled and normal children. *Neuropsychologia*, 22, 73–77.

Mattingly, I. (1972). Reading, the linguistic process and linguistic awareness. In J. Kavanagh & I. Mattingly (Eds.), *Language by ear and by eye*. (pp. 133–147). Cambridge, MA: MIT Press.

Mayall, K., Humphreys, G., Mechelli, A., Olson, A. & Price, C. (2001). The effects of case mixing on word recognition: Evidence from a PET study. *Journal of Cognitive Neuroscience*, 13, 844–853.

Meredith, M. & Stein, B. (1986). Spatial factors determine the activity of multisensory neurones in cat superior colliculus. *Brain Research*, 365, 350–354.

Morais, J., Bertelson, P., Cary, L. & Alegria, J. (1986). Literacy training and speech segmentation. *Cognition*, 24, 45–64.

Muter, V., Hulme, C., Snowling, M. & Stevenson, J. (2004). Phonemes, rimes, vocabulary, and grammatical skills as foundations of early reading development: Evidence from a longitudinal study. *Developmental Psychology*, 40, 665–681.

Muter, V., Hulme, C., Snowling, M. & Taylor, S. (1998). Segmentation, not rhyming, predicts early progress in learning to read. *Journal of Experimental Child Psychology*, 71, 3–27.

Nicholson, R. & Fawcett, A. (1993). Children with dyslexia classify pure tones slowly. *Annals of the New York Academy of Science*, 682, 387–389.

Nicholson, R. & Fawcett, A. (1994). Reaction times and dyslexia. *Quarterly Journal of Experimental Psychology: Human Perception and Performance*, 47, 29–48.

Nittruoer, S. (1999). Do temporal processing deficits cause phonological processing problems? *Journal of Speech Language and Hearing Research*, 42, 925–942.

Olson, R. & Datta, H. (2002). Visual-temporal processing in reading disabled and normal twins. *Reading and Writing*, 15, 127–149.

Olson, R., Forsberg, H., Wise, B. & Rack, J. (1992). Measurement of word recognition, orthographic and phonological skills. In G.R. Lyon (Eds.), *Frames of reference for the assessment of learning disabilities: New views on measurement issues.* (pp. 243–277). Baltimore: Paul Brooks.

Pammer, K., Hansen, P., Holliday, I. & Cornelissen, P. (forthcoming). Attentional shifting and the role of the dorsal pathway in visual word recognition.

Pammer, K. & Kevan, A. (forthcoming). The contribution of visual sensitivity, phonological processing and non-verbal IQ to children's reading.

Pammer, K., Lavis, R. & Cornelissen, P. (2004). Visual encoding mechanisms and their relationship to text presentation preference. *Dyslexia*, 10, 77–94.

Pammer, K., Lavis, R., Hansen, P. & Cornelissen, P. (2004). Symbol-string sensitivity and children's reading. *Brain and Language*, 89(3), 601–610.

Pammer, K., Lavis, R., Cooper, C., Hansen, P. & Cornelissen, P. (forthcoming). Symbol-string sensitivity and adult performance in lexical decision. *Brain and Language*.

Pammer, K. & Wheatley, C. (2001). Isolating the M(y)-cell response in dyslexia using the spatial frequency doubling illusion. *Vision Research*, 41, 2139–2147.

Pourtois, G. & de Gelder, B. (2002). Semantic factors influence multisensory pairing: A transcranial magnetic stimulation study. *Neuroreport*, 13, 1567–1573.

Ramus, F., Rosen, S., Dakin, S.C., Day, B.L., Castellote, J.M., White, S. & Frith, U. (2003). Theories of developmental dyslexia: Insights from a multiple case study of dyslexic adults. *Brain*, 126, 841–865.

Reed, M. (1989). Speech perception and the discrimination of brief auditory cues in reading disabled children. *Journal of Experimental Child Psychology*, 48, 207–292.

Salmelin, R., Service, E., Kiesila, P., Uutela, K. & Salonen, O. (1996). Impaired visual word processing in dyslexia revealed with magnetoencephalography. *Annals of Neurology*, 40, 157–162.

Shankweiler, D., Crain, S., Katz, L., Fowler, A., Liberman, A., Brady, S. Thornton, R., Lundquist, E., Dreyer, L., Fletcher, J., Stuebing, K., Shaywitz, S. & Shaywitz, B. (1995). Cognitive profiles of reading disabled children: Comparisons of language skills in phonology, morphology, and syntax. *Psychological Science*, 6, 149–156.

Slaghuis, W., Twell, A. & Kingstone, K. (1996). Visual and language processing disorders are concurrent in dyslexia and continue into adulthood. *Cortex*, 32, 413–438.

Snowling, M. (2000). *Dyslexia*. Oxford: Blackwell.

Spigelman, M. (1969). Effects of age of onset and length of blindness on auditory spatial learning in the rat. *Canadian Journal of Psychology*, 23, 292–298.

Stein, J. (2001). The magnocellular theory of dyslexia. *Dyslexia*, 7, 12–36.

Stuart, G.W., McAnally, K.I. & Castles, A. (2001). Can contrast sensitivity functions in dyslexia be explained by inattention rather than a magnocellular deficit? *Vision Research*, 41(24), 3205–3211.

Talcott, J., Witton, C., McLean, M., Hansen, P., Rees, A., Green, G. & Stein, J. (2000). Dynamic sensory sensitivity and children's word decoding skills. *Proceedings of the National Academy of Sciences*, 97, 2952–2957.

Tallal, P. (1980). Auditory temporal precision, phonics and reading disabilities in children. *Brain and Language*, 9, 182–198.

Tallal, P. & Stark, R. (1982). Perceptual/motor profiles of reading disabled children with or without concomitant oral language deficit. *Annals of Dyslexia*, 32, 163–176.

Tarkiainen, A., Cornelissen, P.L. & Salmelin, R. (2002). Dynamics of visual feature analysis and of object-level processing in face versus letter-string perception. *Brain*, 125, 1125–1136.

Tarkiainen, A., Helenius, P., Hansen, P.C., Cornelissen, P.L. & Salmelin, R. (1999). Dynamics of letter string perception in the human occipitotemporal cortex. *Brain*, 122, 2119–2131.

Vidyasagar, T.R. (1978). Possible plasticity in the rat superior colliculus. *Nature*, 275, 140–141.

Vidyasagar, T.R. (1979). Functional changes in the mammalian subcortical structures. PhD doctoral dissertation, University of Manchester, UK.

Vidyasagar, T.R. (1991). Interactions between visual and other sensory modalities and their development. In J.R. Cronly-Dillon (Ed.), *Vision and visual dysfunction ii; development and plasticity of the visual system*. Basingstoke: Macmillan.

Vidyasagar, T.R. (1999). A neuronal model of attentional spotlight: Parietal guiding the temporal. *Brain Research Reviews*, 30, 66–76.

Vidyasagar, T.R. (2001). From attentional gating in macaque primary visual cortex to dyslexia in humans. *Progress in Brain Research*, 134, 297–312.

Vidyasagar, T.R. (forthcoming). Attentional gating in primary visual cortex: A physiological basis for dyslexia. *Perception*.

Vidyasagar, T.R. & Pammer, K. (1999). Impaired visual search in dyslexia relates to the role of the magnocellular pathway in attention. *Neuroreport*, 10, 1283–1287.

Wagner, R. & Torgeson, J. (1987). The nature of phonological processing and its causal role in the acquisition of reading skills. *Psychological Bulletin*, 101, 192–212.

Watanabe, J. & Iwai, E. (1991). Neuronal activity in visual, auditory and polysensory areas of the monkey temporal cortex during visual fixation task. *Brain Research Bulletin*, 26, 583–592.

Watson, B. & Miller, T. (1993). Auditory perception, phonological processing and reading ability/disability. *Journal of Speech and Hearing Research*, 36, 850–863.

Wilkins, A., Huang, J. & Cao, Y. (2004). Visual stress theory and its application to reading and reading tests. *Journal of Research in Reading*, 27(2), 152–162.

Witton, C., Stein, J., Stoodley, C., Rosner, B. & Talcott, J. (2002). Separate influences of acoustic AM and FM sensitivity on the phonological decoding skills of impaired and normal readers. *Journal of Cognitive Neuroscience*, 14, 866–874.

Witton, C., Talcott, J., Hansen, P., Richardson, A., Griffiths, T., Rees, A., Stein, J. & Green, G. (1998). Sensitivity to dynamic auditory stimuli predicts nonword reading in both dyslexic and normal readers. *Current Biology*, 8, 791–797.

Wurtz, R. & Albano, J. (1980). Visual-motor function of the primate superior colliculus. *Annual Review of Neuroscience*, 3, 189–226.

8

The effect of print size on reading speed in dyslexia

Beth A. O'Brien, J. Stephen Mansfield and Gordon E. Legge

Developmental dyslexia, a learning disability specific to reading, affects an estimated 5% of children in school. Reading requires processing of both the visual information from the page and the linguistic information that the print represents. Over a century of research on causal factors in developmental dyslexia has emphasised either one or the other of these processes, beginning with theories of visual causation. Morgan (1896) coined the inability to read in children as 'congenital word blindness', while Orton (1928) described the phenomenon of 'strephosymbolia' (twisted symbols), where children could read mirror-image writing more easily. The current view of dyslexia holds that reading failure is caused by a linguistic deficit in coding phonemes (individual speech sounds) within words, and thereby in accessing and manipulating these phonemic codes as required on a wide range of tasks (phonological processing) (Snowling, 2000). This view holds that a phonological processing deficit impedes a child's ability to develop phoneme awareness, to learn grapheme-phoneme correspondence rules, and to decode words (Liberman et al., 1974; Stanovich & Siegel, 1994). The theory accounts for many cases of developmental dyslexia, but there are individuals with dyslexia who do not demonstrate a severe phonological deficit (Wolf & Bowers, 1999; Lovett, Steinbach & Frijters, 2000). Also, remediation programmes aimed at training phonological skills are often but not entirely successful (Lyon & Moats, 1997; Torgesen, 2000). This suggests a need for alternative or additional accounts of causal factors in dyslexia.

Recent evidence shows that subtle impairments in visual processing characterise some individuals with dyslexia. Specifically, impaired processing is found for low spatial and high temporal frequency visual stimuli (Lovegrove et al., 1980; Martin & Lovegrove, 1987; Talcott et al., 1998; but see also Skottun, 2000; Walther-Muller, 1995). The most robust of these findings indicates a particular problem with visual motion processing (Cornelissen et al., 1994; Demb et al., 1998; Talcott, Hansen, Elikem & Stein, 2000; Everatt, Bradshaw & Hibbard, 1999). Low spatial frequency, high temporal frequency and motion information are carried primarily via one of two parallel retino-cortical pathways in the human visual system: the magnocellular pathway. Thus, a unifying theory of visual factors in dyslexia holds that there is a magnocellular channel deficit. Neuroanatomic (Galaburda & Livingstone, 1993; Livingstone, Rosen, Drislane & Galaburda, 1991) and fMRI (Eden, van Meter, Rumsey, Maisog & Zeffiro, 1996; Demb, Boynton & Heeger, 1997) evidence consistent with this hypothesis corroborates the perceptual findings. Yet it is still unclear whether these visual deficits represent a correlate or a cause of reading problems. A direct causal link between vision and dyslexia is suggested by findings and observations where reading under demanding visual conditions, such as with small print, leads to declines in reading performance by dyslexic individuals (Cornelissen, Bradley, Fowler & Stein, 1991; Skottun, 2001).

Cornelissen et al. (1991) found that reading errors decreased with larger print size for reading disabled children with poor binocular control, suggesting a causal link between a stressed visual system and reading impairment. Our previous study (O'Brien, Mansfield & Legge, 2000) also implicated a potential effect of print size, where dyslexic readers require larger print sizes than normal readers to achieve their maximum reading speed. The print size effect was observed between subjects where the group difference in reading speed was greatest with small print, but the number of participants with repeated measures data across print sizes was too small to warrant a firm conclusion. Skottun (2001) noted the importance of demonstrating a parametric dependence of dyslexic reading on a visual variable, and pointed to this potential print size effect in our data. Such an effect would support a link between vision and dyslexia because a purely phonological explanation would not predict an effect of print size.

It is possible that larger print size facilitates dyslexic reading by increasing the visibility of spatial frequencies critical for letter recognition (Solomon & Pelli, 1994) or reading (Legge, Pelli, Rubin & Schleske, 1985). In addition, it is possible that dyslexic readers require a wider spatial-frequency bandwidth for reading than the two cycles per letter measured by Legge et al. (1985). For example, with larger letters, more distinguishing letter features may be available within the two cycle/character critical bandwidth for reading. Dyslexic readers may require more or different sets of features to distinguish between letters within words either because they are less efficient at picking up this visual information than skilled readers, or because their memory store of letter templates to match to incoming information is less well established. Other related factors that could be ameliorated with larger print include lateral masking ('crowding') effects, that may be greater in dyslexic readers (e.g. Geiger & Lettvin, 1987, but see also Klein et al., 1990), or differences in visual span, that is, the number of letters recognisable in a glance (Legge, Ahn, Klitz & Luebker, 1997; Legge, Mansfield & Chung, 2001).

An alternative account of observed print size effects is that they could result from a general magnocellular deficit, which has been proposed to interfere with letter position coding (Cornelissen et al., 1998a, 1998b). The magnocellular channel provides the primary input to the dorsal occipito-cortical pathway, the so-called 'where' pathway that carries information about an object's position in space (Mishkin, Ungerlieder & Macko, 1983). For reading, fidelity of the magnocellular channel should help to localise correctly the serial position of letters within words, and a dysfunction could lead to improper letter localisation and therefore reading errors (Cornelissen & Hansen, 1998). In this case, it may not be the visibility of certain letter features, but instead their relative position within words that is affected by the size of the letters. It could be that deficient position signals have a bigger impact for very small letters whose relative position is harder to identify, and so may result in poorer reading performance with small print.

A magnocellular dysfunction in dyslexic reading has also been related to deficits in visual attention (Iles, Walsh & Richardson, 2000; Pammer & Wheatley, 2001). This theory proposes specific problems with serially focusing attention, either through rapid attentional capture or with attentional disengagement (Valdois, Bosse & Tainturier, 2004). In this regard, Pammer, Lavis, Hansen and Cornelissen (2004) found evidence that problems with attentional focusing contribute to anomalies in relative position coding in dyslexia. Specifically, they found that accurate symbol string recognition was negatively affected by adjacent symbol reversals. Thus, while attentional disturbances could affect reading in their own right, visual attention deficits may manifest as letter position coding errors as well.

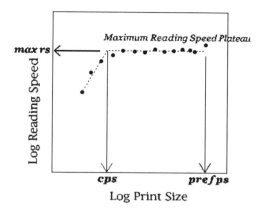

Figure 1. Diagram of reading speed-by-print size curve, showing a two-limb fit with parameters of maximum reading speed for large print sizes (*max rs*), and critical print size (*cps*), below which reading speed drops off dramatically.

Note: Also depicted is the preferred print size supporting the single fastest reading speed (*pref ps*) on the reading speed plateau.

To study in detail the trend that we found previously for group differences of print size effects on reading performance, we compared reading rates as a function of print size for groups of children with and without dyslexia. We measured reading rate across a range of twelve print sizes from -0.2 to 1.0 logMAR (corresponding to a range of 20/12 to 20/200 Snellen letter sizes, or 0.037 cm to 0.582 cm in x-height values) for each individual, and fit the reading rate by print size curves with a two-limb fit that has been found to characterise skilled reading (Mansfield, Legge & Bane, 1996). The two-limb fit captures how reading rates are typically constant across a range of large print sizes, then drop off rapidly below a critical print size (for example, see Figure 1).

If dyslexic readers have a magnocellular deficit that impacts letter position coding, we would expect to see a threshold effect of print size, where letter position coding is accurate and contributes to word recognition only above that threshold, and position coding breaks down for very tiny letters. Our method also allowed us to investigate the alternative possibility that dyslexic readers have a preferred print size that facilitates faster reading, rather than the normal broad range, possibly related to idiosyncrasies in their sensitivity to different spatial frequencies.

Method

Participants

Thirty-four children (22 dyslexic and 12 non-dyslexic) between 6.3 and 10.4 years of age participated in the study. The children were recruited from first to fourth grade classrooms at public schools in the vicinity of Boston, Massachusetts. Classroom teachers identified children who were either struggling readers or who were average readers in their class. Screening measures, including standardised reading and brief intelligence tests, were administered to all children. The children with dyslexia made up a sub-set of children taking part in a larger-scale intervention project (Morris, Wolf & Lovett, 1996) and they satisfied exclusionary criteria of being primary English speakers, and being free of any neurological or psychological disorders and visual or hearing impairments. They met either a low achievement or a discrepancy eligibility criterion of developmental dyslexia. Low achievement was defined as scoring one standard deviation below the norm on either the Woodcock Reading Mastery Test-Revised (WRMT-R) (Woodcock, 1987) Basic Skills or Total Reading clusters, or on the average of the WRMT-R Word Identification, Word Attack and Passage Comprehension sub-tests and the Wide Range Achievement Test-3 (WRAT-3) (Wilkinson, 1983) Reading sub-test. A discrepancy was defined as a significant difference of at least one standard deviation between achievement on any of these three composite reading scores (WRMT-R Basic Skills, Total Reading or the average score described above) and ability (based on Full Scale IQ from either the Kaufman Brief Intelligence Test (KBIT) (Kaufman & Kaufman, 1990), the Wechsler Intelligence Scale for Children (WISC-III) (Wechsler, 1991) or the Wechsler Abbreviated Scale of Intelligence (WASI) (Wechsler, 1999)).[1] Six children met a low achievement criterion, six met a discrepancy criterion and ten met both criteria. The non-dyslexic children were administered the WASI and the same WRMT-R sub-tests as the children with dyslexia. Non-dyslexic children scored within the normal range on these reading measures. Table 1 provides each participant's grade, age, gender, IQ and reading scores.

Because the dyslexic children's reading ability was generally one or more years below their grade level, the non-dyslexic comparison group was chosen to match them with regard to reading level instead of grade level in school. Thus, the non-dyslexic group was younger (Mean age $= 7.6$, Mean grade level $= 2.0$) than the dyslexic group (Mean age $= 8.9$, Mean grade level $= 2.8$) ($F_{(1,32)} = 21.4$, $p < 0.01$ for age, and $F_{(1,32)} = 6.5$, $p = 0.02$ for grade). There was overlap in the ages and grade levels between the groups: dyslexic children were enrolled in Grades 2 to 4 and non-dyslexic children were enrolled in Grades 1 to 3. Comparison between both reading matched and grade matched controls could thereby be made for some of the children in the dyslexic group. Therefore, data for the groups are presented both by chronological grade and reading grade equivalent levels (based on word identification scores from the WRMT-R). While grade level differed between the groups, word reading grade equivalent level did not differ ($F_{(1,32)} = 0.4$, $p = 0.53$, non-dyslexic Mean $= 2.6$ ($SE = 0.87$), dyslexic Mean $= 2.8$ ($SE = 0.66$)). Likewise, word identification raw scores did not differ between the groups ($F_{(1,32)} = 2.6$, $p = 0.12$, non-dyslexic Mean $= 44.7$ ($SE = 4.82$), dyslexic Mean $= 52.1$ ($SE = 2.24$)).

Procedure

Children were asked to read aloud sentences presented as black print on white paper. Each sentence was printed on its own page in a flip book. The sentence was presented by flipping the page after the child indicated that he/she was ready. Sentences were constructed so that all had 60 characters, including spaces between words and at the end of each line, formatted into three lines of left-right justified text in Times-Roman font, similar to the MNREAD sentences of Mansfield, Legge and Bane (1996) (see Appendix). Sentences were presented at a viewing distance of 40 cm. This was maintained by verifying the viewing distance throughout the reading trials. A black card extending 40 cm from the flip book was placed on the table at which the children sat. The edge of the black card was aligned with the child's face, and they were told to keep their head in place 'in line with the card', just as they would keep their feet at the free-throw line when playing basketball. Any trials where the children leaned over the line were rerun with a different sentence. Thirteen levels of print size were presented in descending order

Table 1. Age, grade, gender, IQ and reading measures for each participant (ND = non-dyslexic, D = dyslexic).

Subj.	Grade	Age (yrs)	Gender	FSIQ	VIQ	NVIQ	WRMT-R Basic Skill	Criterion (dyslexia)
ND1	1	6.9	M	107$_a$	108	104	95	none
ND2	1	6.6	M	107$_a$	95	118	107	none
ND3	1	6.8	F	88$_a$	98	83	98	none
ND4	2	7.7	F	91$_a$	100	86	102	none
ND5	2	7.9	F	102$_a$	101	102	94	none
ND6	2	7.8	F	82$_a$	80	86	100	none
ND7	2	7.6	F	96$_a$	93	99	105	none
ND8	3	8.3	M	98$_a$	109	86	105	none
ND9	3	8.2	F	94$_a$	99	90	99	none
ND10	3	8.7	F	91$_a$	94	90	96	none
ND11	3	8.5	M	93$_a$	108	81	106	none
ND12	1	6.3	F	97$_a$	95	99	111	none
D1	3	9.5	F	84$_b$	79	93	84	LA
D2	3	9.6	F	102$_b$	101	103	81	BOTH
D3	3	9.1	F	106$_b$	110	102	85	DISC
D4	2	8.8	F	95$_b$	92	99	82	BOTH
D5	3	9.3	M	103$_b$	107	98	87	DISC
D6	4	10.0	F	91$_b$	93	91	85	LA
D7	3	8.8	M	117$_b$	110	123	89	DISC
D8	4	10.0	F	97$_b$	99	95	86	BOTH
D9	4	10.0	F	120$_b$	112	125	85	DISC
D10	3	9.3	M	78$_b$	84	75	83	LA
D11	4	10.4	M	108$_c$	109	106	76	BOTH
D12	2	8.2	M	83$_c$	92	77	76	BOTH
D13	2	8.8	M	97$_a$	96	98	75	BOTH
D14	2	8.1	M	94$_a$	82	108	78	BOTH
D15	2	7.9	M	92$_a$	89	96	86	LA
D16	2	8.5	F	81$_a$	80	86	73	BOTH
D17	3	9.2	M	108$_a$	98	117	79	BOTH
D18	2	7.5	M	129$_a$	133	119	95	BOTH
D19	3	9.2	F	88$_a$	89	91	85	LA
D20	2	8.1	F	104$_a$	105	103	93	DISC
D21	2	8.1	M	89$_a$	98	84	84	LA
D22	2	8.0	M	98$_a$	102	93	88	DISC

Notes: IQ measures include full-scale (FSIQ), verbal (VIQ) and non-verbal (NVIQ) quotients based on the WASI$_a$, WISC-III$_b$, or KBIT$_c$. Basic Skill reading scores from the WRMT-R are compound standard scores from the Word Identification and Word Attack sub-tests. For participants with dyslexia, definitional criteria are also given (LA = low achievement criterion met, DISC = discrepancy criterion met, BOTH = both low achievement and discrepancy criteria were met).

ranging from 1.0 to -0.2 logMAR in 0.1 logMAR steps – i.e., from 0.582 to 0.037 cm x-heights corresponding to Snellen ratios from 20/200 to 20/12. There were two to three trials per print size.

Children read a practice sentence first, and were told that the letters would get smaller on each trial. They were instructed to read each sentence as quickly as they could, and to read as many words as they could see even if they thought they were guessing. Time to read each sentence was recorded with a stopwatch, commencing when the page was flipped and finishing when the child completed reading the last word. Reading errors were noted and used to calculate reading rates as correctly read words per minute. Sessions were also audio-taped to verify reading errors.

Results

Individual data

Each participant's raw data was plotted as reading rate (correct words read per minute) as a function of print size. These data were fit with a two-limb function, where a flat portion signified maximum reading speed above a critical print size, and where reading speed dropped off rapidly below the critical print size (CPS). The individual plots yielded maximum reading speeds and critical print sizes for each individual. Examples of typical individual reading speed by print size plots in Figure 2 show that the two-limb function provided a good fit to dyslexic as well as non-dyslexic readers, supporting the hypothesis that dyslexic print size-by-reading rate curves follow the typical two-limbed form. Estimates of goodness of fit for the two-limb function did not differ between groups (RMS error, $p = 0.58$), so the two-limb function provided an equally good fit for both groups. R-squares for all fits were significant ($p < 0.05$) with the exception of one non-dyslexic child (ND7). Inspection of this child's data indicated that her print size-by-reading speed plot did show the typical two-limb shape. One dyslexic participant's (D18) print size-by-reading speed plot did not show the typical two-limb shape; his reading speed was fairly flat across the range of print sizes. Examination of the two-limb fit parameters revealed that this child was an outlier with regard to critical print size. This participant's critical print size was more than three standard deviations above the group mean, and was estimated to be higher than the largest print size tested. This participant's data was therefore not included in the group analyses.

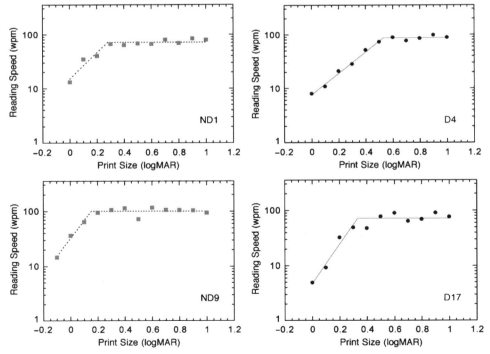

Figure 2. Examples of individual reading speed-by-print size curves shown with two-limb fits for two non-dyslexic and two dyslexic readers.

Maximum reading speed and critical print size were compared between dyslexic and non-dyslexic groups. To determine whether a specific print size facilitated dyslexic reading exclusively, the fastest single reading speed upon the maximum reading speed plateau was obtained for each participant. The print size at which this fastest rate occurred and the magnitude of its difference from the plateau was compared between groups.

Group comparisons

Our primary interest was to investigate visual factors in dyslexic reading independent of general reading ability level. To this end the groups were selected to have comparable reading level skills, and they therefore differed in age (the dyslexic group was older). In addition, we used word reading scores (WRMT-R word identification raw scores) as a covariate in the between group analyses of print size to statistically control for reading skill. We also report separate tests covarying age and IQ, since IQ has been found to account for sensory detection threshold differences in reading disability (Hulslander et al., 2004).

MANCOVAs were run on two sets of dependent variables: (1) those from the two-limb fits (maximum reading speed, critical print size), and (2) those from the point of the single fastest reading speed (the print size supporting the fastest rate, and its difference from the reading speed plateau). Each analysis used a between factor of group (dyslexic versus non-dyslexic) and covaried word identification scores.

For the first MANCOVA, the omnibus effect for group was significant (Wilk's Lambda $F_{(1,29)} = 11.2$, $p < 0.001$). Subsequent univariate tests revealed significant group differences in maximum reading speed (adjusted means of 109.1 wpm ($SE = 5.7$) versus 81.9 wpm ($SE = 4.2$) for non-dyslexic and dyslexic groups, respectively) ($F_{(1,30)} = 14.1$, $p = 0.001$), and critical print size (adjusted means of 0.136 logMAR ($SE = 0.04$) versus 0.258 logMAR ($SE = 0.03$) for non-dyslexic and dyslexic groups respectively) ($F_{(1,30)} = 7.0$, $p = 0.013$). This 0.122 log unit difference in critical print size corresponds to a factor of 1.32 difference in critical print sizes: that is, the dyslexic group required letters that were 32% larger than the controls to achieve their fastest reading speeds. Group means are presented by grade level (Table 2) and by reading grade equivalent (Table 3). It should be noted that critical print size differs from reading acuity, which is the smallest letter size for which one can read anything at all. The groups' reading acuities, as determined with a letter-by-letter method described in Mansfield, Legge and Bane (1996), also differed with word identification covaried ($F_{(1,30)} = 10.4$, $p < 0.01$).

Individual maximum reading speed and critical print size data are plotted as histograms by group, grade and grade equivalent in Figure 3. Interestingly, the histograms show the trend across all the subjects of a decrease in critical print size with grade level. For older children, the threshold for attaining maximum reading rates was lower (i.e. occurred at smaller print sizes). The critical print size distributions for the dyslexic group were shifted to higher thresholds (i.e. larger print) when compared to the controls of either the same chronological grade or reading grade level. In some cases, this shift to a higher critical print size for dyslexic readers was related to a shallower slope on the descending limb of the curve fit. A between-group ANCOVA with the word identification covariate showed a significant group difference in slopes ($F_{(1,30)} = 4.2$, $p = 0.04$, mean slopes of 5.2 ($SE = 0.67$) and 3.5 ($SE = 0.50$) for non-dyslexic and dyslexic groups, respectively). As Figure 4 shows, the group difference in slopes occurs primarily for early readers at word reading levels equivalent to Grades 1 and 2.

Table 2. Means (standard deviations) of two-limb fit parameters by group and grade level. Maximum Reading Speed is reported in words per minute, and critical print size and reading acuity in logMAR units.

Grade	Maximum reading speed		Critical print size		Reading acuity	
	Dyslexic	Non-dyslexic	Dyslexic	Non-dyslexic	Dyslexic	Non-dyslexic
1		61.97 (40.5)		0.237 (0.13)		0.206 (0.17)
2	62.45 (28.8)	102.56 (23.9)	0.302 (0.15)	0.177 (0.15)	0.237 (0.18)	0.036 (0.09)
3	107.17 (27.3)	124.94 (26.9)	0.201 (0.16)	0.090 (0.07)	0.015 (0.9)	− 0.035 (0.06)
4	112.87 (14.5)		0.176 (0.10)		0.006 (0.09)	

Table 3. Means (standard deviations) of two-limb fit parameters by group and reading grade equivalent (based on word identification scores).

READING GRADE EQUIV.	Maximum reading speed		Critical print size		Reading acuity	
	Dyslexic	Non-dyslexic	Dyslexic	Non-dyslexic	Dyslexic	Non-dyslexic
1	23.34	44.88 (26.6)	0.452	0.295 (0.06)	0.685	0.263 (0.15)
2	81.46 (29.3)	102.56 (23.9)	0.265 (0.16)	0.177 (0.15)	0.135 (0.18)	0.036 (0.09)
3	118.16 (28.6)	112.43 (8.5)	0.168 (0.07)	0.098 (0.06)	− 0.023 (0.04)	0.004 (0.03)
4	117.25 (7.5)	163.31	0.100 (0.08)	0.028	− 0.053 (0.04)	− 0.120

With age and full-scale IQ entered as covariates into the MANCOVA investigating the two-limb fit parameters, the same pattern of results emerges where the groups differ significantly in maximum reading speed and critical print size. When IQ alone is covaried in the MANCOVA, the group differences are no longer significant. This follows the findings of Hulslander et al. (2004), where full-scale IQ accounted for the relation between auditory and visual processing with word reading. Here, though, IQ was not significantly correlated with either maximum reading speed or critical print size over the whole group. Within the dyslexic group the two-limb fit parameters did not differ between groups with or without an IQ-achievement discrepancy or between groups of low achievers versus average achievers. Comparing the dyslexic children who met a low achievement criterion only with those who met a discrepancy criterion only and those who met both criteria showed that those meeting both criteria had the highest critical print sizes (Mean = 0.306), followed by the discrepancy only group (Mean = 0.202) and then the low-achievement only group (Mean = 0.179). Thus, the group with lower IQ, the low achievement group, also had the lowest critical print size of dyslexic sub-groups. So a lower IQ does not appear to account for higher critical print size.

The second MANCOVA revealed no significant group differences for either the print size supporting the fastest reading speed or the magnitude of the difference between the single fastest reading speed and the speed on the plateau. This was true when the magnitude of the reading speed difference was normalised according to one's maximum rate on their plateau (determined from the two-limb fits) or to the standard deviation of speeds about their plateau. In other words, the group effect was not significant when the magnitude difference was entered in words per minute, as a percentage of the plateau speed or in individual standard deviation units. In fact, the group means tend in the opposite direction than predicted: the non-dyslexic mean shows larger increases from the reading speed plateau (26.1 wpm ($SE = 2.7$)) than the dyslexic mean (22.6 wpm

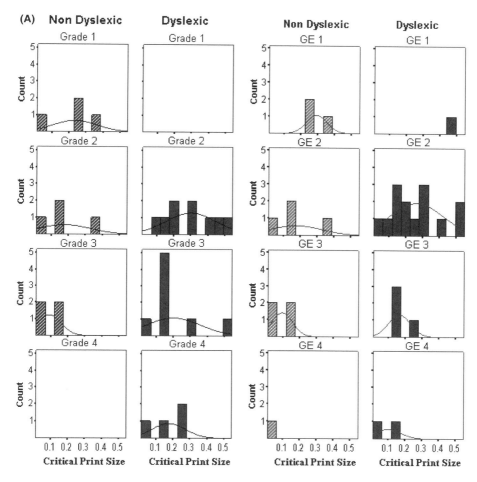

Figure 3a. Histograms of individual data from the two-limb fits.

Notes: Plots of (A) critical print size (logMAR) and (B) maximum reading speed (wpm) are shown separately for group by grade level (left columns) and for group by reading grade equivalent (GE) (based on word identification scores) (right columns). Grades corresponded to the following ages: Grade 1 (age 6), Grade 2 (ages 7 and 8), Grade 3 (ages 8 and 9), Grade 4 (age 10).

($SE = 2.0$)). This same pattern of results was obtained when age and full-scale IQ were entered as covariates instead of word identification scores.

Lastly, we investigated the relationship between maximum reading speed and critical print size to see whether those dyslexic children with more severe reading difficulty (e.g. those with the slowest reading rates) also had larger critical print sizes. Across all participants, maximum reading speed and critical print size were significantly correlated ($r = -0.436$, $p = 0.01$), but only remained significant within the non-dyslexic group ($r = -0.818$, $p = 0.001$), and not the dyslexic group ($r = -0.227$, $p = 0.32$) (see Figure 5). Screening for apparent outliers revealed only two participants (one dyslexic and one non-dyslexic) with residuals above two standard deviations. Removing both of these individuals from the analysis did not change the pattern of the outcome: the non-dyslexic correlation was significant ($r = -0.865$, $p < 0.001$), and the dyslexic correlation was not

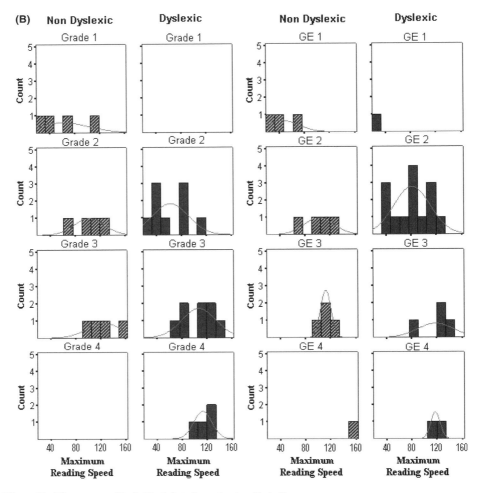

Figure 3b. Histograms of individual data from the two-limb fits.

($r = -0.424$, $p = 0.06$), although there was a trend. The correlation for non-dyslexics was still significantly larger than that for the dyslexics (z' difference $= 2.01$, $p < 0.05$).

Discussion

Dyslexic and non-dyslexic children demonstrated similar profile shapes of reading rate across print size, profiles that follow the typical two-limb shape found previously for adults (Mansfield, Legge & Bane, 1996). We found a similar consistency of curve profiles between dyslexic and non-dyslexic readers when we measured reading rates by luminance contrast of text and background (O'Brien, Mansfield & Legge, 2000). Thus, print size and print contrast are visual variables for which dyslexic reading speed exhibits the same qualitative dependence – a two-limb shape that typifies skilled reading.

Although the dyslexic profiles had the normal shape, two characteristics of the two-limb fits did differ for the dyslexic readers. As expected, their maximum reading speed along the plateau was slower than that of the non-dyslexic readers even though they were

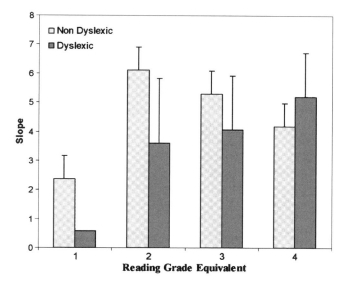

Figure 4. Group means of slopes from the descending limb of two-limb functions, shown by reading grade equivalent (based on word identification scores).

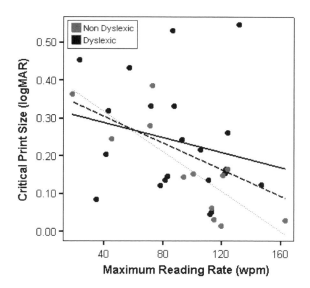

Figure 5. Regressions of critical print size on maximum reading speed for all subjects (dashed line), and for dyslexic (solid line) and non-dyslexic (dotted line) groups.

older and with control for word identification skill. Also, their critical print sizes were larger than those of the controls, indicating that they needed larger print to support maximum reading rates. The group difference in critical print size was partially due to a difference in slopes of the descending portion of the two-limb fits. Dyslexic readers' shallower slopes were moderately correlated with larger critical print sizes ($r = -0.58$).

These results confirm the hypothesis that dyslexic print size-by-reading rate curves have the typical two-limbed form but larger critical print sizes, and refute the alternative hypothesis of a monotonic increase of dyslexic reading rates with increasing print size. What could theoretically account for these results? Reading words with very small letters may prove difficult either because the letters are hard to identify or because it is hard to determine where they appear in the word. Models of reading hold that both letter identification and letter position coding play important roles in word identification (e.g. Adams, 1979; Estes & Brunn, 1987). Thus, slow, inaccurate word identification with small letters could be due to either compromised letter identification or letter position coding.

Letter recognition and reading normally require a critical spatial frequency bandwidth. The idea that dyslexic readers need larger print to compensate for a higher or broader spatial frequency bandwidth for reading does not account for the findings, since one would expect reading performance to keep improving with increasing print size if this were the case. Likewise, the idea that dyslexic readers may have a particular print size where reading performance peaks, due to differential sensitivity to specific spatial frequencies, was also not borne out. There were no points above critical print size where reading was more efficient for the dyslexic readers.

Letter recognition alone is not sufficient for word identification and reading; rather inter-letter effects also need to be taken into account. Knowing the position of a letter relative to the other letters in a word is necessary for correct word identification; for example, distinguishing the orthographic input of 'trap' versus 'tarp' or 'part' requires correctly locating the spatial arrangement of the letters in the word. The magnocellular channel may carry a code for the relative position of each letter in the word; for instance, [t-1], [r-2], [a-3], [p-4]. This channel may contain more noise in dyslexic readers, so the numbers for 'r' and 'a' in our example may contain some uncertainty (e.g. for position 2 in the word there is a 60% chance it is the 'r' that I saw and a 40% chance it is the 'a'). Cornelissen and Hansen (1998) describe how relative letter position information is contained within an intermediate spatial scale of the visual stimulus (i.e. the print), while information about whole words and letter features is carried by coarse and fine scales, respectively.

For very tiny print, the fine spatial scale must become too small to resolve critical features, so letters cannot be identified and the acuity limit is reached. Just above this point, letters can be resolved but may not be ordered correctly because of noise (spatial uncertainty) in the codes for spatial position. Theoretically, greater relative position noise in dyslexia may contribute to slow reading in general, and could cause dyslexic reading to be more susceptible to deterioration with small print: meaning dyslexic readers should have slower maximum reading speeds and higher critical print sizes. The present results are consistent with a dyslexic magnocellular-letter position coding deficit.

Other related accounts of inter-letter effects on word reading include crowding, visual attention and visual span. Crowding, or lateral masking, refers to the hindering of letter recognition when a letter is flanked by other letters. The difference in curve shape for dyslexic readers could be because of greater susceptibility to crowding effects, especially if their recognition of isolated letters is already inaccurate or slow. Indeed, previous studies have found greater crowding effects for dyslexic readers (Atkinson, 1999; Geiger & Lettvin, 1987). Klein and D'Entremont (1999) found greater interference between far flankers than near ones for dyslexics, which they attributed to differences in visual attentional filtering. While it is unclear how visual attention differences per se could account for the present print size effect in dyslexia, two theories are relevant. First, visual attention could be the cognitive module that mediates between magnocellular function at the physiological level and position coding for letters in words (e.g. see Pammer et al., 2004). Second, visual attention may impact the visible window of text while reading.

Ans, Carbonnel and Valdois (1998) developed a connectionist model of reading that uses a visual attention window, wherein maximal parallel processing occurs, and which is modified in size based on reading mode. The attentional window in this model can be narrowed to focus on smaller portions of orthographic input if needed. This notion of a reader's attentional control over the number of letters processed at a glance may be related to the concept of visual span, the number of letters one can recognise at a glance (O'Regan, Levy-Schoen & Jacobs, 1983). Legge et al. (1997, 2001, 2002) systematically studied visual span size with regard to print size, and found that visual span decreases with very small and very large letters, and that reading speed covaries with the size of the visual span. Normally, smaller visual spans (in characters) are found for print sizes smaller than the critical print size. The present finding of a difference in curve shape for dyslexic readers could be because of a difference in their visual span. That is, we would predict that dyslexic visual spans may continue to increase with increasing print size to a somewhat larger print size (corresponding to the increased critical print size), and the size of the visual span may be smaller than normal even above the critical print size. These potential differences in visual span may be related to inter-letter effects such as crowding or attentional resolution.

While each of these theoretical accounts – position coding, crowding, visual attention or visual span – could contribute to the present print size effect for dyslexic readers, the theories are not mutually exclusive; rather they are likely to be related. For example, imprecise letter position coding could result from attentional disturbances or increased crowding effects in dyslexia. Huckauf and Heller (2002) demonstrated that crowding effects could be explained by position uncertainty rather than interactions of adjacent letter forms. Teasing apart letter position coding and crowding effects on dyslexic reading would require further study by independently manipulating print size and letter spacing. Furthermore, both position uncertainty and crowding effects may contribute to the extent of one's visual span for reading.

It is also possible that a magnocellular deficit could be manifest as slower reading with small text in the present study because of oculomotor factors. The magnocellular visual pathway has neural connections with areas involved in eye-movement programming (e.g. the superior colliculus). Because reading, as in the present study, requires a succession of saccadic eye movements, a magnocellular deficit could have an impact at this level instead of or in addition to a letter-position coding deficit. Producing eye movements within text with small print may be especially difficult, as Kowler and Anton (1987) found that very small saccades may take longer to produce. The present study cannot speak to this possibility. An investigation comparing print size effects of text presentations with and without required eye movements (e.g. normal page-formatted text versus rapid serial visual presentation (RSVP)) would be required to differentiate these effects.

Because the dyslexic group was older in the present sample, one could speculate that the characteristic differences of the two-limb curves result from a general developmental lag, where dyslexic readers behave like younger non-dyslexic readers with regard to having slower maximum reading rates and higher critical print sizes. That the groups still differed when reading level was controlled runs counter to this claim. We chose to 'equate' the reading groups on isolated word identification, although other factors may be developmentally relevant as well. Furthermore, a developmental lag model would be strongly supported if the dyslexic and non-dyslexic data fell on the same critical-print size-by-maximum-reading-rate regression line, but this was not the case either. The dyslexic group showed a lack of a correlation between these variables, whereas the non-dyslexic group showed a fairly strong correlation. This implies some de-coupling of the maturational influences that normally tie the two variables together. Here, the slowest dyslexic readers did not necessarily require larger print size thresholds to attain their maximum reading speed, whereas slower non-dyslexic readers did.

One might also expect that if general intelligence accounts for sensory processing differences in dyslexia, then those with lower IQ would show the greatest impact on sensory processing (i.e. they would have higher critical print sizes). However, this did not appear to be the case with the group we tested. It was the children with higher IQ and an IQ-achievement discrepancy who actually had the highest critical print sizes.

Lastly, it is of interest in understanding the development of normal reading behaviour that the non-dyslexic group showed effects of age on critical print size as well as maximum reading speed. Increasing reading rates with age conforms to previous findings of a linear increase between 10 and 20 wpm per grade (Carver, 1990; Tressoldi, Stella & Faggella, 2001). We are not aware of any previous research findings showing the developmental change in critical print size. Our data showed that critical print size decreases with age, suggesting younger children need larger print to optimise reading performance. It is noteworthy that reading materials for early, very young readers generally have larger print than texts for older children. We also found a negative correlation between reading speed and critical print size, showing that in general slower non-dyslexic readers required larger print size to support their maximum reading speed. The finding that dyslexic readers require larger print size to attain their maximum reading speed has implications for the type of print that educators select for these children (e.g. see Hughes & Wilkins (2002) regarding general recommendations for print size and spacing in children's books for group reading).

Acknowledgements

This work was supported in part by NIH Grants HD30970 and EY 02934. We wish to thank the families, teachers and schools of our participants for their co-operation and support. We also thank the anonymous reviewers for their helpful comments.

Note

1. All children with dyslexia were administered the KBIT at screening and either the WISC-III or the WASI after screening as part of their participation in the intervention project. Although the KBIT shows high correlation with the two Wechsler measures of intelligence (0.78 (Prewett, 1995), and 0.89 (Hayes, Reas & Shaw, 2002), respectively), the Wechsler scales show higher validity than the KBIT in clinical samples (Chin et al., 2001; Thompson, Brown, Schmidt & Boer, 1997). Therefore these measures are reported for the dyslexic group and were used to calculate discrepancy scores. KBIT scores are reported for two children whose WISC-III or WASI scores were not obtained.

References

Adams, M.J. (1979). Models of word recognition. *Cognitive Psychology*, 11(2), 133–176.

Ans, B., Carbonnel, S. & Valdois, S. (1998). A connectionist multi-trace memory model of polysyllabic word reading. *Psychological Review*, 105, 678–723.

Atkinson, J. (1993). Vision in dyslexics: Letter recognition, acuity, visual crowding, contrast sensitivity, accommodation, convergence and sight reading music. In S.F. Wright & R. Groner (Eds.), *Facets of dyslexia and its remediation*. Amsterdam: Elsevier Science.

Carver, R.P. (1990). *Reading rate: A review of research and theory*. San Diego: Academic Press.

Chin, C.E., Ledesma, H.M.L., Cirino, P.T., Sevcik, R.A., Morris, R.D., Frijters, J.C. & Lovett, M.W. (2001). Relation between Kaufman Brief Intelligence Test and WISC-III scores of children with RD. *Journal of Learning Disabilities*, 34(1), 2–8.

Cornelissen, P., Bradley, L., Fowler, S. & Stein, J. (1991). What children see affects how they read. *Developmental Medicine and Child Neurology*, 33, 755–762.

Cornelissen, P.L., Richardson, A.L., Mason, A., Fowler, M.S. & Stein, J.F. (1994). Contrast sensitivity and coherent motion detection measured at photopic luminance levels in dyslexics and controls. *Vision Research*, 35, 1483–1494.

Cornelissen, P.L., Hansen, P., Gilchrist, I., Cormack, F., Essex, J. & Frankish, C. (1998a). Coherent motion detection and letter position encoding. *Vision Research*, 38, 2181–2191.

Cornelissen, P.L., Hansen, P., Hutton, J., Evangelinou, V. & Stein, J. (1998b). Magnocellular visual function and children's single word reading. *Vision Research*, 38, 471–482.

Cornelissen, P.L. & Hansen, P.C. (1998). Motion detection, letter position encoding, and single word reading. *Annals of Dyslexia*, 48, 155–188.

Demb, J.B., Boynton, G.M. & Heeger, D.J. (1997). Brain activation in visual cortex predicts individual differences in reading performance. *Proceedings of the New York Academy of Sciences*, 94, 13363–13366.

Demb, J.B., Boynton, G.M., Best, M. & Heeger, D. (1998). Psychophysical evidence for a magnocellular deficit in dyslexics. *Vision Research*, 38, 1555–1559.

Eden, G.F., van Meter, J.W., Rumsey, J.W., Maisog, J. & Zeffiro, T.A. (1996). Functional MRI reveals differences in visual motion processing in individuals with dyslexia. *Nature*, 382, 66–69.

Estes, W.K. & Brunn, J.L. (1987). Discriminability and bias in the word-superiority effect. *Perception and Psychophysics*, 42(5), 411–422.

Everatt, J., Bradshaw, M.F. & Hibbard, P.B. (1999). Visual processing and dyslexia. *Perception*, 28(2), 243–254.

Galaburda, A.M. & Livingstone, M.S. (1993). Evidence for a magnocellular defect in developmental dyslexia. In P. Tallal, A.M. Galaburda, R.R. Llinas & C. von Euler (Eds.), *Temporal information processing in the nervous system*. Annals of the New York Academy of Sciences, 682, 70–82.

Geiger, G. & Lettvin, J.Y. (1987). Peripheral vision in persons with dyslexia. *New England Journal of Medicine*, 316, 1238–1243.

Hays, J.R., Reas, D.L. & Shaw, J.B. (2002). Concurrent validity of the Wechsler Abbreviated Scale of Intelligence and the Kaufman Brief Intelligence Test among psychiatric inpatients. *Psychological Reports*, 90(2), 355–359.

Huckauf, A. & Heller, D. (2002). What various kinds of errors tell us about lateral masking effects. *Visual Cognition*, 9(7), 889–910.

Hughes, L.E. & Wilkins, A.J. (2002). Reading at a distance: Implications for the design of text in children's big books. *British Journal of Educational Psychology*, 72(2), 213–226.

Hulslander, J., Talcott, J., Witton, C., DeFries, J., Pennington, B., Wadsworth, S., Willcutt, E. & Olson, R. (2004). Sensory processing, reading, IQ, and attention. *Journal of Experimental Child Psychology*, 88, 274–295.

Iles, J., Walsh, V. & Richardson, A. (2000). Visual search performance in dyslexia. *Dyslexia*, 6, 163–177.

Kaufman, A.S. & Kaufman, N.L. (1990). *Kaufman brief intelligence test*. Circle Pines, MN: American Guidance Services.

Klein, R.M., Berry, G., Briand, K., D'Entremont, B. & Farmer, M. (1990). Letter identification declines with increasing retinal eccentricity at the same rate for normal and dyslexic readers. *Perception and Psychophysics*, 47, 601–606.

Klein, R.M. & D'Entremont, B. (1999). Filtering performance by good and poor readers. In J. Everatt (Ed.), *Reading and dyslexia: Visual and attentional processes*. New York, NY: Routledge, Taylor & Francis Group.

Kowler, E. & Anton, S. (1987). Reading twisted text: Implications for the role of saccades. *Vision Research*, 27, 45–60.

Legge, G.E., Ahn, S.J., Klitz, T.S. & Luebker, A. (1997). Psychophysics of reading – XVI. The visual span in normal and low vision. *Vision Research*, 37(14), 1999–2010.

Legge, G.E., Lee, H.-W., Owens, D., Cheung, S.-H. & Chung, S.T.L. (2002). Visual span: A sensory bottleneck on reading speed. *Journal of Vision*, 2(7), 279.

Legge, G.E., Mansfield, J.S. & Chung, S.T.L. (2001). Psychophysics of reading – XX. Linking letter recognition to reading speed in central and peripheral vision. *Vision Research*, 41, 725–743.

Legge, G.E., Pelli, D.G., Rubin, G.S. & Schleske, M.M. (1985). Psychophysics of reading – I. Normal vision. *Vision Research*, 25(2), 239–252.

Liberman, I.Y., Shankweiler, D., Fischer, F.W. & Carter, B. (1974). Explicit syllable and phoneme segmentation in the young child. *Journal of Exceptional Child Psychology*, 18, 201–212.

Livingstone, M.S., Rosen, G.D., Drislane, F.W. & Galaburda, A.M. (1991). Physiological and anatomical evidence for a magnocellular deficit in developmental dyslexia. *Proceedings of the National Academy of Sciences (USA)*, 88, 7943–7947.

Lovegrove, W.J., Martin, F., Blackwood, M. & Badcock, D. (1980). Specific reading difficulty: Differences in contrast sensitivity as a function of spatial frequency. *Science*, 210, 439–440.

Lovett, M.W., Steinbach, K.A. & Frijters, J.C. (2000). Remediating the core deficits of developmental reading disability: A double-deficit perspective. *Journal of Learning Disabilities*, 33(4), 334–358.

Lyon, G.R. & Moats, L.C. (1997). Critical conceptual and methodological considerations in reading intervention research. *Journal of Learning Disabilities*, 30, 578–588.

Mansfield, J.S., Legge, G.E. & Bane, M.C. (1996). Psychophysics of reading – XV: Font effects in normal and low vision. *Investigative Ophthalmology & Visual Science*, 37(8), 1492–1501.

Martin, F. & Lovegrove, W.J. (1987). Flicker contrast sensitivity in normal and specifically disabled readers. *Perception*, 16, 215–221.

Mishkin, M., Ungerlieder, L.G. & Macko, K.A. (1983). Object vision and spatial vision: Two cortical pathways. *Trends in Neuroscience*, 1010, 3323–3334.

Morgan, W.P. (1896). Word blindness. *British Medical Journal*, 2, 1378.

Morris, R., Wolf, M. & Lovett, M. (1996). *The treatment of developmental reading disabilities*. HD 30970.

O'Brien, B.A., Mansfield, J.S. & Legge, G.E. (2000). The effect of contrast on reading speed in dyslexia. *Vision Research*, 40, 1921–1935.

O'Regan, J.K., Levy-Schoen, A. & Jacobs, A.M. (1983). The effect of visibility on eye-movement parameters in reading. *Perception and Psychophysics*, 34, 457–464.

Orton, S.T. (1928). Specific reading disability – Strephosymbolia. *Journal of the American Medical Association*, 90, 1095–1099.

Pammer, K. & Wheatley, C. (2001). Isolating the M(y)-cell response in dyslexia using the spatial frequency doubling illusion. *Vision Research*, 41, 2139–2147.

Pammer, K., Lavis, R., Hansen, P. & Cornelissen, P. (2004). Symbol-string sensitivity and children's reading. *Brain and Language*, 89, 601–610.

Prewett, P.N. (1995). A comparison of two screening tests (the Matrix Analogies Test–Short Form and the Kaufman Brief Intelligence Test) with the WISC-III. *Psychological Assessment*, 7(1), 69–72.

Skottun, B.C. (2000). The magnocellular deficit theory of dyslexia: The evidence from contrast sensitivity. *Vision Research*, 40, 111–127.

Skottun, B.C. (2001). Is dyslexia caused by a visual deficit? *Vision Research*, 41, 3070.

Snowling, M.J. (2000). *Dyslexia* (2nd edn). Malden, MA: Blackwell Publishers.

Solomon, J.A. & Pelli, D.G. (1994). The visual filter mediating letter identification. *Nature*, 369, 395–397.

Stanovich, K.E. & Siegel, L.S. (1994). Phenotypic performance profile of children with reading disabilities: A regression-based test of the phonological-core variable-difference model. *Journal of Educational Psychology*, 86(1), 24–53.

Talcott, J.B., Hansen, P.C., Elikem, L.A. & Stein, J.F. (2000). Visual motion sensitivity in dyslexia: Evidence for temporal and motion energy integration deficits. *Neuropsychologia*, 38, 935–943.

Talcott, J.B., Hansen, P.C., Willis-Owen, C., McKinnell, I.W., Richardson, A.J. & Stein, J.F. (1998). Visual magnocellular impairment in adult developmental dyslexics. *Neuro-ophthalmology*, 20, 187–201.

Thompson, A., Browne, J., Schmidt, F. & Boer, M. (1997). Validity of the Kaufman Brief Intelligence Test and a four-subtest WISC-III short form with adolescent offenders. *Assessment*, 4(4), 385–394.

Torgesen, J.K. (2000). Individual differences in response to early interventions in reading: The lingering problem of treatment resisters. *Learning Disabilities Research & Practice*, 15(1), 55–64.

Tressoldi, P.E., Stella, G. & Faggella, M. (2001). The development of reading speed in Italians with dyslexia: A longitudinal study. *Journal of Learning Disabilities*, 34(5), 414–417.

Valdois, S., Bosse, M. & Tainturier, M. (2004). The cognitive deficits responsible for developmental dyslexia: Review of evidence for a selective visual attentional disorder. *Dyslexia*, 10, 339–363.

Walther-Muller, P.U. (1995). Is there a deficit of early vision in dyslexia? *Perception*, 24, 919–936.

Wechsler, D. (1991). *Wechsler Intelligence Scale for Children* (3rd edn). Boston, MA: The Psychological Corporation.

Wechsler, D. (1999). *Wechsler Abbreviated Scale of Intelligence*. Boston, MA: The Psychological Corporation.

Wilkinson, G.S. (1993). *Wide Range Achievement Test – 3*. Wilmington, DE: Wide Range Inc.

Wolf, M. & Bowers, P. (1999). The 'double-deficit hypothesis' for the developmental dyslexias. *Journal of Educational Psychology*, 91(3), 1–24.

Woodcock, R. (1987). *Woodcock Reading Mastery Test*. Circle Pines, MN: American Guidance Service.

Appendix

logMAR	List 1	List 2	List 3
1.0	The three elephants in the circus walked around very slowly	The two friends did not know what time the play would start	
0.9	An old man took a picture of my sister and her little puppy	She wanted to show us the new toys she got for her birthday	
0.8	Ten different kinds of flowers grow by the side of the road	The father gave his children some fruit for lunch every day	We could not guess what was inside the big box on the table
0.7	Please do not make noise while they are reading their books	The snow fell softly this morning before our family woke up	The mother told her son that she wanted him to go to school
0.6	Many people came to help us clean the place after the party	The teacher wanted the children to learn how to draw a boat	Put your first name on this paper if you will help tomorrow
0.5	We like to listen to music when we are eating our breakfast	She gave a glass of water to her mother before going to bed	We sometimes take long walks together if it is warm outside
0.4	My brother was not feeling very well so he did not go today	Everyone wanted to go outside when the rain finally stopped	He could see a bird outside if he looked through his window
0.3	They were not able to finish playing the game before dinner	Three of my friends had never been to a circus before today	Three of my closest friends are going to visit him tomorrow
0.2	My grandfather has a large garden with fruit and vegetables	My mother loves to hear the young girls sing in the morning	My father takes me to school every day in his big green car
0.1	The young boy held his hand high to ask questions in school	I do not understand why we must leave so early for the play	My father asked me to help the two men carry the box inside
0.0	It is more than four hundred miles from my home to the city	They would love to see you during your visit here this week	He told a long story about ducks before his son went to bed
− 0.1	The teacher showed the children how to draw pretty pictures	The old man caught a fish here when he went out in his boat	My brother wanted a glass of milk with his cake after lunch
− 0.2	There are two dogs and three cats in the park near my house	Our mother tells us that we should wear heavy coats outside	Our father wants us to wash the clothes before he gets back

9

The relationship between dyslexia and Meares-Irlen Syndrome

Isla Kriss and Bruce J.W. Evans

Meares-Irlen Syndrome (MIS) is a condition characterised by symptoms of visual stress and visual perceptual distortions which are alleviated by individually prescribed coloured filters. The syndrome (previously known as Scotopic Sensitivity Syndrome) can occur in good readers but is said to be particularly prevalent in people diagnosed with dyslexia (Irlen, 1997). There is a large body of literature on MIS, reviewed by Evans (2001), and to date there have been two rigorous double-masked randomised placebo controlled trials (Wilkins et al., 1994; Robinson & Foreman, 1999). These trials support the existence of this syndrome and validate the treatment with individually prescribed coloured filters. In particular, both randomised controlled trials demonstrate that the benefit from coloured filters is idiosyncratic and specific: different people need different colours and the colour needs to be defined with some degree of precision. This accounts for a great deal of controversy in the literature: studies using individually prescribed filters tend to be positive whilst those that test all participants with the same colour, or with a very limited range of colours, tend to be negative (Evans, 2001).

The first double-masked randomised placebo-controlled trial found that individually prescribed coloured filters (precision tinted lenses) brought about a significant reduction in symptoms of eyestrain and headache compared with control lenses of a similar but different colour (Wilkins et al., 1994). The lenses were prescribed using an instrument, the Intuitive Colorimeter, that had been developed by Wilkins and patented by the Medical Research Council (Wilkins, Nimmo-Smith & Jansons, 1992).

The second double-masked randomised-controlled trial investigated the effects of coloured filters on reading speed, accuracy, comprehension and self-perception of academic ability, with the widely used Neale Analysis of Reading Test (Robinson & Foreman, 1999). A total of 113 participants were divided into three groups either using placebo filters, standard blue filters or optimal (individually prescribed) filters. Compared with the other groups, the group using optimal filters increased markedly in reading accuracy and comprehension, but not in speed (see below). This study used the Irlen system (Irlen, 1991).

An audit of a clinical population found that one-and-a-half years after patients had been prescribed precision tinted lenses, 73% were still using them on a daily basis (Evans et al., 1999). In the open trial of precision tints by Maclachlan et al. (1993), a similar figure of 81% was obtained. Patients' perceptions of the benefit they received from their precision tints compared favourably with other interventions, with nearly 80% reporting that tints improved their problems or difficulties (Evans et al., 1999).

The aetiology of MIS has been reviewed elsewhere (Evans, 2001; Wilkins, 2003). Although many theories have been proposed, few can account for the individual and sometimes precise nature of the tints required. The most plausible explanation at present relates to pattern glare (Wilkins et al., 1984) and cortical hyperexcitability (Wilkins, Huang & Cao, 2003). Striped patterns can be unpleasant to look at and some people experience eyestrain and visual perceptual distortions when viewing these. In fact, these symptoms are remarkably similar to those reported by people with MIS. Some people with photosensitive epilepsy are particularly prone to these symptoms, as are others with migraine, and the mechanism for these symptoms is likely to be a hyperexcitability of the visual cortex (Huang, Cooper, Satana, Kaufman & Cao, 2003). Lines of print on a page form a striped pattern, which can have the spatial properties that may cause pattern glare (Wilkins & Nimmo-Smith, 1984). It seems likely that this mechanism is responsible for at least some patients' symptoms of 'visual stress' when reading, which characterise MIS. The peak responses of some colour sensitive areas of the visual cortex are spatially arranged in the order of the hues of coloured stimuli (Xiao, Wang & Felleman, 2003) and this could account for the benefit from specific coloured filters. Recent research suggests that individually prescribed coloured filters can also help people with visually precipitated migraine (Wilkins, Patel, Adjamian & Evans, 2002) and epilepsy (Wilkins et al., 1999).

An initial system for prescribing tinted lenses by non-eyecare professionals (Irlen, 1991; Evans & Drasdo, 1991) has been supplemented by the Wilkins/MRC system mentioned above (Wilkins, Nimmo-Smith & Jansons, 1992). This is now widely used in the UK by optometrists in primary care practice and by some orthoptists and optometrists in secondary-care hospital eye departments. The Wilkins/MRC system was used in the present research and is described in more detail below.

Detection of Meares-Irlen Syndrome

The possible presence of MIS in an individual is sometimes indicated by a recollection of symptoms experienced during reading. However, there are limitations to the use of symptoms for the detection of MIS (Jeanes et al., 1997): symptoms may be exaggerated (for example, by suggestible children), some children fail to recognise symptoms until they have been eliminated because to the child the symptoms are 'normal' and the symptoms of MIS are non-specific. This last point is important since the symptoms of MIS can be caused by a variety of other visual problems (Evans, 2005). Although symptoms should never be ignored, these limitations restrict their potential use in screening for MIS and most screening programmes use coloured overlays.

Coloured overlays are transparent plastic sheets that are placed on the page to allow a comparison of text that is covered by an overlay with text that is uncovered. Both of the major systems (Evans, 2001) that are used for treating MIS in the UK use coloured overlays in this way (Irlen & Lass, 1989; Wilkins, 1994). The protocol that is typically followed (Lightstone & Evans, 1995) starts with a screening test using coloured overlays, which is usually administered by teachers or optometrists. The coloured overlays in the Wilkins/MRC system were designed to sample comprehensively and systematically CIE 1976 UCS chromaticity (Wilkins, 1994). If children express a preference for a coloured overlay then this preference is tested in one of two ways: voluntary sustained use or an immediate improvement in rate of reading. To meet the criterion of voluntary sustained use, the person is issued with their preferred coloured overlay and invited to use the overlay for reading, if it is found to be helpful. Instructions are given that if the overlay is still being used after a half to one school term then the child should seek further testing. To test for an immediate benefit in rate of reading, the Wilkins Rate of Reading Test is used and this is described below (Wilkins, Jeanes, Pumfrey & Laskier, 1996).

Whichever criterion is used, people who demonstrate a benefit from an overlay ultimately may be tested with the Wilkins/MRC Intuitive Colorimeter. This is an instrument which allows the very precise determination of the optimal specification for tinted lenses and it is used in conjunction with a range of precision tinted lenses to prescribe tinted spectacles (Wilkins, Milroy et al., 1992). People almost invariably report more benefit from precision tinted lenses than from coloured overlays because precision tinted lenses are easier to use (e.g. with white boards and when writing) and because the colour can be prescribed with more precision.

The Wilkins Rate of Reading Test (WRRT)

Wilkins developed the Rate of Reading Test (WRRT; see Figure 1) in order to isolate and measure the effect of visual factors on reading (Wilkins et al., 1996). Most reading tests are designed to evaluate high-level reading skills, but not the contribution of visual factors to reading: the WRRT evaluates this aspect. For example, the Neale Analysis of Reading Test (Neale, 1997), which revealed an improvement from coloured overlays in reading accuracy and comprehension but, surprisingly, not speed (Robinson & Foreman, 1999), uses relatively large text and widely spaced lines. The WRRT uses smaller, closely spaced text and consists of words that occur with a very high frequency in the English language, which should be familiar to children aged 7 years and above. The WRRT is scored for reading rate and errors, and is simple as far as cognitive and language skills are concerned. The text size and spacing has been selected to make it well suited to detecting visual problems.

Diagnosis and prevalence of Meares-Irlen Syndrome

Both methods of detecting MIS described above have been used to diagnose the condition. The prevalence will, of course, vary with the criteria that are used. A problem with diagnosing MIS (Evans & Joseph, 2002) is that there is likely to be a continuum ranging from people who experience no help from coloured filters, through those who show a mild benefit, to the more severe cases who may experience a marked reduction in symptoms and a very marked improvement in reading performance.

Studies have shown that, using the sustained voluntary use criterion, the prevalence of MIS in unselected school populations is approximately 20% (see Table 1). Jeanes and colleagues showed that children who demonstrated sustained voluntary use of their

come see the play look up is cat not my and dog for you to
the cat up dog and is play come you see for not to look my
you for the and not see my play come is look dog cat to up
dog to you and play cat up is my not come for the look see
play come see cat not look dog is my up the for to and you
to not cat for look is my and up come play you see the dog
my play see to for you is the look up cat not dog come and
look to for my come play the dog see you not cat up and is
up come look for the not dog cat you to see is and my play
is you dog for not cat my look come and up to play see the

Figure 1. A passage from the Wilkins Rate of Reading Test (reproduced with permission of Prof Arnold Wilkins and of i.o.o. Sales Ltd, London).

Table 1. Prevalence of Meares-Irlen Syndrome in unselected populations.

Study	Sample	Criterion	Proportion (%)
Wilkins et al. (1996; Fig. 3)	77 unselected children, aged 8–11 yrs	initially selected an overlay to use	49
		>5% faster at WRRT	20
		sustained (8 weeks) voluntary use	20
		sensitivity of 5% criterion for sustained use	73
		specificity of 5% criterion for sustained use	90 (74)
Jeanes et al. (1997)	152 unselected children, aged 5–11 yrs	initially selected an overlay to use	53
		sustained (3 month) voluntary use	36
		sustained (10 month) voluntary use	24
Wilkins et al. (2001; Table 3 & Fig. 7)	426 unselected children, aged 6–8 yrs	initially selected an overlay to use	60
		>5% faster at WRRT	36
		>25% faster at WRRT	5
		sustained (8 months) voluntary use	31
		sensitivity of 5% criterion for sustained use	68
		specificity of 5% criterion for sustained use	79 (50)
Evans & Joseph (2001)	113 unselected university students, aged 18–44 yrs	Initially selected an overlay	88
		>5% faster at WRRT	34
		>25% faster at WRRT	2

Source: (modified after Evans and Joseph, 2001).
Notes: The proportion column gives the proportion of the full study population who meet the adjacent criterion. Sensitivity is defined as the percentage of the full study population who chose an overlay and continued to use it – who initially showed an improvement of >5% in the rate of reading. Specificity is defined as the percentage of the full study population who either did not choose an overlay or did not continue to use one – who did not initially show an improvement of >5% in the rate of reading. An alternative method, used by Wilkins et al. (2002, Fig. 7) and included here in parentheses, defines specificity as the percentage of participants who chose an overlay but did not continue to use it – who did not initially show an improvement of >5% in the WRRT.

overlay showed a mean improvement of 14% in reading speed with the WRRT (Jeanes et al., 1997). The WRRT predicts the children who subsequently will use their overlay, and does so before they have become acquainted with its use (Wilkins et al., 1996). Two single-masked randomised placebo-controlled trials confirmed that the benefit in rate of reading with overlays is not attributable to placebo effects (Bouldoukian, Wilkins & Evans, 2002; Wilkins & Lewis, 1999).

Several studies have calculated the prevalence of MIS in unselected samples, for example by screening large groups of unselected children in schools (Jeanes et al., 1997; Wilkins et al., 1996; Wilkins, Lewis, Smith, Rowland & Tweedie, 2001). These studies are summarised in Table 1, which gives figures for prevalence according to various diagnostic criteria. Table 1 also includes one study of adult university students which suggests that the prevalence in adults is similar to that in children (Evans & Joseph, 2002).

Although there is now good evidence for the prevalence of MIS in the general population, we know of no previously published studies that have determined the prevalence of MIS in people diagnosed with dyslexia. Irlen has claimed that MIS has a prevalence of 12–14% in the general population, and 46% in those with dyslexia, but no data or diagnostic criteria were given to support this statement (Irlen, 1997). A PubMed search for the keywords *dyslexia* AND (*Meares-Irlen Syndrome* OR *Irlen Syndrome* OR *Scotopic Sensitivity Syndrome*) revealed only four papers, none of which gave estimates of prevalence. The aim of the present study is to compare the prevalence of MIS in a cross-sectional sample of dyslexic and control children.

Method

The study was a 2 × 2 mixed factorial design experiment, with dyslexic and control group being the between-participants variable and testing with and without overlay being the within-participants variable.

Participants

Sixty-four children were tested, 32 in the dyslexic group and 32 controls. The groups were matched for age and gender so that, in each group, the mean age was 9.4 years and the age range was 7–12 years, with 21 males and 11 females in each group. Participants were recruited from various state schools and dyslexia clubs; socio-economic background was loosely matched by the area in which the participants lived. During the process of informed consent it was made clear that the research did not constitute an 'eye test' and did not detract from the need for routine eye care.

Selection criteria for all participants were as follows: aged between 7–12 years and able to read the 15 words in the WRRT. An additional criterion for the dyslexic group was a diagnosis of dyslexia by an educational psychologist. Teachers selected control participants as having no suspicion of dyslexia and a reading age that is not significantly worse than that predicted for their age and intelligence. Intelligence was not formally assessed in the study, but teachers were asked to select children whose intelligence was within the average range. No other criteria were applied in selecting participants and children who had received previous optometric treatment, including coloured filters, were neither actively sought nor excluded. Care was taken to ensure that subject sources did not attempt to select children whom they felt may, or may not, have a visual problem.

Procedure

Participants were tested with the Intuitive Overlays (Wilkins, 1994), as described in the test instructions (Wilkins, 2001). The test used the following colours: rose, lime green, blue, pink, yellow, aqua, purple, orange, mint green and grey. They were presented in this order to avoid presenting similar or complementary colours one after the other. Double overlays were also investigated, so that a total of 30 colours were presented. The effect of the chosen overlay was assessed with the WRRT (Wilkins et al., 1996) as specified in the test instructions (Wilkins, 1996).

Participants were asked to wear during the testing any glasses that were usually worn for reading. In each situation where testing took place (typically a normally illuminated classroom), care was taken to avoid glare from the windows and overhead lights, and to ensure that the room was fairly quiet and that there were no distractions during the test procedure. Participants were shown a sheet of paper with 15 high frequency English words, as used in the WRRT, but in large type. They were asked to read these aloud, and were corrected if they made errors. Participants who produced errors after re-reading the list of words were excluded from the experiment, as they would not be able to read the same words in the WRRT. All participants who demonstrated a preference for an overlay, or for a combination of overlays, were tested with the WRRT with and without their chosen overlay.

In the administration of the WRRT, participants were asked to read the text aloud as quickly as possible and without errors. The subject was asked to read the first three lines of passage B or C (selected at random) as a practice trial, without any overlay. The goal of this practice attempt was to familiarise the subject with the task of reading randomly ordered text. The participant was presented with version A of the test with the small typeface, unless they were unable to read it or it caused discomfort. If this happened then there was a larger version of the test that would have been used, although this was not found to be necessary for any of the participants. The selected overlay or combination of overlays was placed on the text, and the stopwatch was started as the participant was instructed to begin. As the participant was reading, each error was noted by marking the score sheet above the word that was misread. The participant was stopped after one minute and the score sheet was marked to indicate how far they had read. If they finished the passage before the minute was up, then the number of seconds taken was noted. The process was repeated with version B and no overlay, then with version C again without an overlay and lastly version D with the overlay.

Results

Overlays chosen

Table 2 shows the number of participants choosing each colour or combination of overlay. More members of the control than the dyslexic group selected overlays, but the difference between the two groups was not statistically significant (Fisher's exact test, 2-tailed, $p = 0.20$). It is interesting that a marked number of participants in both groups selected mint-green overlays.

WRRT results

The Rate of Reading test was scored according to the test instructions: the number of errors was subtracted from the total amount of words read in one minute. The mean was found of scores on tests A and D, which were read with an overlay. Tests B and C were read without an overlay and the mean of these two scores was also calculated. An inspection of the frequency distributions for these four variables (WRRT mean result with overlay and mean result without overlay in each group) revealed data that approximated normal distributions, but were slightly skewed towards lower values in the dyslexic group. Kolmogorov-Smirnov tests showed that these distributions were not significantly different from a normal distribution, suggesting that parametric ANOVA is appropriate. As a precaution, a key analysis below is confirmed with a non-parametric test.

Figure 2 is a scatter plot showing the WRRT results for each participant, labelled to identify members of the dyslexic and control groups. Points above the diagonal represent faster reading with the overlay than without, which is particularly apparent for the dyslexic group. The improvement with an overlay does not seem to be related to reading speed.

Table 2. Number of participants choosing each colour or combination of overlay.

Colour of overlay	Dyslexic group	Control group
None	5	1
Rose	0	0
Lime green	1	0
Blue	1	0
Pink	2	0
Yellow	0	2
Aqua	1	2
Purple	0	2
Orange	2	2
Mint green	9	12
Grey	3	9
Mint & lime green	4	0
Double grey	1	0
Purple & pink	1	0
Double mint green	1	0
Double lime green	1	0
Aqua & mint green	0	1
Double orange	0	1
Total	32	32

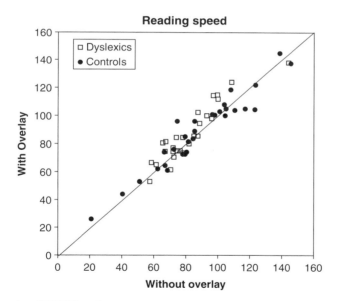

Figure 2. Scatter plot of WRRT results.

Note: Each point is a participant: filled circles are control participants and unfilled squares are dyslexic participants.

Table 3 and Figure 3 show the descriptive statistics for the WRRT results. Only participants who chose an overlay are included in these analyses. Children in the control group have slightly higher scores than the dyslexic group, both with and without

Table 3. Descriptive statistics for WRRT results.

Mean Score	N	Mean with overlay	Standard deviation	Mean without overlay	Standard deviation
Dyslexic group	27	86.91	20.31	82.00	18.31
Control group	31	87.37	27.13	86.90	28.46

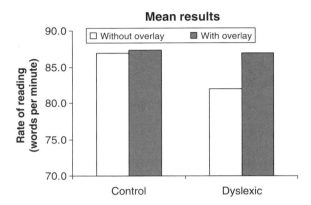

Figure 3. Comparison of mean WRRT results for dyslexic and control groups with and without overlays.

overlays. Also, there is a difference between the mean test scores with and without the overlay for the controls of only 0.47, compared with 4.91 for the dyslexic group.

Using a repeated measures analysis of variance (ANOVA), the effect of group was not significant ($p = 0.67$), but the effect of overlay was significant ($p = 0.009$). There was a significant interaction between overlay and group ($p = 0.031$). The effect of overlay was further investigated with the non-parametric Wilcoxon signed ranks test. The effect of the overlay on WRRT results reached significance in the dyslexic group ($p = 0.005$) but not in the control group (0.75).

Calculation of prevalence

As noted in the introduction, various criteria have been used to estimate the prevalence of MIS, and prevalence will inevitably vary with the criterion. Indeed, we think it likely that MIS exists on a continuum. An increase on WRRT with an overlay of $>5\%$ is commonly used as a criterion (Table 1). However, according to Jeanes et al. (1997) an increase of about 8% in rate of reading with the overlay indicates a likelihood of prolonged use of the coloured overlay, and thus could be used as an indicator of MIS. Figure 4 shows these two criteria and an additional criterion of $>10\%$. A $>25\%$ criterion is not included because none of the dyslexic group and only one of the control group read $>25\%$ faster with their overlay: in view of the number of participants and the previous data for the $>25\%$ criterion (Table 1) this is not surprising.

It should be noted that, in contrast to the preceding section but in common with some previous studies, the total number of participants in each group (32) is used as the denominator in prevalence calculations. In other words, it is assumed that participants

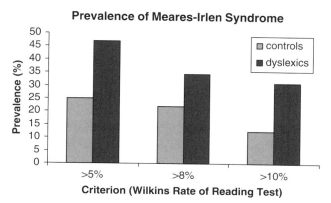

Figure 4. Comparison of prevalence of MIS in dyslexia and control groups, for various diagnostic criteria (see text for explanation).

Table 4. The number of lines skipped by dyslexic and control participants.

Number of lines skipped	Dyslexic group	Control group
1	2	7
2	5	2
3	0	3
4	0	1
6	1	0
7	0	1
Total	8	14

who did not report a benefit from any overlay would have failed to show an improvement greater than the relevant criterion.

It was found that 11 out of the 32 (34%) in the dyslexic group had an increase of $>8\%$ on the rate of reading test with the overlay, compared with 7 out of the 32 (22%) in the control group. The prevalence for a $>5\%$ criterion is 47% in the dyslexic group and 25% in the control group; and for the $>10\%$ criterion is 31% in the dyslexic group and 12.5% in the control group. The odds ratios and associated 95% confidence limits were calculated (Garb, 1996) from the data represented in Figure 4. The odds ratio is 2.6 (95% confidence interval 0.9–7.3) for the $>5\%$ criterion, 1.8 (0.6–5.4) for the $>8\%$ criterion and 3.0 (0.8–10.3) for the $>10\%$ criterion. In view of the fact that the lower 95% confidence intervals did not exceed 1.0, it is not surprising that comparisons of the proportion of dyslexic and non-dyslexic participants with MIS did not reach significance for each of the three criteria in Figure 4 (chi-square test, $p > 0.065$).

Analysis of WRRT errors

The WRRT results for each participant were inspected to look for common errors made by each group. Table 4 shows the number of participants that skipped lines whilst performing the WRRT.

Although Table 4 shows that the dyslexic group were more likely to skip lines, only two of the participants who skipped two lines met the $>8\%$ criterion for MIS. In the control group, four participants who skipped lines met the $>8\%$ criterion. Two only skipped one line, one skipped three lines and the fourth skipped seven lines.

Discussion

Our data support previous studies that have shown MIS to be prevalent in the general population. We found a higher prevalence of MIS in dyslexia, but chi-squared analyses of the proportion of each group with MIS did not reach significance. In participants who chose a coloured overlay, there was a significant improvement in rate of reading with the preferred overlay in the dyslexic group but not in the control group.

The diagnostic criterion most commonly used in the literature (Table 1) is the $>5\%$ faster criterion. Using this, our control group had a prevalence of MIS of 25% which is higher than the 20% obtained in a study of 77 unselected children aged 8–11 years (Wilkins et al., 1996), but less than the 33% obtained with 426 unselected children aged 6–8 years (Wilkins et al., 2001) and the 34% in a sample of adult university students (Evans & Joseph, 2002). Clearly, this is a fairly 'easy' criterion to pass, and we wonder whether the $>10\%$ criterion might be more appropriate. As we point out below, there is a need for research on which criterion best predicts sustained use of precision tinted lenses, which can be thought of as the 'gold standard' treatment for MIS.

The results differ from the estimates of prevalence provided by Irlen, but it is difficult to comment on this because Irlen did not provide any data or diagnostic criteria (Irlen, 1997). However, Irlen's figure for the non-dyslexic population of 12–14% is most similar to the prevalence that we obtained in our non-dyslexic group (12.5%) for the criterion of $>10\%$ faster. This criterion was associated with a prevalence in our dyslexic group of 31%, which is lower than Irlen's prediction of 46%. People with a combination of dyslexia and MIS might be especially likely to consult Irlen Institutes because they would be likely to have more problems at school. If Irlen's estimates are based on her clinical experience at the Irlen Institutes, then this could perhaps have led to an overestimation by Irlen of the prevalence within the dyslexic population. Care was taken in our study to ensure that the participants were not pre-selected as having (or not having) visual symptoms.

Although both groups read faster with overlays than without (Figure 3), the improvement was much greater in the dyslexic group and only reached significance in this group. This might indicate that it is especially important to treat MIS in people with dyslexia. It could be argued that people with dyslexia and MIS have two burdens when they read: the visual perceptual distortions of MIS (Wilkins et al., 2001) and the phonological processing deficits associated with dyslexia (Snowling, 1997). The symptoms of MIS are relatively easy to treat and if they are just one difficulty among those experienced by a child who has dyslexia then it would seem particularly appropriate to prescribe coloured filters in addition to treating the dyslexia. We would therefore argue that children who report reading difficulties of any type ought to be screened for MIS, and indeed for other visual problems as well (Evans, 2001).

Observations on overlay testing

In the control group, a majority of 12 (37.5%) participants selected a mint green overlay, and nine (28%) selected a grey overlay. Also, in the dyslexic group mint green had the highest number of selectors at nine (28%), whereas only three (9%) selected the grey overlay. It is worth noting that both overlays were presented at the end. It is possible that participants could see from the pile that there were not many overlays left, and therefore thought in order to complete the task successfully they must select an overlay (even though it was made clear at the outset that not everyone selects an overlay and it may not aid their reading). A way of dealing with this effect would be by concealing the pile so that the participants are not aware of when the overlays are going to stop being presented. It would be interesting for further research to study the effect of the order of testing.

It is also interesting to note that all apart from one of the controls selected an overlay, in comparison to five of the dyslexics who did not select any. It was made clear to all participants prior to testing that overlays do not help everyone, and that they may not have an advantageous effect on their reading. Other factors that may have encouraged participants to select an overlay when not needed are: novelty reasons and aesthetic reasons (children may have merely picked their favourite colours). The higher number of dyslexic children who did not select an overlay may be due to them responding more honestly, being less susceptible to suggestibility or being more used to formal assessment procedures. This problem could be resolved by introducing a placebo overlay as in some previous studies (Evans & Joseph, 2002; Tyrrell, Holland, Dennis & Wilkins, 1995).

Double overlays also seemed to cause some confusion. Mint green again featured in the majority of double overlay combinations: four dyslexic participants selected the lime and mint green combination, one selected double mint green, and another aqua and mint green. In two cases participants decided that the double overlay was better than the single, but when asked directly whether it was actually clearer and easier to read with the single or the double they chose the single. Perhaps these participants thought that they were expected to find two overlays better than one. Recently, a computerised version of the overlay test has been produced which may overcome the possible problems outlined in this section of order of testing and combining overlays (Thomson, 2002b).

Analysis of WRRT errors

It might have been expected that the dyslexic group would have made more errors in the form of skipping lines during the WRRT. This was not the case: the control group skipped more lines. It might also be thought that more people with MIS would skip lines, since this is thought to be an indicator of MIS (Evans, 2001; Irlen, 1991; Wilkins, 2003). This was not found either: only four out of fourteen of the control group and two out of eight in the dyslexic group who skipped lines were found to have MIS (using the $>8\%$ faster criterion). This may be because of the small size of the text and/or close line spacing. Another explanation might be the presence of visual problems other than MIS, as discussed below.

Limitations

MIS, in common with many other conditions, lacks a completely objective diagnostic test. However, it is interesting to note that a recent review and survey of the criteria that optometrists use when prescribing for low refractive errors revealed an even less desirable situation (O'Leary & Evans, 2003). In most cases, practitioners simply rely on symptoms in deciding whether to prescribe. With MIS, symptoms are one factor but in addition precision tinted lenses are only prescribed after either an immediate improvement in visual performance with the WRRT or a sustained benefit from coloured overlays, which are an inexpensive intervention. Attempts have been made to find additional tests for MIS (Wilkins & Lewis, 1999), and a new pattern glare test might provide useful additional information (Stevenson and Evans, forthcoming). A recent study showed that the Developmental Eye Movement test is, like the WRRT, another useful tool to evaluate the effect of coloured overlays (Northway, 2003).

Several studies of MIS, including the present study, have concentrated on the effect of coloured overlays. Overlay testing is well suited to research as it is both rapid and designed to be easily used in the classroom. The current 'gold standard' treatment is precision tinted lenses that have been individually prescribed after systematic testing with a wide and comprehensive range of colours, for example using the Intuitive Colorimeter (Wilkins & Sihra, 2000). This instrument is quite widely used clinically (Lightstone, 2000) and has been used in double-masked randomised controlled trials of the use of coloured filters in MIS (Wilkins et al., 1994) and migraine (Wilkins et al., 2002). It has also been demonstrated that coloured lenses should be prescribed using a method that leaves the patient colour adapted (e.g. the Intuitive Colorimeter): tinted lenses should not be prescribed to match overlay colour (Lightstone, Lightstone & Wilkins, 1999). However, there is a lack of research on the system as a whole, using coloured overlays, the WRRT, the Intuitive Colorimeter and precision tinted lenses. For example, it would be interesting to investigate which of the diagnostic criteria in Table 1 best predicts sustained voluntary use of precision tinted lenses.

The present study did not include an optometric assessment. It is therefore quite likely that some of the participants had uncorrected errors of refraction, binocular co-ordination and accommodation. These problems affect a significant number of unselected school-children and are often undetected (Thomson, 2002a). Binocular instability and accommodative insufficiency are correlates of dyslexia, although these problems are not usually marked enough to have a significant impact on reading-like tasks (Evans, Drasdo & Richards, 1994a, 1994b). Similarly, although binocular vision and accommodative deficits are also weakly correlated with MIS, these problems are unlikely to account for the benefit from coloured filters in many cases and are unlikely to have a marked effect on the proportion of subjects reading >5% faster with their overlay (Evans, 2001; Evans, Busby, Jeanes and Wilkins, 1995; Evans et al., 1996; Scott et al., 2002). Nonetheless, we would stress that in the usual clinical protocol (Evans, 2005; Evans et al., 1999; Lightstone & Evans, 1995) it is recommended that children should have a full optometric assessment at the earliest possible stage of the investigation of any visual factors that may be contributing to reading or other academic difficulties (Evans, 2001).

Problems encountered with the WRRT were minor. One occasional difficulty was following the children's reading when they skipped many words or lines, or when words were mis-read or added. This could be overcome by tape recording the assessment process (Jeanes et al., 1997). In some cases even though participants were aware that the text had no meaning they would give meaning to two words in a row, such as reading: 'look cat see my dog', instead of what was written in the prose: 'look cat see my and dog'. This would suggest that some readers find it hard to not process words semantically and try and make sense out of a nonsense passage. Other common mistakes included 'my' misread as 'me', and 'is' as 'it'.

Educational implications

Professionals involved in the diagnosis and treatment of children and adults with reading disabilities should be aware of the possible beneficial effects that coloured filters can have. Knowledge of the main symptoms of MIS is important: sore, tired eyes and headaches when reading; blurred and unstable (e.g. moving, flickering) images of letters and words; and sensitivity to excessive light. Students who may benefit from the use of overlays can be identified and referred for further assessment by a teacher or eye-care practitioner who screens with coloured overlays. Even if there is no evidence of reading problems in normal readers, it is possible that many will benefit from the use of overlays and it is hoped that screening for this condition will become more widespread. These symptoms can be caused by other conditions (Evans, 2005), so a full eye examination is important in addition to screening for the effect of coloured filters.

The visual problems assessed by this experiment are not seen as the primary symptoms of dyslexia. Indeed, our results suggest that MIS and dyslexia are separate conditions, which may be present in isolation or sometimes coexist in the same individual. It is recognised that even if overlays help a person with dyslexia to read, the person will probably still experience other difficulties. Reading is a complex activity that involves many visual and cognitive factors. Even social and meta-cognitive factors can have an influence on how a child learns to read and consequently views their reading ability. The diagnosis and treatment of MIS and dyslexia are completely different. Most certainly, coloured filters are not a treatment for dyslexia.

Our results add to the growing evidence (Table 1) suggesting that MIS is surprisingly common and affects many so-called normal readers. Our data suggest that the prevalence of MIS may be a little higher in dyslexic than in non-dyslexic children, although this difference did not reach significance in our samples of 32 dyslexic and 32 control participants. Studies that set out to investigate MIS by studying a group of dyslexic or reading disabled participants are likely to include many participants who do not have MIS. Studies of MIS or the use of coloured filters should use one of the two widely used methods of detecting the condition that are outlined in the introduction.

Acknowledgements

We thank the children who participated in the study, who willingly and enthusiastically gave their time. We are grateful to the teachers without whose help the study would not have been possible, and the children's parents for giving consent. We also thank Sarah Grogan and Arnold Wilkins for helpful comments on earlier drafts describing this work.

References

Bouldoukian, J., Wilkins, A.J. & Evans, B.J.W. (2002). Randomised controlled trial of the effect of coloured overlays on the rate of reading of people with specific learning difficulties. *Opthalmic & Physiological Optics*, 22, 55–60.

Evans, B.J.W. (2001). *Dyslexia and vision*. London: Whurr.

Evans, B.J.W. (2005). Case reports: The need for optometric investigation in suspected Meares-Irlen syndrome or visual stress. *Opthalmic & Physiological Optics*, 25, 363–370.

Evans, B.J.W., Busby, A., Jeanes, R. & Wilkins, A.J. (1995). Optometric correlates of Meares-Irlen Syndrome: A matched group study. *Opthalmic & Physiological Optics*, 15, 481–487.

Evans, B.J.W. & Drasdo, N. (1991). Tinted lenses and related therapies for learning disabilities – a review. *Opthalmic & Physiological Optics*, 11, 206–217.

Evans, B.J.W. & Joseph, F. (2002). The effect of coloured filters on the rate of reading in an adult student population. *Opthalmic & Physiological Optics*, 22, 535–545.

Evans, B.J.W., Drasdo, N. & Richards, I.L. (1994a). Investigation of accommodative and binocular function in dyslexia. *Opthalmic & Physiological Optics*, 14, 5–19.

Evans, B.J.W., Drasdo, N. & Richards, I.L. (1994b). Refractive and sensory visual correlates of dyslexia. *Vision Research*, 34, 1913–1926.

Evans, B.J.W., Patel, R., Wilkins, A.J., Lightstone, A., Eperjesi, F., Speedwell, L. & Duffy, J. (1999). A review of the management of 323 consecutive patients seen in a specific learning difficulties clinic. *Opthalmic & Physiological Optics*, 19, 454–466.

Evans, B.J.W., Wilkins, A.J., Brown, J., Busby, A., Wingfield, A.E., Jeanes, R. & Bald, J. (1996). A preliminary investigation into the aetiology of Meares-Irlen Syndrome. *Opthalmic & Physiological Optics*, 16, 286–296.

Garb, J.L. (1996). *Understanding medical research*. Boston, MA: Little, Brown & Company.

Huang, J., Cooper, T.G., Satana, B., Kaufman, D.I. & Cao, Y. (2003). Visual distortion provoked by a stimulus in migraine associated with hyperneuronal activity. *Headache*, 43, 664–671.

Irlen, H. (1991). *Reading by the colours: Overcoming dyslexia and other reading disabilities by the Irlen method*. New York: Avery.

Irlen, H. (1997). Reading problems and Irlen Coloured Lenses. *Dyslexia Review*, Summer, 4–7.

Irlen, H. & Lass, M.J. (1989). Improving reading problems due to symptoms of scotopic sensitivity syndrome using Irlen lenses and overlays. *Education*, 109, 413–417.

Jeanes, R., Busby, A., Martin, J., Lewis, E., Stevenson, N., Pointon, D. & Wilkins, A. (1997). Prolonged use of coloured overlays for classroom reading. *British Journal of Psychology*, 88, 531–548.

Lightstone, A. (2000). The Intuitive Colorimeter and the prescribing of coloured lenses. *Optician*, 220, 26–33.

Lightstone, A. & Evans, B.J.W. (1995). A new protocol for the optometric management of patients with reading difficulties. *Opthalmic & Physiological Optics*, 15, 507–512.

Lightstone, A., Lightstone, T. & Wilkins, A. (1999). Both coloured overlays and coloured lenses can improve reading fluency, but their optimal chromaticities differ. *Opthalmic & Physiological Optics*, 19, 279–285.

Maclachlan, A., Yale, S. & Wilkins, A. (1993). Research note: Open trial of subjective precision tinting. *Opthalmic & Physiological Optics*, 13, 175–178.

Neale, M.D. (1997). *Neale Analysis of Reading Ability – Revised: Manual for Schools*. Windsor: NFER-Nelson.

Northway, N. (2003). Predicting the continued use of overlays in school children – a comparison of the Developmental Eye Movement test and the Rate of Reading test. *Opthalmic & Physiological Optics*, 23, 457–464.

O'Leary, C.I. & Evans, B.J.W. (2003). Criteria for prescribing optometric interventions: Literature review and practitioner survey. *Opthalmic & Physiological Optics*, 23, 429–439.

Robinson, G.L. & Foreman, P.J. (1999). Scotopic sensitivity/Irlen Syndrome and the use of coloured filters: A long-term placebo-controlled and masked study of reading achievement and perception of ability. *Perceptual & Motor Skills*, 88, 35–52.

Scott, J.C., McWhinnie, H., Taylor, L., Stevenson, N., Irons, P., Lewis, E., Evans, M., Evans, B. & Wilkins, A. (2002). Coloured overlays in schools: Orthoptic and optometric findings. *Opthalmic & Physiological Optics*, 22, 156–165.

Snowling, M.J. (1997). Phonological skills, dyslexia and learning to read. *Dyslexia Review*, 8, 4–7.

Stevenson, S.J. & Evans, B.J.W. (forthcoming). A normative study of the Pattern Glare Test.

Thomson, D. (2002a). Child vision screening survey. *Optician*, 224, 16–20.

Thomson, D. (2002b). The city coloured overlay screener. *Optometry Today*, November 15, 40–43.

Tyrrell, R., Holland, K., Dennis, D. & Wilkins, A. (1995). Coloured overlays, visual discomfort, visual search and classroom reading. *Journal of Research in Reading*, 18, 10–23.

Wilkins, A. (1994). Overlays for classroom and optometric use. *Opthalmic & Physiological Optics*, 14, 97–99.

Wilkins, A.J. (1996). *Wilkins Rate of Reading Test: Instructions for use*. London: i.o.o. Sales Ltd.

Wilkins, A.J. (2001). *Intuitive overlays: Instructions for use*. London: i.o.o. Sales Ltd.

Wilkins, A.J. (2003). *Reading through colour. How coloured filters can reduce reading difficulty, eye strain, and headaches*. Chichester: John Wiley & Sons.

Wilkins, A.J. & Lewis, E. (1999). Coloured overlays, text and texture. *Perception*, 28, 641–650.

Wilkins, A.J. & Nimmo-Smith, I. (1984). On the reduction of eyestrain when reading. *Opthalmic & Physiological Optics*, 4, 53–59.

Wilkins, A.J. & Sihra, N. (2000). Industrial applications: A colorizer for use in determining an optimal ophthalmic tint. *Colour: Research & Application*, 26, 246–253.

Wilkins, A.J., Nimmo-Smith, I. & Jansons, J.E. (1992). Colorimeter for the intuitive manipulation of hue and saturation and its role in the study of perceptual distortion. *Opthalmic & Physiological Optics*, 12, 381–385.

Wilkins, A., Huang, J. & Cao, Y. (2003). Visual stress theory and its application to reading and reading tests. *Journal of Research in Reading*, 27, 152–162.

Wilkins, A., Nimmo-Smith, I., Tait, A., McManus, C., Della-Sala, S., Tilley, A., Arnold, K., Barrie, M. & Scott, S. (1984). A neurological basis for visual discomfort. *Brain*, 107, 989–1017.

Wilkins, A., Milroy, R., Nimmo-Smith, I., Wright, A., Tyrrell, R., Holland, K., Martin, J., Bald, J., Yale, S., Miles, T. & Noakes, T. (1992). Preliminary observations concerning treatment of visual discomfort and associated perceptual distortion. *Opthalmic & Physiological Optics*, 12, 257–263.

Wilkins, A.J., Baker, A., Smith, S., Bradford, J., Zaiwalla, Z., Besag, F.M., Binnie, C.D. & Fish, D. (1999). Treatment of photosensitive epilepsy using coloured glasses. *Seizure*, 8, 444–449.

Wilkins, A.J., Evans, B.J.W., Brown, J., Busby, A., Wingfield, A.E., Jeanes, R. & Bald, J. (1994). Double-masked placebo-controlled trial of precision spectral filters in children who use coloured overlays. *Opthalmic & Physiological Optics*, 14, 365–370.

Wilkins, A.J., Jeanes, R.J., Pumfrey, P.D. & Laskier, M. (1996). Rate of Reading Test: Its reliability, and its validity in the assessment of the effects of coloured overlays. *Opthalmic & Physiological Optics*, 16, 491–497.

Wilkins, A.J., Lewis, E., Smith, F., Rowland, E. & Tweedie, W. (2001). Coloured overlays and their benefit for reading. *Journal of Research in Reading*, 24, 41–64.

Wilkins, A.J., Patel, R., Adjamian, P. & Evans, B.J.W. (2002). Tinted spectacles and visually sensitive migraine. *Cephalalgia*, 22, 711–719.

Xiao, Y., Wang, Y. & Felleman, D.J. (2003). A spatially organized representation of colour in macaque cortical area V2. *Nature*, 421, 535–539.

10

Visual stress in adults with and without dyslexia

Chris Singleton and Susannah Trotter

The view that visual factors are involved in dyslexia has a long and controversial history. The current predominant theory – which is so well supported that it could be said to have acquired the status of orthodoxy – is that dyslexia is caused by a genetically-based anomaly in neurological systems sub-serving phonological processing (see Ramus, 2001, 2003; Snowling, 2000; Stanovich, 2000; Vellutino, Fletcher, Snowling & Scanlon, 2004). Since the 1970s, steadily accumulating evidence has enabled the phonological theory to eclipse other theories, many of which saw dyslexia as a deficit in visual processing of some kind. In his comprehensive landmark analysis, Vellutino (1979) observed: 'Taken together, the impressions derived from the studies attempting both direct and indirect tests of perceptual deficit explanations of reading disability lead to the conclusion that the evidence in support of such explanations is uniformly weak' (pp. 183–184). Vellutino's conclusion marked the demise of a variety of classic theories of dyslexia that assumed a fundamental visual-perceptual dysfunction, stretching back to the pioneers Morgan (1896) and Hinshelwood (1917) – both of whom adopted Kussmaul's (1877) term 'word blindness' as a label for the condition – and including luminaries such as Orton (1925, 1937), Bender (1956) and Frostig and Maslow (1973).

A significant shortcoming of early visual-perceptual theories of dyslexia was that remediation addressing the hypothesised root of the problem – visual-perceptual dysfunction – by means of activities such as visual discrimination training and visual-motor practice, was found to have little benefit in comparison with approaches that tackled the dyslexic reading difficulties more directly (see Hammill, Goodman & Wiederholt, 1974; Hartman & Hartman, 1973). However, during the 1980s and 1990s an alternative remediation for visually-based reading problems began to gain currency. Observations by Meares (1980) and Irlen (1983), that the use of coloured acetate overlays and filters can help a large proportion of children and adults who experience symptoms of eye strain and visual perceptual distortions when reading, gave rise to a new syndrome in the literature. Often called 'Meares-Irlen syndrome', this condition has also been known by several other labels (e.g. 'visual discomfort'; 'scotopic sensitivity syndrome'), and for simplicity and consistency it will be referred to here as 'visual stress'.[1] Conlon (Conlon et al., 1998, 1999) has noted the clustering of somatic symptoms (such as sore, tired eyes and eye-strain) and perceptual effects (such as illusions of colour, shape and motion) in some individuals when exposed to bright or flickering light and/or grating patterns (such as may be created by lines of text on a page). Conlon (2000) argues that this symptom cluster, which she calls 'visual discomfort', can be a cause of reading problems. This observation was made earlier by Irlen (1991), who claimed that 12% of the general population experiences these symptoms, but in people with dyslexia the incidence is 65%, suggesting a strong relationship. In a later article, Irlen (1997) stated that 12–14% of the general population suffer from visual stress, a figure that rises to 46% of those diagnosed with dyslexia, attention deficit disorder and other specific learning difficulties. Despite these claims, the exact nature of the relationship between visual stress and dyslexia still remains unclear.

A possible theoretical explanation for the beneficial effects of colour in cases of visual stress began to emerge when a number of studies reported evidence of impairment in the magnocellular visual system in people with dyslexia (e.g. Cornelissen et al., 1994; Livingstone et al., 1991; Lovegrove, 1991; Lovegrove, Martin & Slaghuis, 1986). The magnocellular (transient) visual system comprises a fast pathway that processes rapid changes in the visual scene, while its counterpart – the parvocellular (sustained) system – is a slower pathway responsible for more detailed, stable visual perception. In normal vision, the two systems work in parallel in a co-ordinated fashion to facilitate detailed visual perception under conditions of almost constant eye movement that continually alters the image on the retina. If one part of the system is dysfunctional it is not unreasonable to anticipate problems in smooth and efficient processing of text. The magnocellular impairment in cases of dyslexia is slight, not found in all dyslexics, and has been disputed (see Scheiman, 1994; Skotton, 2000; Stein, Talcott & Walsh, 2000). Nevertheless, these findings suggested a convenient model for linking dyslexia with anomalies of eye movement control (see Evans, Drasdo & Richards, 1996; Stein, 2001; Stein & Talcott, 1999; Stein & Walsh, 1997) and hence many researchers have gone further by suggesting that visual stress could be encompassed within this theoretical framework (e.g. Irlen, 1994; Lehmkule, 1993; Livingstone et al., 1991; Sloman, Cho & Dain, 1991; Sloman et al., 1995; Williams, Lecluyse & Rock-Faucheux, 1992). Although the precise mechanisms involved have yet to be elucidated, the magnocellular system remains one of the prime candidates to explain how coloured filters and overlays might affect the reading process (Chase et al., 2003; Edwards et al., 1996; Irlen, 1997; Robinson & Foreman, 1999).

However, until the 1990s, when Wilkins and his colleagues (Evans et al., 1995, 1996; Wilkins et al., 1994) began to investigate visual stress using placebo-controlled studies, both the existence of the syndrome and the credibility of treatment using coloured filters were still regarded with suspicion by members of the medical and educational professions. The lack of a convincing theoretical explanation for the purported benefits of colour further hardened scientific and professional scepticism (see Evans, 1997a; Evans & Drasdo, 1991). The work of Wilkins and his colleagues not only provided scientific evidence for the therapeutic effect of coloured filters but also established an alternative theoretical basis for understanding visual stress (for reviews see Evans, 2001; Wilkins, 1995, 2003). According to this view, the symptoms of visual stress are attributable to cortical hyper-excitability caused by pattern glare. Visual grating patterns that can evoke seizures in people with photosensitive epilepsy and trigger migraine headaches can also produce perceptual distortions in normal individuals (Wilkins, 1995). The visual grating created by moving the eyes across lines of print, especially where the pattern is glaring (i.e. lines of dark black text on a bright white page), could generate similar physiological effects. Associations have also been reported in migraineurs between the location of headaches (left or right hemisphere), visual aura preceding headaches (left or right visual field) and the location of perceptual distortions (Wilkins et al., 1984). Maclachan, Yale and Wilkins (1993) found that children who find colour helpful are twice as likely to have migraine in the family as those who show no benefit.

Wilkins (1995, 2003) speculates that since the wavelength of light is known to affect neuronal sensitivity (Zeki, 1983) the use of colour could reduce over-excitation, thus reducing perceptual distortions and headaches when reading.

Wilkins (2003) dismisses the competing theory, which holds that visual stress is attributable to deficits in the magnocellular system. First, he points out that this theory is presently unable to account for the large individual differences in colour optimal for reading. Second, he argues that earlier beliefs that visual stress was associated with dyslexia have become doubtful, since just as many individuals who do not have dyslexia have been found to benefit from colour as those who do have dyslexia. Third, children with visual stress show normal flicker perception (Evans, Drasdo & Richards, 1996). Fourth, visual stress sufferers who regularly use coloured lenses have not been found to have deficiencies in visual-motor tasks believed to be sub-served by the magnocellular system (Simmers et al., 2001). A study by Evans et al. (1995) also failed to find convincing evidence that transient system activity (as measured by eye-movement control) was a credible explanation for reported benefits of colour. However, current knowledge does not enable us to rule out with any confidence the possibility of a relationship between magnocellular deficits and pattern glare/cortical hyperexcitability (see Evans, 2001).

One major implication of Wilkins' cortical hyper-excitability theory is that visual stress is regarded as independent of dyslexia, even though in some individuals the two conditions may be seen to have symptoms in common. Wilkins (2003) concludes that a diagnosis of dyslexia does not make it more likely that reading will be improved by use of coloured filters. The evidence for this comes chiefly from a study by Grounds and Wilkins (cited in Wilkins, 2003), in which four different groups were compared: children with dyslexia, a chronological-age matched group without dyslexia, a group of younger children matched on reading-age group to the dyslexic group and a group of children of low general ability who were similar chronological age and reading age to the dyslexic group. No difference was found between these four groups with respect to the proportion who benefited from overlays. However, Kriss and Evans (2005) found the incidence of visual stress was somewhat higher (37.5%) in children with dyslexia than in children with normal reading (25%). Arguably, the problem centres largely on how visual stress is defined and measured, an important issue that will be returned to later in this article.

Most studies of visual stress have focused on children; few have examined this phenomenon in adults. Robinson and Conway (2000) reported on a small-scale study that found benefits of Irlen filters in adults who experienced visual stress. Evans and Joseph (2002) carried out a more extensive study with 113 unselected university students who were assessed using Intuitive Overlays (I.O.O Marketing, London). The Intuitive Overlays assessment pack includes nine different-coloured acetate overlays plus one grey overlay. These are employed successively, in pairs, with the person being assessed required to judge which of each pair is more comfortable for reading text when viewed through the overlays, until a clear preference emerges (or, in some cases, no preference). For further details, see Wilkins (2003). Since there are no standard criteria for classifying visual stress, it is not possible to give an overall incidence figure for Evans and Joseph's sample. However, the following data give an impression. Some visual perceptual distortions of text were found to be much more common than others: 24% blurring; 16% doubling; 12% jumping; 6% changing size; 3.5% fading or disappearing. Other reported symptoms included: sore or tired eyes when reading (13% moderately; 4% often);

frequently rubbing eyes 20%; skips, re-reads or omits words or lines 35%. Among the 81 students who experienced headaches, 44% reported that these were associated to some degree with reading. However, Evans and Joseph (2002) note that their study did not include an optometric eye examination and therefore some of their participants' symptoms might be attributable to conventional optometric factors such as refractive errors or orthoptic anomalies.

Evans and Joseph (2002) found that in the Intuitive Overlay assessment, 100 (88%) of their total sample were able to choose a coloured overlay that had an immediately positive effect on their perception of text. In the *Rate of Reading Test*, 68% of these students read faster with their chosen overlay than without it. The overall change in reading speed for the group was only 3.8%, but nevertheless this was still highly significant, and there was considerable individual variation. Two of the students read more than 25% faster with the overlay. When the 13 students who did not choose an overlay were administered the *Rate of Reading Test* using the control overlay (grey), only 38.5% read faster with the overlay than without and over this group as a whole the difference in rate of reading for the two conditions was not significant. Using the criterion advocated by Wilkins et al. (1996) – i.e. more than 5% improvement in rate of reading – Evans and Joseph concluded that more than one-third of the sample showed significant benefits when using coloured overlays. However, the sample used in Evans and Joseph's study might not be regarded as entirely representative because two-fifths of the students had experienced difficulties of some kind at school, most commonly with reading, writing, spelling and/or maths. This might have inflated the number of those who benefited from the overlays, although it should be noted that only two of the 113 had diagnosed dyslexia, an incidence which is a little lower than expected but not outside the range found in universities (see Singleton, 1999). Additionally, 36% did not have English as their first language (although all spoke fluent English).

The results of the study by Evans and Joseph suggest that the prevalence of visual stress in the adult population is similar to that reported in children. Jeanes et al. (1997) found that 53% of a normal sample of 152 primary school children (5–11 years) reported beneficial perceptual effects when using overlays, and three months later more than half of these children (36% of the sample) were still using them (these were mostly the children with relatively poor reading). Ten months later the proportion of children still using the overlays had dropped to 24%. In other words, at least 20% of children may be expected to show long-term benefits of use of coloured overlays. Wilkins et al. (2001) found that out of an unselected sample of 77 children aged 8–11 years, 60% chose an overlay and 31% of all the children in the study were still using it voluntarily after eight months. In a double-blind placebo-controlled study, Robinson and Foreman (1999) examined the effects of using coloured filters on reading speed, accuracy and comprehension with a sample of 113 children with reading difficulties. Over a 20-month period the treatment groups made significantly greater gains in reading accuracy and comprehension, but not speed. The authors suggested that coloured filters can reduce the distracting effect of perceptual distortions allowing greater attention to be given to processing text, rather than concentrating on individual words. However, why this failed to produce an increase in reading speed (which is generally found in other studies) is difficult to explain.

The present study sought to clarify the relationship between visual stress and dyslexia by comparing the reading performance of dyslexic and non-dyslexic adults with, and without, colour. In order to examine visual stress independently of dyslexia and of the benefits of colour on reading, it was essential to have a clear method of measuring susceptibility to visual stress. This was achieved by means of a rating scale called the *Visual Processing Problems Inventory* (VPPI; Singleton, in preparation) which comprises 24 questions relating to symptoms of visual stress when reading. Each question is rated on a 5-point scale from 0 ('never') to 4 ('always'), giving a wide range of possible scores (0 to 96). The VPPI can be subdivided into 14 'critical' questions that relate specifically to the perceptual distortions that characterise visual stress and 10 'non-critical' questions that relate to symptoms that are often reported in cases of visual stress, but which could also be a result of other causes. In the present study, both groups were selected so that half the participants exhibited high susceptibility to visual stress on the VPPI and half had low susceptibility to visual stress.

Method

Participants

The participants in this study were 20 university students (10 male, 10 female); mean age 21.55 years (*SD* 3.93 years). Ten of the participants had received a formal diagnosis of dyslexia by an educational psychologist and were recruited via the disabilities service of their university (the dyslexic group). The other ten participants were selected from several samples of students whose VPPI scores were already known as they had taken part in previous research studies (the non-dyslexic group). Within each group, five had low scores on the critical items of the VPPI ('low visual stress') and five had high scores on the critical items of the VPPI ('high visual stress'). As part of the selection procedure, groups were matched for reading accuracy using the WRAT–3 Reading Test (see below), and there were no significant differences between the groups in age. All participants spoke English as their first language and all reported that their vision was either normal or appropriately corrected.[2]

Apparatus and materials

Intuitive Colorimeter (Wilkins, Nimmo-Smith & Jansons, 1992). This is a box in which text can be placed and illuminated by light of varying colour. The subject views the text through a window while the three determinants of colour (hue, saturation and brightness) can be adjusted independently in order to find the precise location in colour space that is most comfortable for the person when reading.

Visual Processing Problems Inventory [VPPI] (Singleton, unpublished). The VPPI comprises 24 questions relating to symptoms of visual stress, which can be subdivided into 14 'critical' questions concerning experience of perceptual distortions when reading (e.g. 'Does the print seem to move about when you read'; 'Does the print become fuzzy or blurry when you read?') and 10 'non-critical' questions that relate to other symptoms (e.g. 'Do you lose your place when reading?'; 'Are you easily distracted when reading?'). Each question is rated on a 5-point scale from 0 ('never') to 4 ('always'), so the total score range is 0–96. In a previous, unpublished study of the VPPI with 142 unselected university students, the mean score was 25.3 (*SD* 11.9; lowest score 0; highest score 75), with an approximately normal distribution of scores.

Wide Range Achievement Reading Test, 3rd edition [WRAT–3 Reading] (Wilkinson, 1993). This is a 40-item test of oral reading of individual words out-of-context.

Wilkins Rate of Reading Test [WRRT] (Wilkins et al., 1996a). This test requires speeded oral reading of a passage of text comprising 15 common words which are repeated in random order. In order to increase the degree of difficulty the text is printed in a small typeface, closely spaced. There is a choice of two typefaces of different size and the smallest was used for this study. When carrying out a test–retest study (as in this case), a different order of words is used for the two assessments. Scores are reported in number of words reading correctly per minute. The test is designed to be a sensitive measure of visual skills involved in reading as the words are extremely familiar and no semantic factors are involved (see Wilkins et al., 1996b). Several studies have shown that reading rate of children who show long-term benefits from coloured overlays is significantly greater with an overlay (Wilkins et al., 2001; Jeanes et al., 1997).

Procedure

The participants were first assessed using the Intuitive Colorimeter to determine the most comfortable colour for reading, and an optimal colour was found for all participants. Colour selection showed the usual individual specificity reported by Wilkins and others in the field, and no trend in optimal colour could be discerned other than the fact that the dyslexics with high visual stress tended to choose more highly saturated colours. All participants were then administered the Wilkins Rate of Reading Test in the Intuitive Colorimeter under two conditions: with their optimal colour, and without (white light). Order effects were controlled for by counterbalancing across the sub-groups. (Note that this design varies from that advocated in the test manual, which is an ABBA design.)

Results

In all analyses, two-tailed tests of probability were used.

In the participant selection process, the groups were matched for reading accuracy using the WRAT–3 Reading Test. The results are shown in Table 1. No significant differences were found between the dyslexic and the non-dyslexic groups, nor between the high visual stress and low visual stress groups, and there was no significant interaction between the variables. Inspection of the standard deviations indicates that the sample was fairly homogeneous with respect to reading accuracy, which was an intentional feature of the design in order to eliminate reading accuracy as a possible confound in the study.

The participants had been selected so that half had high susceptibility to visual stress and half had low susceptibility to visual stress. However, had this selection been made on the basis of overall VPPI scores, there was a risk that causes other than visual stress might have been implicated. Consequently, selection was made on the basis of scores on the critical items of the VPPI, which were more directly connected to the symptoms that characterise the condition. Those in the low visual stress group had VPPI critical items scores of 10 or less, a cut-off that was below the mean score for a sample of 151 non-dyslexic students (12.09; $SD = 8.12$); see Singleton (in preparation) for further details of this study. Those in the high visual stress group had VPPI critical items scores of 20 or greater, a cut-off that was above the mean score for a sample of 50 dyslexic students (16.48; $SD = 9.81$). Hence it was to be expected that both the groups would differ significantly in critical item scores. However, it is of some interest whether the groups also differed significantly in total VPPI scores and in non-critical item scores: in fact, they did.

Table 1. WRAT–3 Reading Test standard scores (and standard deviations).

	All	High visual stress	Low visual stress
Dyslexic	102.6 (10.24)	107.8 (8.20)	97.4 (10.06)
Non-dyslexic	104.4 (6.11)	103.0 (7.38)	105.8 (4.97)
All	103.5 (8.26)	105.4 (7.78)	101.6 (8.69)

Table 2. Mean scores on the Visual Processing Problems Inventory [VPPI] (and standard deviations).

		High visual stress	Low visual stress
Dyslexic	All items (max. score 96)	56.4 (12.70)	25.8 (2.17)
	Critical items (max. score 56)	29.8 (10.23)	5.4 (2.61)
	Non-critical items (max. score 40)	26.6 (5.41)	20.4 (2.60)
Non-dyslexic	All items (max. score 96)	41.8 (5.97)	16.6 (3.91)
	Critical items (max. score 56)	22.2 (5.81)	6.0 (2.55)
	Non-critical items (max. score 40)	19.6 (2.51)	10.6 (2.07)

The means and standard deviations for VPPI scores of the sub-groups are shown in Table 2. It was found that the participants with high visual stress had significantly higher VPPI scores in all categories than those with low visual stress (Total VPPI: $F = 71.7$; $p < 0.001$. Critical VPPI: $F = 54.3$; $p < 0.001$. Non-critical VPPI: $F = 24.7$; $p < 0.001$). These differences held up when the dyslexic and non-dyslexic groups were analysed separately, with $p < 0.001$ in all cases, except for the dyslexic students on non-critical VPPI items, where the significance level dropped to 0.05. Hence among all the dyslexic students in the sample reading problems that might not be directly connected with visual stress were found to be relatively common, although the incidence in those with high visual stress ($M = 26.6$, $SD = 5.41$) was slightly but significantly higher than those with low visual stress ($M = 20.4$, $SD = 2.60$).

Comparing the dyslexic and non-dyslexic groups overall, significant differences in visual stress were found in the VPPI total score ($F = 13.05$; $p = 0.002$) and VPPI non-critical item score ($F = 30.2$; $p < 0.001$), but no significant difference in critical item score. These effects held up when inter-group differences were analysed. Comparing the two high visual stress sub-groups, the dyslexic sub-group had significantly higher VPPI total ($t = 2.33$; $p < 0.05$) and VPPI non-critical scores ($t(8) = 2.63$; $p = 0.03$), but not significantly higher critical scores. Comparing the two low visual stress sub-groups, the dyslexic sub-group also had significantly higher VPPI total ($t = 4.60$; $p = 0.002$) and VPPI non-critical scores ($t = 6.58$; $p < 0.001$), but not significantly higher critical scores. The findings indicate that a good match of groups had been achieved on visual stress indicators but that the dyslexic students experienced significantly more reading problems that were not necessarily directly related to visual stress. There was no significant interaction between the dyslexic and visual stress variables in any of the three VPPI categories.

All groups were found to read faster with optimal colour (see Table 3). However, in all groups except the dyslexic high visual stress group, the mean gains in reading speed were relatively modest at around 3–4%, and non-significant. In the dyslexic high visual stress group there was a mean 16% increase in reading speed when using optimal colour, which was significant ($t = 2.85$; $p = 0.046$). Further analysis of individual results indicates that

Table 3. Wilkins Rate of Reading Test scores in words per minute (and standard deviations) under optimal colour condition and without colour (white light) condition.

	Condition	High visual stress	Low visual stress
Dyslexic	Without colour	119.1 (11.59)	137.0 (45.67)
	With optimal colour	137.70 (15.04)	141.1 (52.66)
Non-dyslexic	Without colour	149.3 (37.56)	158.2 (24.76)
	With optimal colour	155.5 (32.78)	164.7 (22.61)

in the dyslexic high visual stress group all participants showed increases in reading speed, ranging from 5% to 27%, while in the other groups the changes ranged from $+14\%$ to -10%. In fact, two participants showed no change at all in reading speed and two had slightly slower speed in the optimal colour condition. It is also particularly notable that the mean reading speed of the dyslexic high visual stress group in the optimal colour condition (137.7 wpm) was essentially the same as that of the dyslexic low visual stress group when reading without colour (137.0 wpm). Thus while the benefits of colour were not sufficient to raise their reading speed to similar levels as those shown in the non-dyslexic group, nevertheless, effectively, they did bring them up to the same level as other dyslexic students who do not suffer from visual stress.

Discussion

The critical issue in this study is: What is the relationship between visual stress and dyslexia? As outlined in the introduction, this question is complicated by the fact that there at least four different concepts of visual stress: (1) a condition in which unpleasant visual symptoms experienced when reading are reported to be alleviated by use of coloured overlays and filters (also sometimes known as Meares-Irlen Syndrome); (2) a clustering of somatic and perceptual symptoms triggered by bright or flickering light and/or grating patterns (also sometimes known as visual discomfort); (3) cases where an increase in reading speed may be observed when using a coloured overlay for reading, compared with no overlay; and (4) a condition characterised by cortical hyper-excitability, and as such, related to photosensitive epilepsy and migraine. Whilst acknowledging that the statistical relationship between visual stress symptoms and increase in reading speed when using an overlay is relatively weak, a degree of commonality between these different concepts of visual stress is nevertheless apparent. Consequently it is appropriate to treat them as relating to the same underlying condition, at least on the basis of current knowledge, whilst recognising that not all sufferers may experience exactly the same set of symptoms to the same degree or show identical responses to treatment.

In another study (Singleton, in preparation), VPPI scores were found to be significantly higher for a sample of 50 dyslexic compared with 151 non-dyslexic students suggesting that students with dyslexia were more likely to report symptoms of visual stress. However, the difference between the two groups was considerably greater for non-critical items than for critical items, suggesting that the dyslexic and non-dyslexic groups differed more dramatically on factors that were not necessarily related to visual stress than they did on factors that were directly connected with visual stress. Nevertheless, rather than leading to the conclusion that visual stress and dyslexia are completely independent, as preferred by Wilkins (2003), these findings imply a greater likelihood of individuals with dyslexia having visual stress. This conclusion is consistent with recent claims by Grant (2004), who has cited data which indicate that visual stress is much more common in cases of dyslexia amongst university students than previously imagined. Grant, who is a psychologist with many years' experience of assessing students for dyslexia in the UK and who is well known in his field, reported that over the period 2001–2003, of 377 students diagnosed by him as having dyslexia, evidence of visual stress was strongly present in 42% of cases and weakly present in another 34% of cases.

In the present study, the finding that only the dyslexic students with high visual stress showed significant improvements in reading speed when using optimal colour implies a relationship of some sort between dyslexia and visual stress. Had the two factors (dyslexia and visual stress) been entirely independent, one would have predicted that all participants with high visual stress would exhibit a similarly positive benefit of colour (or, alternatively, no effect at all). Visual stress seems to have a particularly pronounced effect on the reading speed of dyslexic students: reading rate without colour for the high visual stress dyslexic group was significantly slower than that of the low visual stress dyslexic group. This effect was not found amongst the non-dyslexic students: reading rate without colour for the high visual stress non-dyslexic group was a little slower than that of the low visual stress non-dyslexic group, but not significantly so. It therefore appears that the combination of dyslexia and high visual stress is particularly detrimental to reading speed, independent of ability to recognise real words. A consequence of this is that untimed tests of reading accuracy will be less helpful in identifying dyslexia in bright, well-educated adults, whereas reading tests that take speed and fluency into account (such as the *Test of Word Reading Efficiency*; Torgeson, Wagner & Rashotte, 1999) are more likely to reveal serious processing difficulties.

Can the present findings be explained simply by differential severity of reading problems across the sub-groups? This is unlikely since the sub-groups did not differ significantly in reading accuracy on WRAT–3, and the high visual stress non-dyslexic sub-group had a similar non-critical VPPI score (19.6) to that of the low visual stress dyslexic sub-group (20.4). In other words, where problems in reading that were not necessarily directly connected to visual stress are concerned, the high visual stress non-dyslexic and the low visual stress dyslexic sub-groups were alike, suggesting that they experienced a similar range of (perceptually unrelated) literacy difficulties to a comparable degree. The only difference between these sub-groups was in degree of visual stress, yet neither showed significant effects of optimal colour on reading rate.

It has frequently been observed that colour is not a universal panacea for visual stress (see Evans, 2001). In the study by Evans and Joseph (2002), 32% of participants did not read any faster with their chosen overlay than without it, and only one-third of their sample demonstrated a significant benefit of overlays, despite 88% of the sample having chosen overlays. Looking at particular symptoms of visual stress in the Evans and Joseph study, of those who experienced a gain in reading rate of greater than 5% when using an overlay, 76% reported sore or tired eyes when reading, 37% reported words blurring when reading and 37% had frequent headaches. Hence although colour is frequently a beneficial treatment for visual stress, it does not seem to work for all sufferers. It is also clear from the Evans and Joseph study that many adults benefit from using coloured overlays when reading, despite lacking reported symptoms of visual stress. These findings call into question the common practice of defining visual stress as a condition that is 'alleviated by the use of individually prescribed coloured filters' (Evans, 1997b, 1997c; Evans & Joseph, 2002; Kriss & Evans, 2005), and which is diagnosed by means of either an immediate improvement on the Wilkins Rate of Reading Test when using a coloured overlay, or sustained voluntary use of an overlay for reading. In the present study, only two of the five students in the high visual stress non-dyslexic group showed increases in reading rate of greater than 5%. Clearly, therefore, relying solely on response to an overlay in order to judge whether or not a person suffered from visual stress would be a questionable practice, as some individuals can experience a range of visual perceptual distortions while reading and yet derive little, if any, benefit from use of a coloured overlay. In this context it is interesting that Wilkins also notes the opposite situation: 'Sometimes individuals who show dramatic improvements in reading fluency with a coloured overlay report no symptoms and show no signs of visual stress ... Whether these individuals have Meares-Irlen syndrome is a question of definition' (2003, p. 18).

By contrast with Grant's (2004) report that over three-quarters of university students with diagnosed dyslexia show significant symptoms of visual stress, Kriss and Evans (2005) report that the prevalence of visual stress in dyslexia is only about 10% higher than its prevalence in non-dyslexic children. On the basis of these results, Kriss and Evans conclude that visual stress and dyslexia 'are separate conditions, which may be present in isolation or sometimes coexist in the same individual' (2005, p. 362). However, in that study visual stress was diagnosed by choice of, and response to, coloured overlays, not by reported symptoms of visual perceptual distortions when reading. Furthermore, Kriss and Evans note that a surprisingly large number of the children in the study chose the mint green overlay, which may indicate that in this particular study factors other than alleviation of visual stress may have played a part in the children's selection. The present study used the Intuitive Colorimeter, which is able to determine optimal colour, rather than coloured overlays, a relatively coarse method that can only approximate optimal colour (Wilkins, 2003).

Recent studies by Grounds and Wilkins (in preparation) have yielded evidence to support a closer relationship between dyslexia and visual processing than was previously suspected. These authors found that the reading rate of dyslexic children aged 12–15 years displays greater slowing over time when compared with control groups. This effect, which seems to be independent of errors in reading, is significantly attenuated by the use of coloured overlays, and also by manipulation of perceptual characteristics of text, such as letter size and spacing. These results suggest that individuals with dyslexia are more sensitive to the visual features of text, and consequently have greater susceptibility to reading-induced fatigue.

At the present time there is no completely objective diagnostic test for visual stress and, certainly, when assessing children, it is recognised that questioning them about suspected visual perceptual symptoms could result in misleading responses. Hence in such cases diagnosis by positive response to the preferred treatment method may be argued to be the next best thing. When assessing adults, however, there is no reason why symptomatology should not be the fundamental basis for initial diagnosis, as is the norm in medical practice. When doing so, however, it should be recognised that the symptoms of visual stress are non-specific, i.e. they can result from a variety of other conditions, including ocular pathology, refractive error, binocular vision anomalies and accommodative anomalies (see Evans, 2001). Many people who have symptoms of visual stress regard them as 'normal' and they may only realise they actually had a problem when they experience the benefits of treatment. Hence not only would it be prudent to refer all cases of suspected visual stress to an eye-care practitioner who can check for undiagnosed conventional visual problems, but also to administer coloured overlay screening to any child or adult who shows signs of dyslexia.

The present study shows that on the basis of reported symptomatology, university students who experience high levels of visual stress are more likely to show improvements in reading rate with optimal colour if they also have dyslexia than if they do not have dyslexia. While that does not demonstrate an aetiological connection between the two conditions, it suggests an interaction that has major implications for diagnosis and treatment, and indicates a need for further research on possible mechanisms of linkage between dyslexia and visual stress, including the magnocelluar system as well as processes involved in visual fatigue. However, it is possible that it is only when reading is difficult (for whatever reason) that the task of reading benefits from treatment of visual stress, facilitating improvements in reading speed. The reading task used in this study was quite brief; longer and more challenging reading tasks, investigated under conditions of optimal colour and without, might yield different outcomes to that reported here, and in such circumstances non-dyslexic participants who report high levels of visual stress might also experience benefits of colour.

Notes

1. The term 'visual stress' has occasionally been used to refer to visual discomfort caused by decompensated heterophoria (latent squints/strabismus); e.g. see Pickwell, Jenkins & Yetka (1987); Yetka, Pickwell & Jenkins (1989). It is not being used in this sense here.
2. It is acknowledged that undetected visual problems may have existed in this sample (see Evans, 2001; Evans & Rowlands, 2004), but it was beyond the scope of the authors to investigate this. The extent to which VPPI results might be confounded by such problems has yet to be assessed.

References

Bender, L.A. (1956). *Psychopathology of children with organic brain disorders.* Springfield, IL: Charles C. Thomas.

Chase, C., Ashourzadeh, A., Kelly, C., Monfette, S. & Kinsey, K. (2003). Can the magnocellular pathway read? Evidence from studies of colour. *Vision Research*, 43, 1211–1222.

Conlon, E. (2000). Visual perceptual problems in reading: Their relationship to reading disability and neural processing. Paper presented to the 6th Irlen International Conference, Australia, July 2000.

Conlon, E., Lovegrove, W., Chekaluk, E. & Pattison, P. (1999). Measuring visual discomfort. *Visual Cognition*, 6, 637–663.

Conlon, E., Lovegrove, W., Hinem, T., Chekaluk, E., Piatek, P. & Hayes-Williams, K. (1998). The effects of visual discomfort and pattern structure on visual search. *Perception*, 27, 21–33.

Cornelissen, P.L., Richardson, A.R., Mason, A., Fowler, M.S. & Stein, J.F. (1994). Contrast sensitivity and coherent motion detection measured at photopic luminance levels in dyslexics and controls. *Vision Research*, 315, 1483–1494.

Edwards, V.T., Hogben, J.H., Clark, C.D. & Pratt, C. (1996). Effects of a red background on magnocellular functioning in average and specifically disabled readers. *Vision Research*, 36, 1037–1045.

Evans, B.J.W. (1997a). Assessment of visual problems in reading. In J.R. Beech & C.H. Singleton (Eds.), *Psychological assessment of reading.* (pp. 102–123). London: Routledge.

Evans, B.J.W. (1997b). Coloured filters and reading difficulties: A continuing controversy. *Optometry and Vision Science*, 74, 239–240.

Evans, B.J.W. (1997c). Coloured filters and dyslexia: What's in a name? *Dyslexia Review*, 9, 18–19.

Evans, B.J.W. (2001). *Dyslexia and vision.* London: Whurr.

Evans, B.J.W., Busby, A., Jeanes, R. & Wilkins, A.J. (1995). Optometric correlates of Meares-Irlen Syndome: A matched group study. *Ophthalmic and Physiological Optics*, 15, 481–487.

Evans, B.J.W. & Drasdo, N. (1991). Tinted lenses and related therapies for learning disabilities: A review. *Ophthalmic and Physiological Optics*, 11, 206–217.

Evans, B.J.W., Busby, A., Jeanes, R. & Wilkins, A.J. (1995). Optometric correlates of Meares-Irlen syndrome: A matched group study. *Ophthalmic and Physiological Optics*, 15, 481–487.

Evans, B.J.W., Drasdo, N. & Richards, I.L. (1996). Dyslexia: The link with visual deficits. *Ophthalmic and Physiological Optics*, 16, 3–10.

Evans, B.J.W. & Joseph, F. (2002). The effect of coloured filters on the rate of reading in an adult population. *Ophthalmic and Physiological Optics*, 22, 535–545.

Evans, B.J.W. & Rowlands, G. (2004). Correctable visual impairment in older people: A major unmet need. *Opthalmic and Physiological Optics*, 24, 161–180.

Evans, B.J.W., Wilkins, A.J., Brown, J., Busby, A., Winfield, A.E., Jeanes, R. & Bald, J. (1996). A preliminary investigation into the aetiology of Meares-Irlen syndrome. *Ophthalmic and Physiological Optics*, 16, 286–296.

Frostig, M. & Maslow, P. (1973). *Learning problems in the classroom: Prevention and remediation*. New York: Grune & Stratton.

Grant, D. (2004). From myths to realities: Lessons to be drawn from over 600 student assessments. Paper presented at the 6th International Conference of the British Dyslexia Association, University of Warwick, March 2004.

Grounds, A.R. & Wilkins, A.J. (in preparation). Separating the visual and semantic factors that affect reading speed in dyslexic children.

Hammill, D., Goodman, L. & Wiederholt, J.L. (1974). Visual-motor processes: Can we train them? *The Reading Teacher*, 27, 469.

Hartman, N.C. & Hartman, R.K. (1973). Perceptual handicap or reading disability? *The Reading Teacher*, 26, 684.

Hinshelwood, J. (1917). *Congenital word-blindness*. London: H.K. Lewis.

Irlen, H. (1983). Successful treatment of learning difficulties. Paper presented at the Annual Convention of the American Psychological Association, Anaheim, California.

Irlen, H. (1991). *Reading by the colours*. New York: Avery.

Irlen, H. (1994). Scotopic sensitivity/Irlen Syndrome: Hypothesis and explanation of the syndrome. *Journal of Behavioural Optometry*, 5, 62 & 65–66.

Irlen, H. (1997). Reading problems and Irlen coloured lenses. *Dyslexia Review*, Spring, 4–7.

Jeanes, R., Busby, A., Martin, J., Lewis, E., Stevenson, N., Pointon, D. & Wilkins, A.J. (1997). Prolonged use of coloured overlays for classroom reading. *British Journal of Psychology*, 88, 531–548.

Kriss, I. & Evans, B.J.W. (2005). The relationship between dyslexia and Meares-Irlen syndrome. *Journal of Research in Reading*, 28(3), 350–364.

Kussmaul, A. (1877). Disturbance of speech. In H. von Ziemssen (Ed.), *Cyclopaedia of the practice of medicine*, vol 14. Translated by J. A. McCreery. New York: William Wood.

Lehmkule, S. (1993). Neurological basis of visual processes in reading. In D. Willows, R. Kruk & E. Corcos (Eds.), *Visual processes in reading and reading disabilities*. (pp. 77–94). New Jersey: Lawrence Erlbaum.

Livingstone, M., Rosen, G.D., Drislane, F. & Calaburda, A. (1991). Physiological evidence for a magnocellular deficit in developmental dyslexia. *Proceedings of the New York Academy of Science*, 88, 7943–7947.

Lovegrove, W. (1991). Spatial frequency processing in normal and dyslexic readers. In J.F. Stein (Ed.), *Vision and visual dysfunction, Vol 13 Visual dyslexia*. London: Macmillan.

Lovegrove, W., Martin, F. & Slaghuis, W. (1986). A theoretical and experimental case for a visual deficit in specific reading disability. *Cognitive Neuropsychology*, 3, 225–267.

Maclachan, A., Yale, S. & Wilkins, A.J. (1993). Open trials of precision ophthalmic tinting: 1-year follow-up of 55 patients. *Ophthalmic and Physiological Optics*, 13, 175–178.

Meares, O. (1980). Figure/ground, brightness contrast, and reading disabilities. *Visible Language*, 14, 13–29.

Morgan, W.P. (1896). A case of congenital word-blindness. *British Medical Journal*, 2, 1378.

Orton, S.T. (1925). 'Word-blindness' in school children. *Archives of Neurology and Psychiatry*, 14, 581–615.

Orton, S.T. (1937). *Reading, writing and speech problems in children*. London: Chapman & Hall.

Pickwell, D., Jenkins, T.C.A. & Yekta, A.A. (1987). Fixation disparity in binocular stress. *Ophthalmic and Physiological Optics*, 7, 37–41.

Ramus, F. (2001). Outstanding questions about phonological processing in dyslexia. *Dyslexia*, 7, 197–216.

Ramus, F. (2003). Developmental dyslexia: Specific phonological deficit or general sensorimotor dysfunction? *Current Opinion in Neurobiology*, 13, 212–218.

Robinson, G.L. & Conway, R.N.F. (2000). Irlen lenses and adults: A small-scale study of reading speed, accuracy comprehension and self-image. *Australian Journal of Learning Disabilities*, 5, 4–12.

Robinson, G.L. & Foreman, P.J. (1999). Scotopic sensitivity/Irlen Syndrome and the use of coloured filters: A long-term placebo-controlled study of reading achievement and perception of ability. *Perceptual and Motor Skills*, 89, 35–52.

Scheiman, M. (1994). Scotopic sensitivity syndrome, reading disability and vision disorders. *Journal of Behavioural Optometry*, 5, 63–67.

Simmers, A.J., Bex, P.J., Smith, F.K.H. & Wilkins, A.J. (2001). Spatiotemporal visual function in tinted lens wearers. *Investigative Ophthamology and Vision Science*, 423, 879–884.

Skotton, B.C. (2000). The magnocellular deficit theory of dyslexia: Evidence from contrast sensitivity. *Visual Research*, 40, 111–127.

Singleton, C.H. (Chair) (1999). *Dyslexia in higher education: Policy, provision and practice* (Report of the National Working Party on Dyslexia in Higher Education). Hull: University of Hull.

Singleton, C.H. (in preparation). A rating scale for the evaluation of symptoms of visual stress in reading.

Sloman, R.T., Cho, H. & Dain, S.J. (1991). Colour-mediated grouping effects in good and disabled readers. *Ophthalmic and Physiological Optics*, 11, 320–327.

Sloman, R.T., Dain, S.J., Lim, H. & May, J.G. (1995). Reading-related wavelength and spatial frequency effects in visual spatial location. *Ophthalmic and Physiological Optics*, 15, 125–132.

Snowling, M.J. (2000). *Dyslexia* (2nd edn). Oxford: Blackwell.

Stanovich, K.E. (2000). *Progress in understanding reading: Scientific foundations and new frontiers*. New York: Guildford Press.

Stein, J.F. (2001). The magnocellular theory of dyslexia. *Dyslexia*, 7, 12–36.

Stein, J.F., Talcott, J.B. & Walsh, V. (2000). Controversy about the visual magnocellular deficit in developmental dyslexics. *Trends in Cognitive Science*, 4, 209–211.

Stein, J.F. & Talcott, J.B. (1999). Impaired neuronal timing in developmental dyslexia – The magnocellular hypothesis. *Dyslexia*, 5, 59–77.

Stein, J.F. & Walsh, V. (1997). To see but not to read: The magnocellular theory of dyslexia. *Trends in Neuroscience*, 20, 147–152.

Torgeson, J.K., Wagner, R.K. & Rashotte, C.A. (1999). *Test of Word Reading Efficiency (TOWRE)*. Austin, TX: Pro-Ed.

Vellutino, F.R. (1979). *Dyslexia: Theory and research*. Cambridge, MA: MIT Press.

Vellutino, F.R., Fletcher, J.M., Snowling, M.J. & Scanlon, D.M. (2004). Specific reading disability (dyslexia): What have we learned in the past four decades? *Journal of Child Psychology and Psychiatry*, 45, 2–40.

Wilkins, A.J. (1995). *Visual stress*. Oxford: Oxford University Press.

Wilkins, A.J. (2003). *Reading through colour*. Chichester: Wiley.

Wilkins, A.J., Evans, B.J.W., Brown, J., Busby, A., Winfield, A.E., Jeanes, R. & Bald, J. (1994). Double-masked placebo-controlled trials of precision spectral filters in children who use coloured overlays. *Ophthalmic and Physiological Optics*, 14, 365–370.

Wilkins, A.J., Jeanes, R.J., Pumfrey, P.D. & Laskier, M. (1996a). *Rate of Reading Test*. London: I.O.O. Marketing.

Wilkins, A.J., Jeanes, R.J., Pumfrey, P.D. & Laskier, M. (1996b). Rate of Reading Test: Its reliability and its validity in the assessment of the effects of coloured overlays. *Ophthalmic and Physiological Optics*, 16, 491–497.

Wilkins, A.J., Lewis, E., Smith, F., Rowland, E. & Tweedie, W. (2001). Coloured overlays and their benefits for reading. *Journal of Research in Reading*, 24, 41–64.

Wilkins, A.J., Nimmo-Smith, I. & Jansons, J.E. (1992). Colorimeter for the intuitive manipulation of hue and saturation and its role in the study of perceptual distortion. *Ophthalmic and Physiological Optics*, 12, 381–385.

Wilkins, A.J., Nimmo-Smith, M.I., Tait, A., McManus, C., Della Sala, S., Tilley, A., Arnold, K., Barrie, M. & Scott, S. (1984). A neurological basis for visual discomfort. *Brain*, 107, 989–1017.

Wilkinson, G.S. (1993). *Wide Range Achievement Test, 3rd edition (WRAT–3)*. Wilmington, DE: Jastak Associates.

Williams, M.C., Lecluyse, K. & Rock-Faucheux, A. (1992). Effective interventions for reading disability. *Journal of the American Optometry Association*, 63, 411–417.

Yekta, A.A., Pickwell, L.D. & Jenkins, T.C.A. (1989). Binocular vision without visual stress. *Optometry and Vision Science*, 66, 815–817.

Zeki, S. (1983). Colour coding in the cerebral cortex: The responses of wavelength-selective and colour-coded cells in monkey visual cortex to changes in wavelength composition. *Neuroscience*, 9, 767–781.

Index